101 GOLF COURSES

101 GOLF COURSES

A tour of the best and most uplifting golf courses in the world

Geoffrey Giles

Bath · New York · Singapore · Hong Kong · Cologne · Delhi · Melbourne

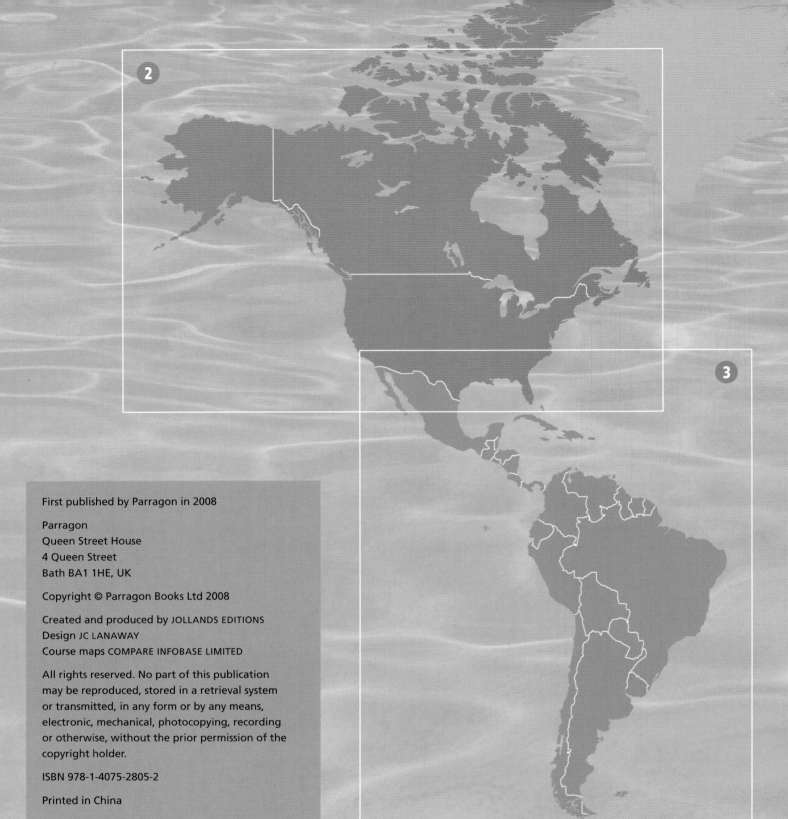

First published by Parragon in 2008

Parragon
Queen Street House
4 Queen Street
Bath BA1 1HE, UK

Copyright © Parragon Books Ltd 2008

Created and produced by JOLLANDS EDITIONS
Design JC LANAWAY
Course maps COMPARE INFOBASE LIMITED

ISBN 978-1-4075-2805-2

Printed in China

PRACTICAL DETAILS

Most of the courses in this book welcome visiting golfers, the exceptions being some private clubs, mainly in the United States and Canada. The famous championship courses are inundated with requests to play, so book well in advance. Club websites will usually include details of fees, availability, handicap restrictions, dress codes, and whether a letter of introduction is required, and many will have an online booking facility.

Distances in the book are given in yards, which are used in North America and—still, despite metrication—by the golfing community in Great Britain.

Scorecards give the hole lengths from the back or championship tees as they were at the time of writing. Note that, for championships, what might be a short par 5 for the members is sometimes re-designated as a long par 4 for competitors. Clubs frequently build new tees or simply remeasure their course, so these distances should only be used as a guideline.

Every effort has been made to check facts thoroughly, but errors may have crept in. The publisher would be grateful for corrections or information helpful for future editions.

▶▶▶ Contents

▶▶▶ Introduction

It was the great English-born American golf course designer Robert Trent Jones who wrote, "The first golf course architect, of course, was the Lord, and he was the best there has ever been." The early golfers of Scotland and the Netherlands played their golf on relatively undefined patches of ground wherever they happened to live. There was no such thing as a typical golf course. And while a few elements of a course have become standardized, there is still no standard golf course.

The Scots became the defining influence on golf when the Honourable Company of Edinburgh Golfers laid down the first set of rules in 1744. In 1754 twenty-two "Noblemen and Gentlemen" gathered in St. Andrews to form the Royal and Ancient Golf Club of St. Andrews (R&A), and the newcomers gradually gained the ascendancy. Their rules dealt mainly with the situations that might occur during the course of a match—the rules of matchplay. You played against each other, not against the course. Medal play would have been unthinkable, because the number of holes per course varied until St. Andrews, which had now reduced its course to one of 18 holes, standardized this number for a round of golf in 1858.

ABOVE The spiritual home of golf, St. Andrews. The R&A does not own the golf courses—the Old Course is one of several run by the Links Management Trust on behalf of the town. Visitors may book online, by post, or by telephone far in advance, take advantage of one of the golf tour operators' packages, or take pot luck in one of the daily ballots.

BELOW Royal County Down, originally laid out by Old Tom Morris over 100 years ago.

In the mid-19th century men began to "design" golf courses. The great players of the day were called upon to lay out the "links" of newly formed golf clubs. Those great players were all Scottish and they all played on the links courses of Scotland, on that strip of unfertile, sandy soil between the beach and the town or farmland. Inevitably they tried to recreate the features that gave their home courses distinction. They looked for green sites in hollows, which would be self-watering with dew, or on humps and hillocks, because they tested technique. Sand exposed by sheep sheltering from the wind or natural erosion had become a common feature of links, and these were replicated by early bunkers.

Today's golf course designers are master craftsmen, and they are doing just what Allan Robertson, Tom Morris and Willie Park did a century and a half ago. They now have the benefit of computer-aided design, sophisticated earthmoving machines, real-estate lawyers, civil engineers, and environmentalists. Given the restraints of what they may be allowed to do, ecologically, and the dire consequences of getting it the tiniest bit wrong, we should rejoice that the greatest players of our day are prepared to emulate Robertson, Morris, and Park.

ABOVE Cape Kidnappers, New Zealand—an example of the work of American designer Tom Doak. Doak has an unerring talent for locating stunning green sites and keeping the golfer thinking until the very last putt has dropped.

FOLLOWING PAGES The humps and hollows of the Old Course, St. Andrews. The crumpled fairways give all manner of different lies and stances, while bunkers litter the place, very often in the most unexpected of places.

▶▶▶ Courses 1–27

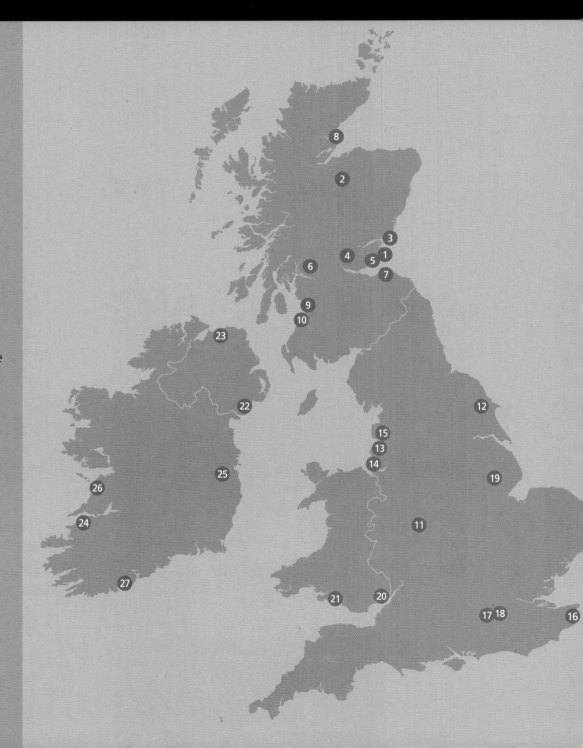

▶▶▶ Great Britain & Ireland

Scotland is the cradle of golf. The game was enjoyed there in the Middle Ages, and it is recorded that golf was played in England in 1608 by Scots attached to the court of King James I of England (James VI of Scotland) at Blackheath. However, golf in the British Isles must be judged by the courses of the 21st century, of which there are about 3,000.

Some of these are historic: the Old Course at St. Andrews, Royal Liverpool, Royal County Down. Some are state of the art: Celtic Manor, the Belfry, the K Club. But it is the quality of the courses that do not make the "Top 10 Charts" that illustrates the strength in depth of golf courses in the U.K. and Ireland.

Nowhere in the world can boast finer—or more profuse—links or heathland courses. Yet there are so many other choice terrains—downland, fenland, moorland, and ancestral parkland. For the most part these have been exploited by the great architects of the Golden Age: Harry Colt, Alister MacKenzie, Herbert Fowler, George Abercromby, Tom Simpson. Contemporary giants have not been slow in following suit.

St. Andrews

The Old Course, St. Andrews, Fife, Scotland

There is no more famous golfing town than St. Andrews. It is, after all, the Home of Golf, and the game has been played there since the 15th century. Overlooking the Old Course is the handsome clubhouse of the Royal and Ancient Golf Club (R&A), a comparative newcomer to St. Andrews having been founded in 1754. Nowadays the R&A governs the game throughout the world, with the exception of North America, and every five years it brings its Open Championship (or British Open, as it is widely known through the golfing world) to the Old Course, producing winners of the caliber of Tiger Woods, Jack Nicklaus, Severiano Ballesteros, and Nick Faldo in recent years and James Braid and Bob Jones in the distant past.

Jones was one of many golfers who found that it takes time to appreciate the many subtleties of the Old Course. It has humps and hollows here, there, and everywhere; hundreds of bunkers, many in the unlikeliest of places, some such as Hell, Strath, Hill, or Road terrifying even the world's greats; huge, rolling greens, all but four of them double greens shared by holes playing in opposite directions; and there is a wealth of history in every blade of grass—all the greats of golf have played here, and the locals will recount tales fantastical of derring-do and catastrophe everywhere on the course. The first-time visitor would be well advised to employ the services of a good local caddie, not only to unravel the mysteries of playing the Old Course but also to share in some of those numerous St. Andrews legends.

BOB JONES AND ST. ANDREWS

Strange to relate, Bob Jones hated the Old Course on his first visit, tearing up his card during the 1921 British Open, but he came to love it as he got to know it better, eventually saying, "I could take out of my life everything except my experiences at St. Andrews and I'd still have a rich, full life." It was on the Old Course in 1930 that Jones won the Amateur Championship, defeating Roger Wethered 7 and 6. In this remarkable year Jones also won the U.S. Amateur at Merion, the U.S. Open at Interlachen and the British Open at Royal Liverpool, a feat unlikely to be repeated, now referred to as the Impregnable Quadrilateral. At the end of that season Jones, at the age of 28, retired from competitive golf, concentrating on his career as a lawyer.

CARD OF THE COURSE

Hole	Distance (yards)	Par
1	376	4
2	453	4
3	397	4
4	480	4
5	568	5
6	412	4
7	390	4
8	175	3
9	352	4
Out	3,603	36
10	380	4
11	174	3
12	348	4
13	465	4
14	618	5
15	456	4
16	423	4
17	455	4
18	357	4
In	3,676	36
Total	7,279	72

LEFT *One of the most famous views in golf, looking over the Swilcan Bridge towards the clubhouse of the R&A.*

BELOW RIGHT *The Road bunker is one of the most feared on the Old Course. Many great players settle for a bogey five rather than risk failing to escape its clutches.*

In the footsteps of the great

There is no simpler drive in golf than that on the 1st hole of the Old Course, or that would be the case if the tee were anywhere else than right in front of the R&A clubhouse. But it is a hugely broad fairway shared with the 18th, and there are no bunkers. However, there is the sinuous Swilcan Burn to be cleared to reach the green. Thereafter the course makes its way out in the shape of a shepherd's crook to the Eden Estuary, turning in a loop before retracing its steps alongside the outward holes on wide shared fairways and greens. The space, which appears to invite uninhibited driving and cavalier approach play, is deceptive. Such are the ingenuities of the course's defenses that how the hole is played from tee to green depends on exactly where the pin is located.

However much you may be enjoying your round you cannot relax until you have passed the 17th, the Road Hole, dominated by the treacherous Road bunker. Get in there and there may be no escape! But all is surely alleviated by the walk up the 18th, the most famous walk in golf.

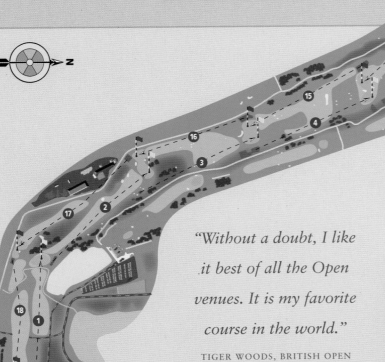

"Without a doubt, I like it best of all the Open venues. It is my favorite course in the world."

TIGER WOODS, BRITISH OPEN
CHAMPION AT ST. ANDREWS IN
2000 AND 2005

BUNKERS—THE STORIES BEHIND THE NAMES

It is said that there are 112 bunkers on the Old Course, which seems a conservative estimate to anyone who has played there. Some of them are in such obscure places that you could never imagine golfers getting into them—but they have! Most also have names. These are some of the more colorful:

CHEAPE'S (2ND HOLE) Named after the Cheape family that owns the nearby Strathtyrum estate. Sir James Cheape bought the Old Course in 1821 to save it from rabbit farmers. His son later sold it to the R&A, which, in turn, sold it to the town. Golfers owe Sir James an enormous debt of gratitude.

CARTGATE (3RD HOLE) Shares its name with the hole itself, so called because of the former cart track that crossed the hole toward the beach.

GINGER BEER (4TH HOLE) Again, a name shared with the hole, referring back to the mid-19th century when "Old Daw" Anderson set up a ginger beer stall there.

SUTHERLAND (4TH/15TH HOLE) Sutherland should not be a factor on the 4th were it not for the difficulties of the right-hand side of the fairway often forcing golfers too far to the left. It was named after one A. G. Sutherland, who is reputed to have had the bunker re-excavated when it was filled in in the 1860s.

COTTAGE (4TH/15TH HOLE) For the same reasons as Sutherland, Cottage should not be a factor on the 4th, but it is. It refers to Pilmour Cottage, which once stood nearby and is now the clubhouse of the Eden Course.

STUDENTS (4TH HOLE) There are two theories behind the naming of these bunkers. It has been said that they refer to the practice of busy students, not having the time for a full round, playing out this far and then turning for home. An alternative suggestion is that these were cosy (and out-of-sight) places for male students to take their lady friends.

SPECTACLES (4TH HOLE) This is exactly what they look like, set at the foot of the ridge crossing this fairway.

COFFINS (6TH/13TH HOLES) You are playing a little extravagantly if you get in these on the 6th hole. They are a threat to all, however, on the 13th. They are so coffin-like that you feel you may be in them forever.

SHELL (7TH HOLE) Apart from the fact that it looks rather like a mussel shell from above, the name refers back to the days when the base of the bunker used to be cockle shells. (If you are wildly off course on the 7th, you might find yourself in Hill or Strath bunkers—leave these for the 11th!)

SHORT HOLE BUNKER (8TH HOLE) Some of the bunker names are rather more prosaic!

KRUGER (9TH HOLE) This is actually two bunkers, built during the Boer War and named after the former president of the Transvaal.

A third bunker, further on, is named Mrs. Kruger. Rumor has it that there is also one named Kruger's Mistress!

STRATH (11TH HOLE) This commemorates the Strath brothers. Andrew won the 1865 British Open. His brother David tied for first place in 1876 but he refused to take part in the play-off, leaving Bob Martin as the champion.

HILL (11TH HOLE) Hill is not far behind Strath in venom. It is cut into the face of the hill on which the 11th green sits.

ADMIRAL'S (12TH HOLE) Sited close to the tee, the bunker is said to have been named after an admiral who, in his 80s, failed to see the sizable bunker as he walked forward from the tee, distracted as he was by a beautiful young lady walking past, wearing, it is said; pillar-box red.

BELOW *Hell Bunker dominates strategy on the 14th hole for handicap golfers. Will the second shot clear it or do you go round the side of it?*

STROKE (12TH HOLE) Get in here and you almost certainly will drop a stroke.

NICK'S (13TH HOLE) The first of several bunkers threatening a pulled drive, presumably named after the devil who put it there.

CAT'S TRAP (13TH HOLE) Invisible from the fairway, the bunker catches your ball as a cat traps a mouse.

WALKINSHAW (13TH HOLE) Named after a local golfer who made a habit of visiting this pot bunker.

LION'S MOUTH (13TH HOLE) Lion's Mouth is another vicious bunker lying in wait beyond Cat's Trap. Perversely, Lion's Mouth is smaller than Cat's Trap.

THE BEARDIES (14TH HOLE) A quartet of bunkers with whiskery grass adorning their lips.

BENTY (14TH HOLE) Benty refers to one of the traditional seaside grasses: Bent.

KITCHEN (14TH HOLE) Kitchen was once known as the Devil's Kitchen because it was a small but deep pot bunker. It has since been enlarged.

HELL (14TH HOLE) One of the best-known bunkers in golf with a vast acreage and a seriously steep face from which escape forward is by no means guaranteed.

GRAVE (14TH HOLE) A small bunker in front of the green, which was formerly coffin-shaped.

PRINCIPAL'S NOSE (16TH HOLE) A set of three bunkers said to represent the prominent nose of the principal of St. Mary's College in the mid-19th century. It is also said to be named after the ugly protuberance from the porch above the doorway of a principal's lodgings in the town.

DEACON SIME (16TH HOLE) Deacon Sime refers to a St. Andrews clergyman who asked for his ashes to be scattered in the bunker, on the premise that he had spent so much of his earthly life in that particular bunker that he might as well spend eternity there as well.

GRANT'S (16TH HOLE) Commemorates a 19th-century captain of the R&A who made a habit of getting into this bunker.

WIG (16TH HOLE) Formerly called Jackson's Wig, recalling the formal dress of golfers in days past. Jackson was a captain of the R&A.

SCHOLAR'S (17TH HOLE) Scholar's is a reminder that the course used to be played in the opposite direction. You were a promising young scholar if you could clear this bunker with your drive.

PROGRESSING (17TH HOLE) You were doing well, but had not yet attained the proficiency of a scholar, if you could clear this bunker.

ROAD (17TH HOLE) The fearsome bunker that eats into the green of the Road Hole, both named after the tarmac road running tight along the right side of the green.

Boat of Garten

Boat of Garten Golf and Tennis Club, Inverness-shire, Scotland

Rarely is golf played in a more beautiful setting than at Boat of Garten. The Cairngorm Mountains provide a breathtaking backdrop before which ribbons of crumpled fairways are threaded through avenues of silver birches, with abundant heather and broom adding swathes of purple and brilliant gold to the more restrained greens and blues of the mountains and Abernethy Forest. Deer and the occasional osprey remind us that this part of Scotland is particularly rich in wildlife, while the puffing of a steam engine on the preserved Strathspey Railway brings a period touch to this very unspoiled corner of the Highlands.

ABOVE *With the backdrop of the Cairngorm Mountains, Boat of Garten is undeniably pretty. It is also immense fun at whatever level you play. This is the 2nd hole.*

In fact it was the coming of the railway in 1863 that put Boat of Garten on the map. The hamlet of Gart, with its ferry across the River Spey, already existed there. The station built to serve the village and ferry took its name, Boat of Garten, from that ferry. With easier access the village grew into a popular retreat for walkers, anglers, and those who valued the crystal-clear mountain air (and, more recently, skiers). It was only a matter of time before there was a golf course.

Modest beginnings

At first, in 1898, the golf course was a simple layout of six holes. A couple of extra holes and tennis courts were constructed later. In due course further land became available, and James Braid was called in to advise on a full 18-hole course. It opened in 1932 and remains almost the same today apart from the recent conversion of two former par 4s into par 5s. Braid was then one of the most sought-after

architects in golf course design and had demonstrated with his alterations to Carnoustie in 1926 that he could produce a course to examine even the world's best players. At 5,876 yards/5,373 m from the very tips, "Boat" is hardly a championship test, yet it is not a pushover for accomplished golfers. The charm of Braid's course is its subtlety, but sloppy golf is rigorously punished, with heather waiting to swallow careless tee shots, well-placed bunkers and many a drop-off to the sides or behind the greens.

Unusually, Boat opens with a short hole. It would normally present no difficulty, but a touch of uncertainty is understandable on the first shot of the day. A straightforward par 4 and another short hole take play to the course boundary, on the other side of which runs the Strathspey Railway. From here on the fairways take on a mischievous, rolling character, often demanding of the golfer the ability to play with the ball above or below the feet from a rising or a hanging lie. The 6th is a particularly fine hole, with a long, slow curving fairway calling for excellent judgment of length and direction from the tee and a green raised above bunkers demanding a perfect second shot. Braid himself championed the 12th hole, perhaps the most handsome of all the holes. Boat keeps one of its toughest holes for the last, with a very testing approach shot to a raised green. After the round, there are few better views to be enjoyed from a clubhouse than those at Boat.

"With scenery like this, does the golf really matter?"

PETER ALLISS,
THE GOOD GOLF GUIDE

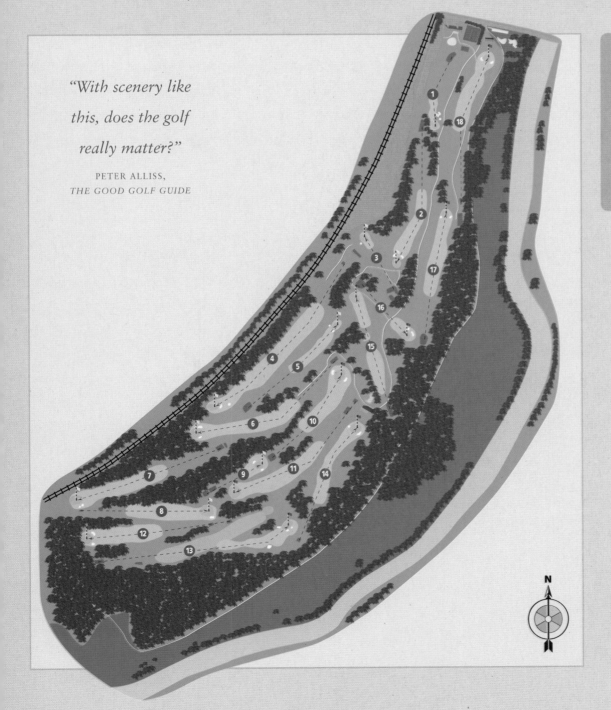

CARD OF THE COURSE

Hole	Distance (yards)	Par
1	189	3
2	360	4
3	163	3
4	514	5
5	301	4
6	403	4
7	386	4
8	355	4
9	154	3
Out	2,825	34
10	271	4
11	379	4
12	349	4
13	473	5
14	323	4
15	307	4
16	168	3
17	344	4
18	437	4
In	3,051	36
Total	5,876	70

N

Carnoustie

Carnoustie

Championship Course, Carnoustie Golf Links, Angus, Scotland

Is Carnoustie the toughest course on the British Open roster? How it was prepared for the 1999 Open in the wind and rain it certainly was, Paul Lawrie's winning score being six over par. It was more sympathetically prepared for the 2007 Open, when Padraig Harrington and Sergio Garcia tied on 277, seven under par, Harrington winning in a four-hole play-off. What most observers were agreed on was that this set-up displayed all the greatness of this historic links, and in particular that there were often two or three different strategies for playing a particular hole, depending on a golfer's strengths and weaknesses, the wind and the weather.

It is not certain when golf began in Carnoustie (probably over 500 years ago) but it was some time around 1842 that Allan Robertson—the pre-eminent golfer at that time—was brought from St. Andrews to lay out a ten-hole course on the Barry Links. Another St. Andrews stalwart, Old Tom Morris, made considerable alterations in 1867, expanding the course to 18 holes, and James Braid made the final significant changes in 1926.

The longest British Open course

Carnoustie hosted its first British Open in 1931, with Scottish-born American Tommy Armour coming from five behind to win—subsequent champions have included Henry Cotton (1937), Ben Hogan (1953), Gary Player (1963), and Tom Watson (1975). As a championship course Carnoustie has always been among the longest. For the 2007 Open it measured a daunting 7,412 yards/6,778 m, the longest ever,

with two par 4s reaching almost 500 yards/457 m in length, yet such is the prowess of contemporary professionals with modern equipment that many forsook their drivers, taking long irons from the tee. They did it for the simple reason that you cannot blast your way round this course. You have to plot your way around it. The bunkers are deep, gathering and perfectly positioned; the rough can be savage; out-of-bounds threatens on several holes; and the Jockie's and Barry burns were brilliantly incorporated into the design, especially on the last two holes.

Jockie's Burn, for instance, limits the length of the tee shot on the challenging 5th, putting pressure on the approach to a multi-level, snaking green, cunningly

bunkered and over 50 yards/46 m deep. Out-of-bounds waits to wreck scores on the long 6th, causing many an errant tee shot to be pushed into the deep rough on the other side.

Of all the hazards it is the Barry Burn that is most feared, very largely because it comes into play viciously on the last two holes, hard on the heels of the 16th, a seriously long par 3 on which only the straightest of tee shots can pierce the bunkered mounds guarding the front of the green. Birdies here are rare, dropped shots frequent. The 17th then strikes out over the burn, which meanders hugely, creating almost an island fairway, with length restricted where the burn crosses the fairway.

Still to come is the scariest drive of them all, back over the Barry Burn to another narrow fairway, once again bounded by the burn. Even after a successful drive, there remains the long second to the green, which lies perilously close to the out-of-bounds fence and is, naturally, only just beyond yet another meander of the dreaded burn. What a tough hole!

LEFT *Barry Burn, snaking across the 17th and 18th. Jean van de Velde's skirmishes with it cost him a seven in the 1999 British Open, when a six would have won it.*

CARD OF THE COURSE

Hole	Distance (yards)	Par
1	406	4
2	463	4
3	358	4
4	412	4
5	415	4
6	578	5
7	410	4
8	183	3
9	478	4
Out	3,703	36
10	466	4
11	383	4
12	499	4
13	176	3
14	514	5
15	472	4
16	248	3
17	461	4
18	499	4
In	3,718	35
Total	7,421	71

▶ Almost 300 young men from Carnoustie and the surrounding area have emigrated to the United States to work as golf professionals. One of the best known was Stewart Maiden, Bob Jones's teacher at the East Lake Club, Atlanta.

▶ The Smith brothers from Carnoustie had an enviable professional record. Alex was twice U.S. Open champion, Willie once, and Macdonald came second to Bob Jones in both the British Open and the U.S. Open in 1930.

▶ Ben Hogan, one of golf's all-time greats, entered only one British Open, in 1953 at Carnoustie. He won the championship by four strokes. It was part of a remarkable run of victories that included the U.S. Masters and the U.S. Open.

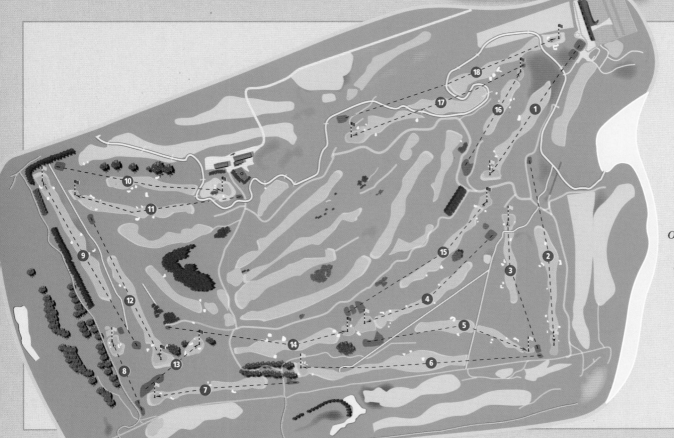

"I love playing over here because it allows you to be creative."
TIGER WOODS

Gleneagles

King's Course, Gleneagles Hotel, Auchterarder, Perthshire, Scotland

When the 2014 Ryder Cup is played in Scotland it will be at Gleneagles. Jack Nicklaus's PGA Centenary Course has the honor of hosting it, having proved its fitness by hosting the annual Johnnie Walker Championship on the European Tour. The enormous hotel, built in the style of a French château and the venue for the 2005 G8 Summit, will then be exactly 90 years old.

ABOVE *The 7th on the King's Course is a tough dogleg, on which the further you aim left to shorten the dogleg the longer you have to drive to clear a ridge.*

Older still are James Braid's two wonderful courses, opened before the hotel, in 1919. The King's and Queen's courses were a vital part of the strategy to attract royalty, nobility, and the merely wealthy to the hotel, the pride and joy of the Caledonian Railway, which was described both as a "Palace in the Glens" and as the "Riviera in the Highlands." Clearly the company's ambitions were well founded, for the hotel remains one of the world's great hotels to this day, and Braid's golf courses are as revered as ever.

Both the King's and the Queen's are serious contenders for the coveted title of the finest inland course in Scotland. Neither course is long enough seriously to challenge today's top players—hence the need for the construction of the PGA Centenary Course—but those who value charm, variety, subtlety, and ingenuity in a golf course in ravishing surroundings can still derive great satisfaction from a round on either, preferably both. And, of course, they are maintained in impeccable condition.

CARD OF THE COURSE

Hole	Distance (yards)	Par
1	362	4
2	436	4
3	374	4
4	466	4
5	178	3
6	480	5
7	444	4
8	178	3
9	409	4
Out	3,327	35
10	499	5
11	230	3
12	442	4
13	464	4
14	309	4
15	459	4
16	158	3
17	377	4
18	525	5
In	3,463	36
Total	6,790	71

Drum Sichty and Kittle Kink

On both courses each hole is named, an old Scottish tradition, and at Gleneagles the holes were named from the outset, not carrying forward some ancient traditional name (for the holes were new) but quite simply to amuse visitors. For the record, "Drum Sichty" is no more than a view of the hills while "Kittle Kink" is a tricky bend. But the names are good ice-breakers between player and caddie, and a good caddie is useful not only in guiding the player through the many problems posed by hilly courses, but also in sharing the finer points of Braid's clever designs with the appreciative golfer.

One of the great delights of the courses is the way the holes follow each other to create an integrated whole, with refreshing change of pace, a good balance of challenges, and a constant sense of development. At a little under 6,000 yards/5,486 m the Queen's Course may seem too short for the accomplished player, but do not be fooled! Seven of the par 4s exceed 400 yards/366 m in length and there are two substantial par 3s, the 14th and 17th. It was a favorite course of Lee Trevino.

In comparison with the Queen's, the King's is said to be more masculine. Sandy Lyle has particular respect for the tough, uphill 4th: in Lyle's opinion, "a first-class hole by any standard." Braid himself considered his favorite hole on the course to be the 13th, another long two-shot hole, appropriately named Braid's Brawest ("Braid's Best"). Everywhere there is a sense of space, the twists and turns of each course giving ever-changing views of the uplifting mountain scenery. These are not so much golf courses as experiences!

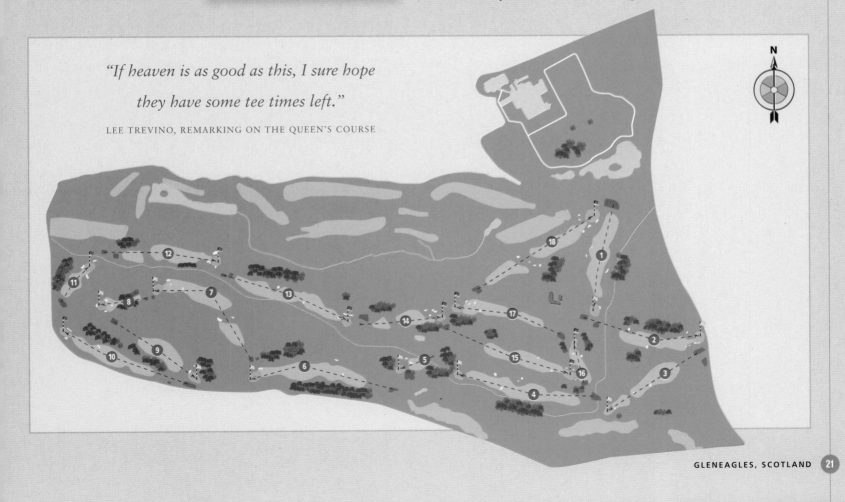

"If heaven is as good as this, I sure hope they have some tee times left."

LEE TREVINO, REMARKING ON THE QUEEN'S COURSE

Kingsbarns

Kingsbarns

Kingsbarns Golf Links, St. Andrews, Fife, Scotland

"Let it not be difficult for the sake of being difficult; rather, let it be interesting and engaging." These are the thoughts of Mark Parsinen, one of the developers of the new course at Kingsbarns, 6 miles/10 km south of St. Andrews on the Fife coast. It has already made a big impression on players and spectators during the annual Dunhill Links Championship, which is played over the three venues of Carnoustie, Kingsbarns, and St. Andrews. There are even calls for it to be added to the British Open roster, which is unlikely given its proximity to St. Andrews.

Although the modern Kingsbarns course was opened as recently as 2000, golf has been played here since 1793. That original course was abandoned in the mid-19th century and turned into farmland. Another course was laid out in 1922, but it, too, foundered when the site was mined to deter invasion at the outbreak of World War II. After the war the land reverted to farming use. Those earlier courses were humble affairs, none being on the scale of today's state-of-the-art Kingsbarns, which is undeniably impressive.

Recreating a links

The architect charged with laying out the new course was an American, Kyle Phillips, working in partnership with Parsinen. He was faced with a mammoth task, for part of the site available was silt and clay, and a great deal of earthmoving was required to redistribute the deep sands from the eastern side of the land equally throughout the course, to build sand dunes from scratch, and to provide rapid-draining soil for the fairways. The views inland from

LEFT *The 12th curves in a long arc beside the beach, which forms part of the Fife Coastal Path.*

BELOW *Golfers on the 15th green, a fine par 3 running hard against the shore.*

the course are nothing special over flattish farmland, so Phillips decided to orientate the course in such a way that the majority of holes would enjoy seascapes, and that those holes that play away from the sea would have dunes or trees as a backdrop. At Kingsbarns the visual aspect of the course is as impressive as the golfing challenge it presents.

On an exposed site such as this the wind is rarely absent, and Phillips allowed for this by providing wide fairways that are themselves a clever part in the design as they offer multiple choices—there are many different ways of playing most holes, depending on the skill of the player and his or her intelligence. Kingsbarns is, then, a welcome change from so many one-dimensional, penal, contemporary designs that call for a specific, perfectly executed stroke on

every shot and, thus, leave no opportunities for invention and individuality.

As early as the first drive of the round a choice can be made, the harder drive to the left leaving an easier approach to the green and vice versa. And what a green it is, seemingly perched on a cliff hanging over the sea! In fact it is one of Phillips's many optical illusions. There is room for several further holes below the green. Nor did Phillips miss any opportunity to route the course along the sea shore, with no fewer than six holes enjoying close proximity to breaking waves. One of those is the majestic 12th, one of the most photographed holes on the links, its curving fairway hugging the rocks and strands for some 600 yards/549 m—a fine golf hole in a magical setting.

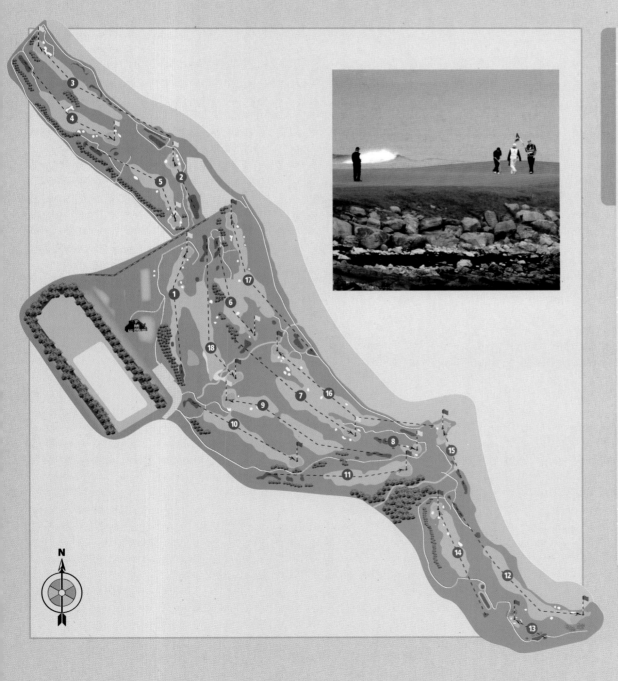

CARD OF THE COURSE

Hole	Distance (yards)	Par
1	414	4
2	200	3
3	516	5
4	408	4
5	398	4
6	337	4
7	470	4
8	168	3
9	558	5
Out	3,469	36
10	387	4
11	455	4
12	606	5
13	148	3
14	366	4
15	212	3
16	565	5
17	474	4
18	444	4
In	3,657	36
Total	7,126	72

Loch Lomond

Loch Lomond

Loch Lomond Golf Club, Luss by Alexandria, Dunbartonshire, Scotland

Every year, in the week before the British Open, eyes turn to Loch Lomond, home of the Scottish Open since 1996. Many of the great names of golf take part in this championship to hone their games for the British Open. To others it represents their last chance to qualify for the big one. For the spectators—and millions who watch on television—it is a rare opportunity to revel in the romantic setting of this very private golf course, set in the historic parkland on the banks of Loch Lomond.

A troubled birth

Loch Lomond was not an instant success. It took years before planning permission was granted and construction could begin. No sooner had ex-Open champion Tom Weiskopf and his design partner, Jay Morrish, completed the course than a recession hit and the receivers were called in. The grass lay fallow. Enter Arizona businessman Lyle Anderson. Weiskopf persuaded him to visit the dormant course. Anderson liked what he saw and agreed to back the venture with cash—lots of it! He now presides over an international club with lavishly appointed facilities, boasting a range of country pursuits, and with two top-class golf courses (the other being Dundonald on the Ayrshire coast).

Eye candy is the bane of much contemporary golf architecture, but at Loch Lomond Weiskopf and Morrish had no need to resort to it. The place is ravishing in its own

right and the architects used the mountain and loch vistas superbly, also utilizing the streams and ponds, marshes, and woodlands as principal elements in the strategy of design. On the 13th, for instance, there is no sight of the Loch, so a funnel of trees is used to lead the eye from the elevated tee along the well-bunkered fairway of this fine par 5, then beyond up into the heather-clad hills.

This is followed by a great spectator hole, the drivable par-4 14th. The safe play is out to the left, on to a fairway with an iron for position, then a simple pitch over a stream and bunker to the green. The daring play is an all-or-nothing shot over a treacherous bog, either on to the green for an eagle putt, or into the bog with a bogey looming.

These are part of a glorious finish, the 17th being a well-defended short hole, and the last hole a strong dogleg where risk-taking is well rewarded, but failure is wretched.

RIGHT *There have been three holes-in-one on Loch Lomond's 17th during the Bell's Scottish Open: Jarmo Sandelin and Mathias Grönberg in 2000 and Peter Lonard in 2003.*

CARD OF THE COURSE

Hole	Distance (yards)	Par	Hole	Distance (yards)	Par
1	425	4	10	455	4
2	455	4	11	235	3
3	510	5	12	415	4
4	390	4	13	560	5
5	190	3	14	345	4
6	625	5	15	415	4
7	440	4	16	495	4
8	160	3	17	205	3
9	345	4	18	435	4
Out	3,540	36	In	3,560	35
			Total	7,100	71

AN "AMERICAN COURSE"

There is no such thing as a stereotypical "American course." (What have TPC at Sawgrass, Merion, and Pinehurst in common other than their world fame? Architecturally there is little similarity.) Yet Europe is flooded with "American-style" courses. Those who know Portugal's Algarve or Andalucía in Spain will instantly recognize one. Loch Lomond is an American-style course—arguably the best in Europe—yet, perversely, it is quite unlike any of the others.

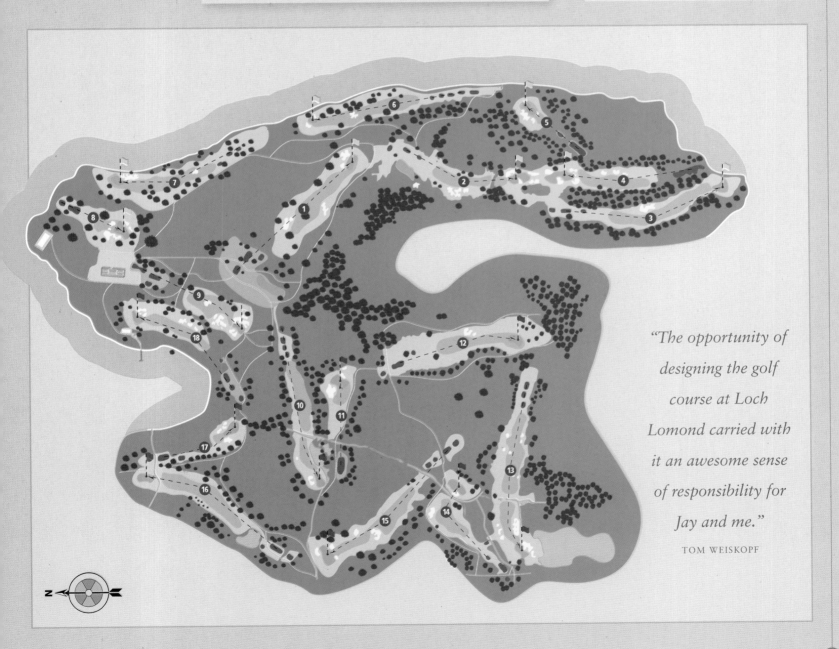

"The opportunity of designing the golf course at Loch Lomond carried with it an awesome sense of responsibility for Jay and me."

TOM WEISKOPF

Muirfield

The Honourable Company of Edinburgh Golfers, Muirfield, Gullane, East Lothian, Scotland

Muirfield is the third home of the Honourable Company of Edinburgh Golfers, who from 1874 began to host the British Open in rotation with Prestwick and St. Andrews. In 1891 they moved from Musselburgh to Muirfield, nearly 20 miles/32 km to the east of Edinburgh, calling on Old Tom Morris to lay out their new course.

Only a year after it opened Muirfield hosted its first (and the club's seventh) British Open. Fourteen further Opens have followed, as well as the Amateur Championship, Senior Open, Ryder Cup, Walker Cup, and Curtis Cup. Some of the greatest names in golf have triumphed at Muirfield, including Vardon, Braid, Hagen, Cotton, Player, Nicklaus, Trevino, Watson, Faldo, and Els—an impressive list.

Tom Morris's layout was unusual for its day in consisting of two contra-rotating loops of nine holes, one inside the other. This meant that the wind would blow from a different direction on almost every hole. The routing remains but little else of Morris's course survives, today's being mostly the work of Harry Colt and Tom Simpson in the 1920s.

BELOW Muirfield's 12th green is slightly raised, with downslopes and bunkers all around, and, as so often on this course, everything is visible as you play your shot.

THE OLDEST GOLF CLUB

Which is the oldest golf club in the world? Royal Blackheath in southeast London is known to have existed in 1608. Golf was certainly played in Scotland in 1457, because King James II of Scotland issued a decree prohibiting it. It was in the Edinburgh suburb of Leith that the Honourable Company first held a competition over its five-hole course in 1744. As the club's records are complete thereafter, the Honourable Company, which gave the game its first set of rules, becomes the oldest club with a complete, continuous history.

The fairest of tests

The course is well respected by top players, particularly for its fairness—there is very little blindness and there are few capricious bounces. It is a notably good test of driving, the rough being particularly grasping, and some of its bunkering can only be described as ferocious! Perhaps of all the Open courses Muirfield has no "stand-out" hole, for it is a very evenly distributed examination of the game, but most players would agree that the 6th, 8th, and 18th are among the best long, two-shot holes in links golf. The 13th, too, is a white-knuckle short hole with a long, narrow green perched above five terrifying bunkers. A brilliant escape from one of these set up Ernie Els's British Open win in 2002.

From the visitor's point of view, it is worth noting that the club does not introduce temporary tees or winter greens in the off season. You get to play the real course, and for a reduced green fee, to boot.

▶ Jack Nicklaus, after winning the 1966 British Open, said, "It is essentially a fair course. It has more definition than any links that the Open is played on." He went on to name the first course he created—in Dublin, Ohio, USA—Muirfield Village.

▶ It was at Muirfield, in 1892, that the British Open was first played over 72 holes. Previously it had been over 36 holes. It was also at Muirfield in 1892 that an entrance fee to play in the British Open was first imposed.

▶ Ben Crenshaw (former U.S. Masters champion and a distinguished golf course architect) praised Muirfield for "its beautiful honesty as a test of golf."

CARD OF THE COURSE

Hole	Distance (yards)	Par
1	448	4
2	351	4
3	378	4
4	213	3
5	560	5
6	468	4
7	185	3
8	443	4
9	508	5
Out	3,554	36
10	475	4
11	389	4
12	381	4
13	191	3
14	448	4
15	415	4
16	186	3
17	546	5
18	449	4
In	3,480	35
Total	7,034	71

"I liked it from the first day I played it."

JACK NICKLAUS,
ON WINNING THE 1966
BRITISH OPEN

Royal Dornoch

Royal Dornoch

Royal Dornoch Golf Club, Dornoch, Sutherland, Scotland

"The most fun I ever had playing golf," was Tom Watson's opinion of Royal Dornoch, an opinion shared by many of the famous golfers who have made the pilgrimage north to Dornoch. They have visited in large numbers because Dornoch is high on the must-play list of all who have an interest in golf course design.

Golf has been played at Dornoch for some 500 years. The present club, with a modest nine-hole course, was founded in 1877, but a more significant date in Dornoch's development was 1883, when John Sutherland was appointed secretary. He it was who brought in Old Tom Morris to extend the course to 18 holes in 1886; who subsequently refined and improved the design; who had the course brought into exemplary condition; who worked to have Dornoch created a Royal club; and who promoted Dornoch in his writings for London periodicals. Sutherland involved his professionals and greenkeepers in the development of the course and one of those was Donald Ross, who subsequently emigrated to the United States where he introduced the concept of Dornoch-style raised greens to American golf design.

Remoteness is a blessing for Dornoch

Because Dornoch is so far from large centers of population it has never hosted important professional tournaments or the British Open. For that reason the course has been spared the incessant lengthening and alterations that are deemed necessary to keep modern professionals in check. Its holes remain as they were intended to be played twenty, thirty, or even fifty years ago, and the visitor today is still required to utilize a whole variety of types of pitch shot to gain access to these brilliantly sited greens. But it is not only on the approach shot that intelligent play is demanded, for the fairways use the natural slopes, humps, and hollows cleverly, calling for precise and thoughtful driving. The wind, too, must be taken into account.

RIGHT The delightful 10th hole at Dornoch, a gentle enough par 3 if you find the green from the tee, but the very devil if you miss.

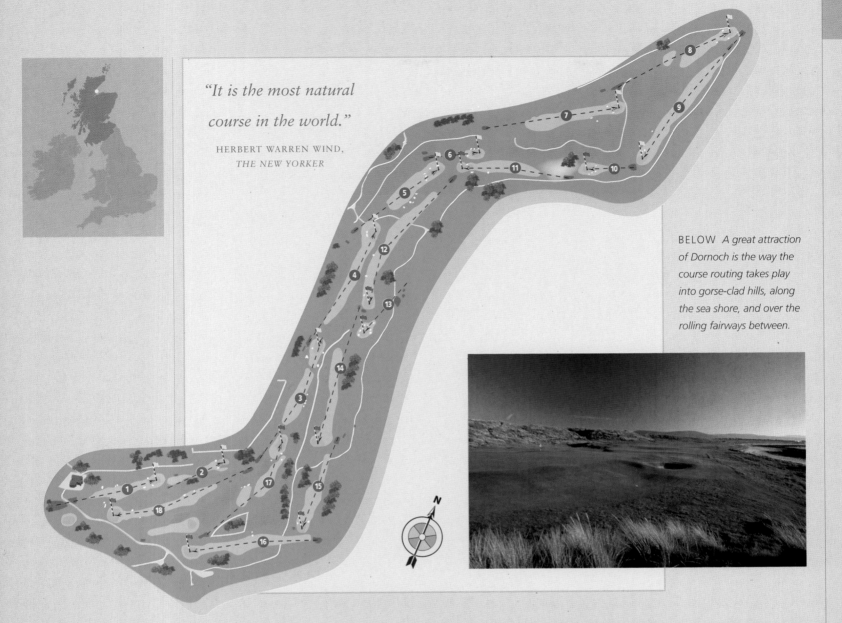

"It is the most natural course in the world."

HERBERT WARREN WIND,
THE NEW YORKER

BELOW *A great attraction of Dornoch is the way the course routing takes play into gorse-clad hills, along the sea shore, and over the rolling fairways between.*

CARD OF THE COURSE

Hole	Distance (yards)	Par	Hole	Distance (yards)	Par
1	331	4	10	177	3
2	184	3	11	450	4
3	414	4	12	507	5
4	427	4	13	180	3
5	354	4	14	445	4
6	163	3	15	358	4
7	463	4	16	402	4
8	437	4	17	405	4
9	529	5	18	456	4
Out	3,302	35	In	3,380	35
			Total	6,682	70

Tom Watson's favorite hole is the 5th, a hole that certainly proves that excessive length is not essential for greatness. The view from the elevated tee is encouraging, the wide fairway some way below awaiting the drive. Yet the green is very long and angled significantly from left to right. The ideal drive, then, is down the left, but this is the side where trouble lurks in the form of a hill covered in gorse, threatening a lost ball. On the right the fairway slopes, guiding the ball inexorably toward a run of bunkers. Even if these are avoided the approach shot must be played across the axis of the narrow, kidney-shaped, putting surface, and there are further bunkers awaiting if that shot is overcooked.

Another of Dornoch's great holes is the bunkerless 14th—Foxy. Everything is governed by a series of dunes, which eat into the fairway from the right, obscuring the green from anywhere other than the extreme left of the fairway. The green is tucked round to the right behind the last of the dunes, broad but shallow, and raised sufficiently to make an approach shot from any length difficult to execute. The 17th, too, is a fine hole, sweeping downhill from the tee, then sharply up to a marvellously located green.

THE LURE OF DORNOCH

John Sutherland, the club's first secretary, was a considerable publicist for Dornoch, writing about it in the *London Daily News* and *Golf Illustrated*. But, unlike many of the great Scottish links that were located near railroads, Dornoch had no railroad until 1902. When the line opened, Sutherland lost no time in alerting golfers all over the country to take the overnight sleeper from London, to play the course the following morning. Among those who visited during these years were the Great Triumvirate: James Braid, Harry Vardon, and J. H. Taylor. Taylor was so thrilled by the course that he arranged to take a fortnight's holiday in Dornoch every year while he was at the peak of his career, so perfect was the course for honing his game. Another who visited, much later, was Ben Crenshaw, who came to Dornoch as part of his preparations for the 1980 British Open, held that year at Muirfield. Asked, when he returned to Muirfield, what he thought of Dornoch, he replied, "Let me put it this way, I nearly did not come back."

RIGHT *The 2nd at Dornoch looks benign enough from here, but get in the front right bunker and you may well have to escape sideways or backward.*

Iain Lowe Photography

Royal Troon

Royal Troon Golf Club, Troon, Ayrshire, Scotland

Troon was already an important sea port on the Firth of Clyde when a railroad was opened from Glasgow in 1840. Soon its beaches and clean air attracted Glaswegians to take vacations there and the wealthy to build big houses. The next railroad station south of Troon was Prestwick, the birthplace of championship golf, and in 1878 it was decided that Troon should have its own golf course.

Land was leased from the Duke of Portland and a five-hole course was created in the area of the present 1st, 2nd, 17th, and 18th holes. That course was extended piecemeal and by 1888 there were 18 holes, stretching to 5,600 yards/ 5,121 m, following much the same route as today's course. Further amendments took place over the years and by 1923 Troon was ready to host its first British Open.

Arnold Palmer was at the peak of his career when he won the British Open at Troon in 1962, yet even with his extraordinary powers of recovery he realized that he should "not get locked into a life and death struggle with the course." The first-time visitor, looking down the opening fairway from the tee, could be forgiven for querying that comment, for everything looks so straightforward and benign. And so it is, for a while.

Increasingly menacing

"As much by skill as by strength" is the club's motto, and the first three holes amble gently alongside the beach, each under 400 yards/366 m in length. Two birdieable par 5s are separated by a charming par 3 on top of the dunes, and everything seems pretty simple so far. The most inviting drive of the round follows at the 7th, but already the mind is sharpening for the mischief of the 8th, the notorious Postage

SOCIAL STATUS

At the end of the 1923 British Open the champion, Arthur Havers, and the runner-up, Walter Hagen, were invited into the clubhouse for the presentation ceremony. Hagen refused to go as none of the other professional golfers had been admitted to the clubhouse during the tournament. He went instead to the pub, where a large number of the spectators joined him.

CARD OF THE COURSE

Hole	Distance (yards)	Par
1	361	4
2	391	4
3	379	4
4	558	5
5	210	3
6	599	5
7	403	4
8	123	3
9	423	4
Out	3,447	36
10	438	4
11	488	4
12	431	4
13	470	4
14	178	3
15	481	4
16	542	5
17	222	3
18	453	4
In	3,703	35
Total	7,150	71

▶ At the age of 71 Gene Sarazen played in the 1973 British Open at Troon and holed his tee shot on the infamous Postage Stamp for an ace in the first round. In the second round he found a bunker off the tee, but then holed his recovery shot.

LEFT *The Postage Stamp was originally played blind to a green on the far side of the dune. The new hole, built in 1909–10, was opened by Harry Vardon, James Braid, J. H. Taylor, and Alex Herd.*

Stamp. It is the shortest hole in British Open golf, but you are either on the minuscule putting surface in one stroke, expecting a birdie, or else, if you missed the green, on a rough-clad hillock, in one of five deep greenside bunkers, or far below the green in a grassy hollow. Escape from any of these is no certainty, as the German player, Hermann Tissies, found to his cost in the 1950 British Open. He finished up with a 15!

It is on the back nine, almost invariably played into the wind, that Troon bares its teeth, starting with an intimidating blind and angled drive to the elusive 10th fairway. The subsequent approach to a pinnacle green is difficult to judge. As for the 11th, it was described by Arnold Palmer as, "The most dangerous hole I have ever seen." The young Jack Nicklaus ran up a 10 on this hole in his first Troon Open, and during the 1997 British Open the hole played to an average of 4.65 shots, easily the hardest on the course. Gorse and the hole's proximity to the railroad track are the principal card wreckers.

The corrugated fairways of the 13th and 15th can be difficult to find and hold, the 17th is particularly tough in any sort of wind, and the 18th green is not one to overshoot, with the indignity of out-of-bounds immediately beyond the putting surface.

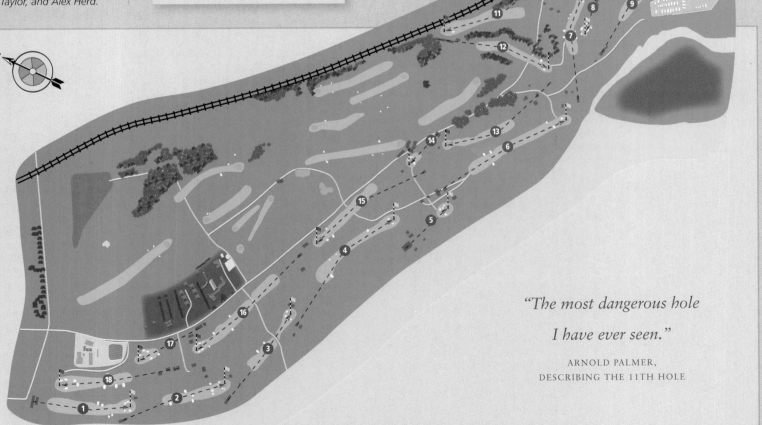

*"The most dangerous hole
I have ever seen."*

ARNOLD PALMER,
DESCRIBING THE 11TH HOLE

Turnberry

Turnberry

Ailsa Course, Westin Turnberry Hotel, Turnberry, Ayrshire, Scotland

Turnberry's Ailsa Course enjoys the most spectacular setting of the half-dozen courses on the British Open roster. Often compared to California's Pebble Beach, it made its Open debut in 1977 and immediately produced a classic. Yet twice in its history this most majestic of courses was on the brink of extinction.

The railroads played an important part in the spread of golf throughout Britain (America, too, for that matter). They were also responsible for the establishment of some of the country's finest hotels, not least Gleneagles, Cruden Bay, and Turnberry. It was in the early 1900s that the Glasgow and South Western Railway negotiated a lease with the Marquis of Ailsa to enable them to construct a hotel at Turnberry. Already in existence on site was the Marquis's private 13-hole course, and a further 13 holes were added so that by 1906

Turnberry could, with justification, call itself a golf resort. It was good enough to host the British Ladies' Championship of 1912, and a promising future seemed certain.

Unfortunately progress was halted by World War I, when the course became an airfield. After that war restoration was undertaken and the thread of development resumed. Worse destruction came in 1939 in the form of a major air base, a vital part of the defense of transatlantic shipping lanes. Surely that was the end for Turnberry.

NAMING OF HOLES

In common with many Scottish courses, Turnberry's holes are named as well as numbered. The 2nd, for instance, is Mak Siccar ("make sure"), the 3rd Blaw Wearie ("out of breath"), 6th Tappie Tourie ("hit to the top"), 10th Dinna Fouter ("don't mess about"), 13th Tickly Tap ("a tricky little hit"), 15th Ca Canny ("take care"), 17th Lang Whang ("good whack").

LEFT *The short 11th, with the lighthouse and Ailsa Craig—the very essence of golf at Turnberry, a scene far removed from the runways of a wartime airfield.*

A remarkable resurrection

It was not the end, however, in the mind of Turnberry's manager, Frank Hole. Despite huge obstacles he managed to garner sufficient compensation from public funds after World War II and enough support from the newly formed British Railways, the hotel's owners, to turn three concrete runways and all their attendant paraphernalia into a golf course worthy of the site. What Scottish designer Philip Mackenzie Ross produced was one of the most visually attractive courses in Scotland.

Turnberry then worked its way up the tournament ladder and in 1977 it got its just reward—its first British Open. It turned out to be one of the greatest of all, the famous "duel in the sun," with Tom Watson and Jack Nicklaus going head-to-head to produce some of the most spectacular golf ever seen, Watson just managing to hold out the battling Nicklaus in a thrilling contest.

It could be argued that the first three holes of the Ailsa Course sail under the radar a little, because the player is already anticipating the stretch of shoreline holes from the 4th to the 11th, unparalleled on British Open courses and worthy of comparison with those famed seaside holes at Pebble Beach. The seascapes are stunning, especially at sunset, but the golf requires full concentration, with a number of holes threaded down valleys between the dunes, others (such as the short 4th and 6th holes) fully exposed to the wind on top of the dunes. Arguably, the curving 8th is the best of these demanding par 4s, but the visitor cannot wait to be photographed on the peninsular 9th tee, the drive being made over sufficient of the ocean toward a distant clifftop fairway to cause trepidation in many an otherwise proficient player.

Perhaps the austerities of postwar Britain suggested to Ross a minimalist approach to bunkering, but this aspect was tightened in preparation for the 2009 British Open, Turnberry's fourth. The second course, renamed Kintyre, has also been almost wholly remodeled by Donald Steel.

▶ In the final round of the 1979 European Open, played at Turnberry, Sandy Lyle birdied six of the first seven holes to establish an eight-shot lead, going on to win the tournament comfortably. The one hole he failed to birdie was the comparatively simple 2nd.

CARD OF THE COURSE

Hole	Distance (yards)	Par
1	350	4
2	430	4
3	462	4
4	165	3
5	442	4
6	231	3
7	529	5
8	431	4
9	454	4
Out	3,494	35
10	452	4
11	174	3
12	446	4
13	412	4
14	449	4
15	209	3
16	409	4
17	497	5
18	434	4
In	3,482	35
Total	6,976	70

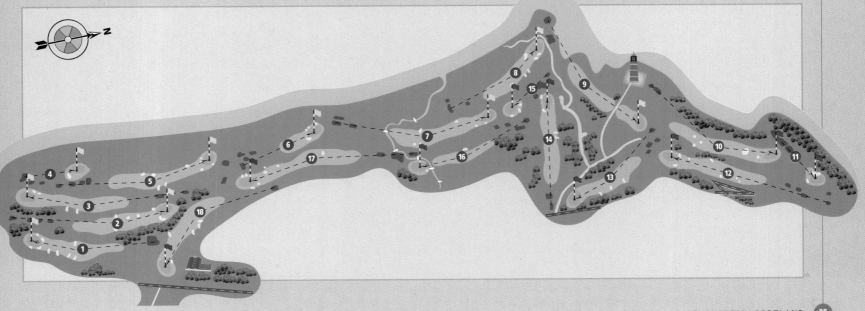

The Belfry

Brabazon Course, The Belfry, Warwickshire, England

The Brabazon boasts a unique record—it is the only course on either side of the Atlantic to have hosted four Ryder Cups, with the Europeans winning in 1985 and 2002, the Americans winning in 1993, and the 1989 match halved. It has, then, been a happy hunting ground for the Europeans.

Driving past the courses (there are three) today, all you can see is a fairly unpromising, flat site with lines of parallel trees indicating where fairways might be located. Had you driven past before the courses were built you would not even have seen the trees, for these were potato fields on cold Midlands clay. The property had none of the qualities you would normally look for in assessing its suitability for golf, and golf of the highest class at that.

The job of creating a silk purse out of a sow's ear fell to Peter Alliss and Dave Thomas, and Thomas has returned over the years to make changes and tweaks to allow the course to keep pace with the prodigious advances in performance of golfers, golf clubs and golf balls, particularly over the past twenty years. Alliss and Thomas created a workmanlike course of good length and plenty of challenge on a remarkably modest acreage.

For most of us the strategy of the Brabazon is about avoiding coming to grief in the many streams and lakes that enter into play on almost every hole. There is some prolific bunkering, too, not least on the short 7th, which, from the tee, suggests something out of Pine Valley. Card-wrecking holes come as early as the 3rd, a reachable par 5 (particularly from the everyday tees) with a corner of a lake to be carried on the way to the green, and we might even fall into the pond on the short 12th simply because it is there. But the holes that expose us all (amateur hacker and world star alike) are the 10th and 18th.

Two world-class holes

The 10th is a very short par 4, which actually gets better the shorter it is played. For the Ryder Cup it is reduced from its full 311 yards/284 m to around 270 yards/247 m. The reason is simple: to tempt the contestants to go for the green from the tee. You could get there with two 9-irons. But what would you not give for a putt for an eagle two? Get it wrong, of course, and you are fishing your ball out of the water or you have bounced off the branches of the green-side trees into perdition.

Perhaps the best is kept for last. This is one of the scariest drives in golf, those needing to attack the hole having to clear as much of the lake on the left as they dare. If that is successful, the second shot is played uphill over a further stretch of lake to an enormously long, three-tiered green. All golfers should play this hole once in their lives if only to understand the courage of those Ryder Cup players who have made par or birdie here under monumental pressure.

BELOW *The tough 473-yard/ 433-m par-4 18th on the Brabazon Course at the Belfry, one of golf's finest finishing holes, involving two nail-biting crossings of the lake.*

RIGHT *The attractive 10th, a siren hole, luring most golfers into an attempt to drive the green, with the capacity to force most of them to reload—three off the tee!*

CARD OF THE COURSE

Hole	Distance (yards)	Par	Hole	Distance (yards)	Par
1	411	4	10	311	4
2	379	4	11	419	4
3	538	5	12	208	3
4	442	4	13	384	4
5	408	4	14	190	3
6	395	4	15	545	5
7	177	3	16	413	4
8	428	4	17	564	5
9	433	4	18	473	4
Out	3,611	36	In	3,507	36
			Total	7,118	72

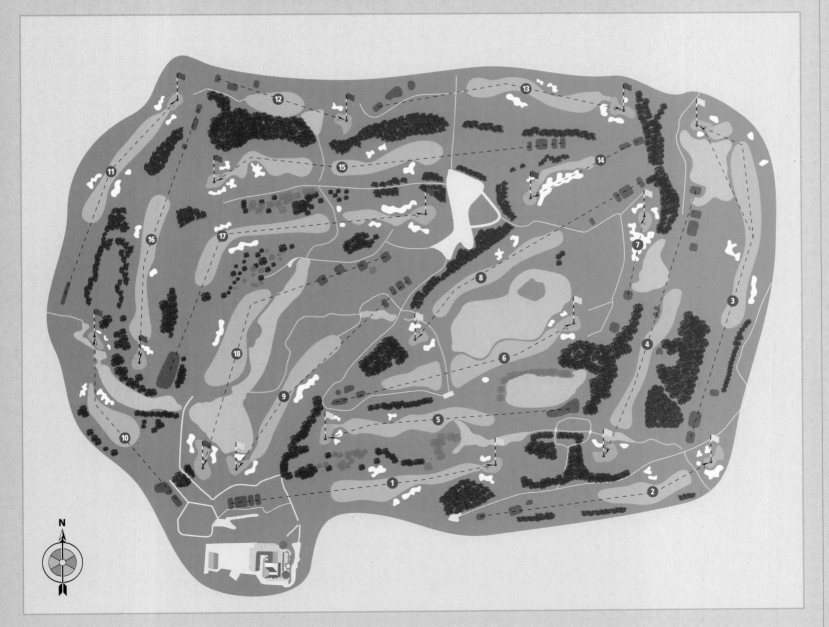

Ganton

Ganton

Ganton Golf Club, Scarborough, North Yorkshire, England

If you had to choose a single golf course to encapsulate all that's good about English golf, Ganton would be as good a choice as any. It's old, founded in 1891; it has hosted many high quality tournaments, amateur and professional; it's a mix of heathland and links golf; it's a traditional club yet warmly hospitable; and it's also a great test of all departments of a player's game.

Driving to the course along the busy York–Scarborough road, you could be forgiven for wondering if this were the right road—it just doesn't look like golfing country. Turn down the lane leading to the club and everything changes, even the quality of the air! There are tantalizing glimpses of immaculate fairways and greens, tall pines, cavernous bunkers, and hostile gorse. Already it is apparent that only the A game will do.

Ganton is a compact course, which helps to ensure that the pace of play is brisk, although the ingenious routing brings golfers together at different stages of their rounds. Ganton members are sociable, taking every opportunity to compare notes on their respective matches.

INLAND LINKS

What sets the course at Ganton apart from its immediate surroundings is the land on which it was built. This used to be the beach, many thousands of years ago, before the sea retreated to where it is today. Beneath the course is a deep layer of sand giving excellent drainage and supporting the sort of crisp turf more usually encountered at the seaside. Ganton plays like a links, firm and fast. The pitch-and-run shot is usually far more effective than the high-hit wedge, especially in a strong wind, funneled through the Vale of Pickering.

RIGHT *Ganton's 14th is one of the finest par 4s under 300 yards/274 m in Britain. The setting, in the Vale of Pickering, makes Ganton one of the loveliest places to play.*

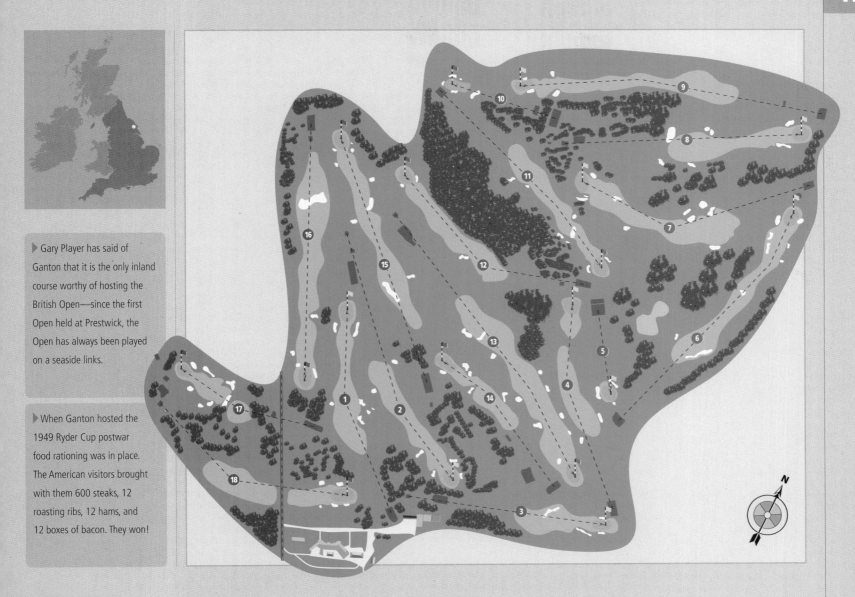

▶ Gary Player has said of Ganton that it is the only inland course worthy of hosting the British Open—since the first Open held at Prestwick, the Open has always been played on a seaside links.

▶ When Ganton hosted the 1949 Ryder Cup postwar food rationing was in place. The American visitors brought with them 600 steaks, 12 roasting ribs, 12 hams, and 12 boxes of bacon. They won!

On the course

The prospect from the 1st tee is inviting, a welcoming fairway rising gently in front of you, before sliding to the right past bunkers to a green, bunkered on either side of the entrance. It is not a difficult hole, but you are immediately aware that sloppy play will not go unpunished. Again, it is the bunkering that keeps you on your toes on the 2nd, and bunkering provides a stiff challenge for those aspiring to drive the 3rd green. From here the course twists and turns over a sequence of delightful holes, meeting the wind from every angle, until on the 14th the course bares its teeth. It may be a short par 4, but it is a brilliant one, tempting bold play and cruelly punishing the inadequate.

Strong hitting is needed to conquer the 15th, and it will be useful on the 16th tee where you are required to clear a monumental quarry of a bunker in mid-fairway. The harder task is positioning the drive correctly to grant an unimpeded approach to the green, raised above bunkers and backed by bright yellow gorse. The 17th is a brutal long short hole (played as a par 4 by visitors), and the round ends with a supremely strategic dogleg. Greed will bring disaster! Then it's time for a drink and a slice of the famous Ganton cake.

CARD OF THE COURSE

Hole	Distance (yards)	Par	Hole	Distance (yards)	Par
1	373	4	10	168	3
2	445	4	11	417	4
3	334	4	12	363	4
4	406	4	13	524	5
5	157	3	14	282	4
6	470	4	15	461	4
7	435	4	16	448	4
8	414	4	17	249	3
9	504	5	18	434	4
Out	3,538	36	In	3,346	35
			Total	6,884	71

Royal Birkdale

Royal Birkdale Golf Club, Southport, Merseyside, England

There is refreshingly little pomp for a club and course with such history. The respect of being chosen for the 100th British Open and a consistent ranking in the U.K. Top 10 are quite sufficient for Royal Birkdale.

A striking sight greets visitors to Royal Birkdale: a white art-deco clubhouse resembling a ship sailing on a tossing sea of sand dunes. It was designed in 1935 to replicate the superstructure of the ocean liners that in those days steamed out from Liverpool in considerable numbers, heading for all corners of the then intact British Empire. Within the clubhouse, however, its creature comforts most definitely belong to the 21st century.

True links golf is played in partnership with nature, and Birkdale's course uses little trickery or human intervention to create its challenges, the difficulties coming instead with subtle design and substantial yardages. Thick rough and willow scrub devour errant shots, and act as a wonderful haven for a wide variety of wildlife. However, the design (evolved over the years by the Hawtree family of golf course architects) is actually very simple: holes weave through valleys between sand hills, creating flat fairways (for a links!)

giving the reward of many yards of roll on a well-struck shot, and a good stance for the next shot. The crests and troughs of that tossing sea of sand dunes are omnipresent, but you are only troubled by them if you stray off line. There are some fine tee and green sites high on them, such as the 11th tee and 12th green.

A long and distinguished championship history

Host to the British Open on nine occasions between 1954 and 2008, Royal Birkdale always proves to be an outstanding venue, with its fair nature rewarding good play, while the sand hills lining the fairways create a set of natural grandstands for spectators, the best of any course on the Open roster. The overriding feedback from every Open is that the course is hard but fair, and it is a consistent favorite with the professionals.

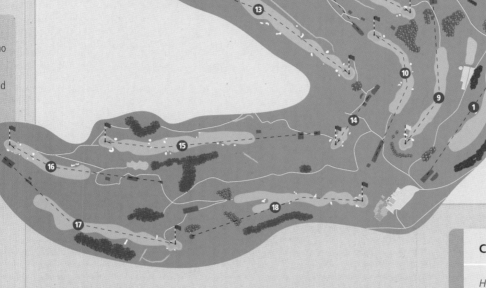

▶ The rough can be brutal for Open week. In 1971 Lee Trevino joked: "... at 15 we put down my bag to hunt for a ball, found the ball, lost the bag!"

LEFT *Overlooking the final green, Royal Birkdale's unique clubhouse resembles an ocean liner, so many of which used to steam past the course on their way out from Liverpool.*

A PROUD MOMENT FOR GOLF

One of golf's great gentlemen, Jack Nicklaus generously conceded a short but missable putt to Tony Jacklin on the 18th green at the climax of the 1969 Ryder Cup at Birkdale, a putt that allowed the home team to tie with the Americans. "I am sure you would have holed, but I was not prepared to see you miss," was Nicklaus's brotherly remark to his opponent.

The difficult 1st, a long, left-hand dogleg, sets the precedent that accurate hitting is key, with out-of-bounds right, the infamous "Jutland" bunker on the left, and characteristic mounds that block approaches to the green from poor positions. Although trees are never a factor in regulation play, they often provide a handsome backdrop, such as when they top the dunes behind the 2nd green, a green cunningly contoured and guarded by pot bunkers.

As with all good designs, planning from the tee is essential to allow the correct approach shot to the green, such as on the tough 6th, on which one must flirt with a huge bunker on the right to leave a decent angle to the elevated green. The holes twist and turn through the dunes allowing the prevailing wind to hit from every angle.

There is good variation to the holes, with short par 4s such as the dogleg 5th and downhill 11th both requiring good management. The greens, which were completely rebuilt by Martin Hawtree in the 1990s, are a fine test, with mounds, hollows, and clever bunkering around them calling for an imaginative short game, summed up by Seve Ballesteros's famous chip-and-run between the bunkers on the 18th in 1976.

CARD OF THE COURSE

Hole	Distance (yards)	Par
1	449	4
2	421	4
3	407	4
4	203	3
5	344	4
6	480	4
7	177	3
8	457	4
9	411	4
Out	3,349	34
10	403	4
11	408	4
12	183	3
13	498	4
14	198	3
15	544	5
16	416	4
17	547	5
18	472	4
In	3,669	36
Total	7,018	70

Royal Liverpool

Royal Liverpool Golf Club, Hoylake, Wirral, England

Founded in 1869, Royal Liverpool (or Hoylake as it is popularly known) is one of England's oldest golf clubs. Golf was first played here alongside amateur horse and pony races, for this was the site of the Liverpool Hunt Club. Naturally, the horses were not expected to charge up and down the sand dunes, so, for the most part, this is an unusually flat course. But appearances can be deceptive, especially here.

In no time at all (1872) Hoylake had attracted its first professional tournament—in fact the first of any significance outside Scotland. The first prize was almost double the prize for the British Open. It attracted a small but distinguished field with Young Tom Morris emerging victorious. Next up was the inaugural Amateur Championship (1885), followed by its first British Open (1897). The winner on this occasion was Royal Liverpool's own Harold Hilton; he and his club companion John Ball were the only amateurs to win the British Open until the emergence of Bob Jones, who won at Hoylake in 1930. This was to become the second leg of his incredible "Impregnable Quadrilateral," when he won the Open and Amateur Championships of the United States and Britain in the same year.

The Open returned to Hoylake several times, but after Roberto de Vicenzo's victory in 1967 there was a lengthy gap until 2006, when Tiger Woods showed everybody else how to play the course.

RIGHT *The 12th green presents a difficult target, raised up on top of the dunes, but it gives wonderful views over the Dee Estuary to the Flintshire hills.*

Woods—the great strategist

As he had done previously at St. Andrews in 2005, Woods analyzed the course from the point of view of his own strengths, deciding that it was too dangerous to use the driver prospectively from the tee. He reckoned that if he played for position rather than length, making sure that his tee shot landed in the best spot from which to approach the green, his long-iron play to the green would get him close to the hole. His approach play that week was imperious.

The order of the holes was altered for the Open, but more usually Hoylake begins with a unique hole, a bunkerless par 4 on which it is possible to drive out of bounds on either side. The green adjoins a "cop" (a grassy bank, typical of Hoylake) which is also out of bounds. Like the first hole, most of the early holes are level, but there is a relentlessness about the probing that never lets up. The wind rarely lets up either.

As the round progresses the character of the course changes gradually until the 8th, when the pitch is made steeply uphill to a rolling green standing on top of the dunes, giving way to a glorious sequence of seaside holes with expansive views. The pick of these must be the 12th, a majestic par 4 beginning with a drive to a low, curving fairway, followed by a long second shot uphill to a brilliantly sited green, repelling all but the finest approaches. Woods solved its problems on the second day of the Open by pitching in for an eagle. His approach, stone dead, on the final afternoon was breathtaking. Great golf on a great course!

▶ For the 2006 Open a number of alterations were made to the course, including a brand new 17th hole (played as the 1st for the championship). The old green was so near to a road that it was not unknown for players to putt out of bounds.

CARD OF THE COURSE

Hole	Distance (yards)	Par
1	429	4
2	372	4
3	528	5
4	202	3
5	453	4
6	423	4
7	198	3
8	534	5
9	393	4
Out	3,532	36
10	448	4
11	198	3
12	456	4
13	161	3
14	554	5
15	459	4
16	560	5
17	454	4
18	436	4
In	3,726	36
Total	7,258	72

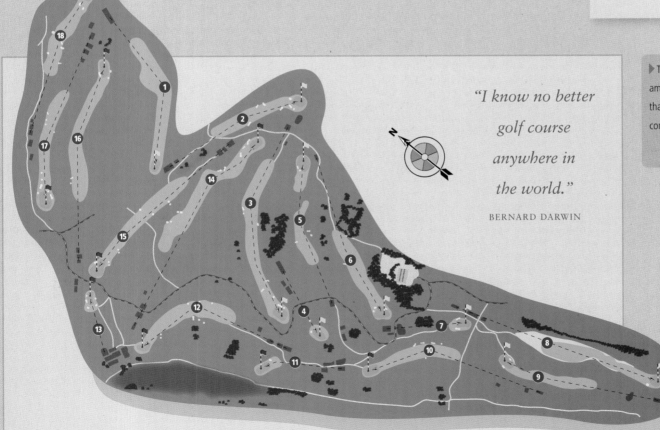

"I know no better golf course anywhere in the world."

BERNARD DARWIN

▶ The 6th hole is unusual among championship courses in that the drive is made over the corner of an orchard.

Royal Lytham

Royal Lytham and St. Annes Golf Club, Lancashire, England

English golf is full of surprises, and one of those surprises has to be Royal Lytham. It lies on a somewhat unprepossessing chunk of land, the Fylde, whose crowning glory is the rather dowdy holiday resort of Blackpool. Hopes are not raised by the immediate surroundings of the club, with neither a sand dune to be seen nor a breaking wave. In fact the club is enclosed by housing and a railroad track. Yet there is no denying that this is one of England's great clubs with one of its finest courses, well worthy of its frequent hosting of the British Open.

Lytham made an auspicious start to its Open career. The year was 1926 and the winner was none other than Bob Jones, the greatest amateur golfer the game has known. No further Opens were held there until after World War II when an illustrious list of champions was produced: Bobby Locke, Peter Thomson, Bob Charles, Tony Jacklin, Gary Player, and Seve Ballesteros (twice). Yet there were no Americans in that group. Amends were made in 1996, 70 years after that first American triumph, when Tom Lehman emerged as champion, reinforced in 2001 when David Duval realized the full potential of his talent.

Each one of those great champions needed abundant grit and determination, for Lytham never lets up. It is a very well-defended course and utterly unforgiving.

EUROPE'S RESURGENCE

When Tony Jacklin won the Open at Lytham in 1969 it proved to be an influential moment in British and European golf, because it signaled the start of a resurgence in self-belief. No longer did the Europeans fear the Americans, Australians, and South Africans who previously had dominated world golf. It paved the way for wins in majors by Sandy Lyle, Ian Woosnam, Seve Ballesteros, Bernhard Langer, José María Olazábal, Nick Faldo, Paul Lawrie, and Padraig Harrington.

Nothing is orthodox at Lytham

That is not to say that Lytham is eccentric—far from it! But it is unusual in opening with a par 3, and to have three par 4s well under 400 yards/366 m on the back nine is far from today's norm. Yet that back nine is fearsome. Scores are made on the way out, more often than not lost on the way home.

Lytham is relentless. For the average player it is probably the most examining of all the Open tests, largely because of its prolific bunkering. As British Open has succeeded British Open and equipment has developed and player prowess grown, new bunkers have had to be added each time in order to stiffen the challenge. The old ones have been left intact. They threaten shots of every length on each hole.

It is an educative experience following great players over the closing holes. Of the 15th hole Jack Nicklaus once exclaimed, "God! It's a hard hole!" The fairway is angled across the line of the drive, narrow and well bunkered. A conservative drive leaves a blind shot, against the wind, to find the green. In 1979 Seve Ballesteros played an amazing recovery shot from a car park to the right of the 16th green for an unlikely birdie on his way to winning the championship. For the rest of us the best approach is from the left.

Bob Jones made an astonishing recovery on the 17th on his final round in 1926, so remarkable a shot that a plaque is set in the ground to the left of the fairway bunkers to commemorate it. With two diagonal lines of bunkers crossing the fairway, the final drive is one of the more nerve-racking in golf, and many a championship has been thrown away on this hole.

LEFT *The clubhouse was built by Woolfall and Eccles of Liverpool, who had recently completed the Royal Liverpool clubhouse. It was to be "a picturesque building, with the introduction of half-timbering."*

CARD OF THE COURSE

Hole	Distance (yards)	Par
1	206	3
2	438	4
3	458	4
4	392	4
5	212	3
6	494	5
7	557	5
8	419	4
9	164	3
Out	3,340	35
10	335	4
11	542	5
12	198	3
13	342	4
14	445	4
15	465	4
16	359	4
17	467	4
18	412	4
In	3,565	36
Total	6,905	71

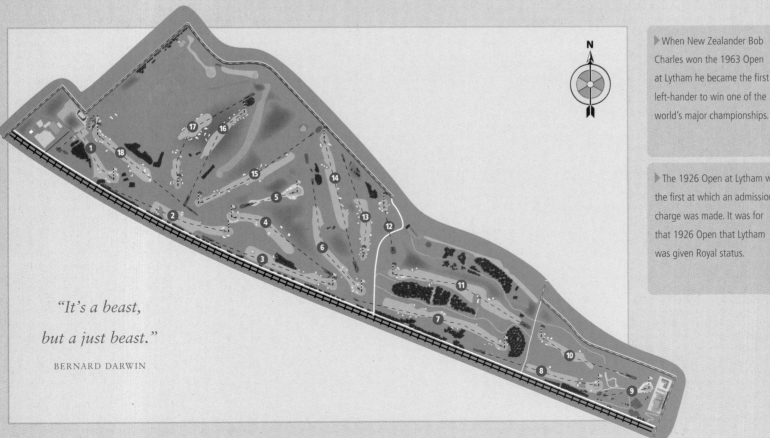

▶ When New Zealander Bob Charles won the 1963 Open at Lytham he became the first left-hander to win one of the world's major championships.

▶ The 1926 Open at Lytham was the first at which an admission charge was made. It was for that 1926 Open that Lytham was given Royal status.

"It's a beast, but a just beast."

BERNARD DARWIN

Royal St. George's

Royal St. George's Golf Club, Sandwich, Kent, England

The British Open was a Scottish monopoly for the first 33 years of its existence, but in 1894 the championship was allowed to be played south of Hadrian's Wall for the very first time. It could hardly have ventured much farther south, for it came to the Kent coast at Sandwich, where the Royal St. George's Golf Club had been established (by two Scotsmen, of course) in 1887.

Our two Scotsmen (Dr. Laidlaw Purves and Henry Lamb) had traveled along much of England's Channel coast in an attempt to find a piece of ground that resembled those of the great links of their native land. They were beginning to despair of ever discovering what they were searching for, when—at Sandwich—they found a wild, tumbling wilderness in which an exciting and exceedingly challenging course could be built.

A natural course

On such land, Purves and Lamb had no need to engage in lengthy earthmoving. It was merely a matter of finding as varied a routing out and back as they could through, across, and along the dunes. They did such a good job that the course follows much the same route today. There have been changes, though, not least the elimination of blind shots and one particularly blind par 3—the Maiden.

RIGHT *The 6th green, right in the heart of some of the finest duneland on earth. Farther along the shore lies Prince's Golf Club, host to the 1932 British Open.*

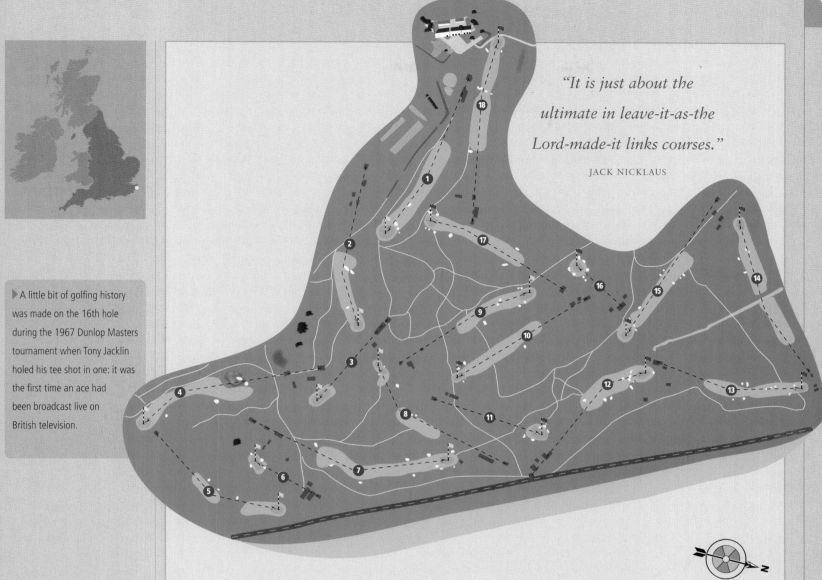

"It is just about the ultimate in leave-it-as-the Lord-made-it links courses."

JACK NICKLAUS

▶ A little bit of golfing history was made on the 16th hole during the 1967 Dunlop Masters tournament when Tony Jacklin holed his tee shot in one: it was the first time an ace had been broadcast live on British television.

CARD OF THE COURSE

Hole	Distance (yards)	Par	Hole	Distance (yards)	Par
1	441	4	10	413	4
2	413	4	11	240	3
3	210	3	12	380	4
4	494	4	13	459	4
5	421	4	14	551	5
6	172	3	15	478	4
7	530	5	16	163	3
8	455	4	17	425	4
9	389	4	18	468	4
Out	3,525	35	In	3,577	35
			Total	7,102	70

Of all the British Open courses it is Sandwich that feels the most removed from everyday life, the clubhouse sitting as it were in the fields at the end of a track. And that sense of remoteness continues on the opening hole, striking out into the wide expanses, long and far. On the 4th the first-time visitor might be somewhat perplexed at the prospect from the tee, for a giant sand dune bars the way to the distant fairway, and in its face are set two of the most fearsome bunkers imaginable. It is the beginning of a wonderful sequence of holes taking play to the sea shore.

There is respite of a kind around the turn, but the run home from the 14th is the stuff of white knuckles. Indeed, that 14th has ruined many an Open aspirant's chances, with an out-of-bounds wall keeping worryingly close company with the fairway all the way to the green. (Prince's Golf Club, venue for the 1932 British Open, won by Gene Sarazen, lies on the other side of that wall.) Sturdy hitting is required to surmount the difficulties of the three remaining long two-shot holes, very exposed to the wind as they are, yet the delicate 16th is no pushover, despite its being the shortest hole on the course.

Sunningdale

Old Course, Sunningdale Golf Club, Berkshire, England

Membership of Sunningdale Golf Club is one of the most sought after in England. First and foremost it is a true members' club, with a wonderful spirit and atmosphere to be found in the clubhouse and on the course. Additionally, Sunningdale is one of those few privileged clubs to possess two equally great courses, the Old and the New. Having been at the forefront of English golf for over a century there is also a great sense of tradition and history.

When golf was first introduced to England in 1608, the game was played on the short, links-like grasses of Blackheath. Scots had brought the game with them when they traveled south with their recently crowned king, James I of England, James VI of Scotland. Hardly surprisingly, they sought the nearest thing they could find to linksland on which to play their golf. Having found Blackheath they did not need to look elsewhere. They had no cause to travel into the county of Surrey, which was then heavily forested with few towns, so they never discovered the golfing potential that awaited some 20 miles/32 km from the center of London.

In fact it was not until the last two decades of the 19th century that golf took root in this part of England, assisted in no small part by the coming of the railroads and the invention of commuting. The mainly professional people who moved into the country from London—the doctors, lawyers, bankers, and stockbrokers—began to establish golf clubs where they lived. To their delight they found that the land here, on a sandbelt stretching from Berkshire through Surrey to Hampshire and West Sussex, could provide them with ideal ground for firm and fast golf, a world away from golfing on the damp and heavy clays of London.

THE PERFECT ROUND

Qualifying rounds for the British Open in 1926 were held at Sunningdale, where Bob Jones recorded a 66 and a 68—a performance described by Bernard Darwin as "incredible and indecent." His 66 (33 out, 33 in) included 33 putts and 33 other shots, and each hole was a three or a four. It was described at the time as the finest round of golf ever shot in Britain.

LEFT *The par-5 10th, one of the most handsome holes on a notably attractive course. Park and Colt used the topography of Sunningdale admirably.*

Sunningdale leads the way

Although there were already a number of established golf courses in the area, Sunningdale set a new standard when it opened for play in 1901, and from the start the whole venture was heavily publicized. The course was designed by the former British Open champion, Willie Park Jr., and he sought to reproduce the features of links golf that had, so far, been largely missing from inland golf in England. Golfers were required to think in a very different way, to plot their way round a series of subtle, not coarse, challenges.

BELOW RIGHT *The 17th hole, and beyond it the 18th, leading to Sunningdale's fine clubhouse. These two strong par 4s provide the climax of an excellent finish.*

CARD OF THE COURSE					
Hole	Distance (yards)	Par	Hole	Distance (yards)	Par
1	494	5	10	478	5
2	489	5	11	325	4
3	319	4	12	451	4
4	161	3	13	185	3
5	419	4	14	509	5
6	415	4	15	226	3
7	402	4	16	438	4
8	182	3	17	421	4
9	273	4	18	432	4
Out	3,154	36	In	3,465	36
			Total	6,619	72

Park was perhaps unlucky in that his design work coincided with the demise of the old guttie ball and the arrival of the new Haskell ball with its increased performance. The club, however, was far from unlucky in having appointed Harry Colt as its inaugural secretary. He it was who rebuilt the course in the 1920s into what we know today, adding the equally good New Course at the same time.

Playing Sunningdale Old Course is a complete experience, with a magical routing making superb use of every natural feature available to the architect to give the golfer pause for thought. These are not greens to be blitzed with lob wedges. Rather, the ball needs to be caressed into and on to the putting surface. There are holes of all lengths and sizes, giving great change of pace and requiring wisdom on every tee, for drive in the wrong area and there is little hope of stopping the next shot on the green. As you would expect at such a club, both Sunningdale courses are always presented in perfect condition.

Wentworth

Wentworth

West Course, Wentworth Club, Virginia Water, Surrey, England

Driving through the vast Wentworth Estate is a voyage of discovery. The mansions of the rich and famous line the lanes and drives, many of them backing on to the fairways of the three golf courses that occasionally cross the roads, causing the driver to stop while a four-ball launches its tee shots on their journeys.

ABOVE *Wentworth's West Course is as visually attractive as it is demanding. It is one of those courses that invites you to play good shots. This is the par-3 2nd.*

The Wentworth Estate came into being in the 1920s through the vision, entrepreneurial skills and extraordinary confidence of a developer—George Tarrant. When it came to constructing the golf courses, Tarrant knew exactly who to use—Harry Colt. Colt and Tarrant had collaborated on a similar scheme some years earlier at St, George's Hill, and the success of both ventures has ensured that both are among the most desirable places to live in the whole London area.

Colt built the East Course in 1924. Today it measures only a little over 6,000 yards/5,486 m, but it is a thoroughly entertaining course and was good enough to host a match between the professionals of America and Great Britain and Ireland in 1926, thus paving the way for the Ryder Cup. The East was also the venue for the inaugural Curtis Cup, between women amateur golfers of the United States and Great Britain and Ireland, in 1932. Second up was the West Course, also Colt-designed, of 1926. There was then a gap of over 60 years until the third course, the Edinburgh, opened in 1990. This was designed by John Jacobs in association with Gary Player and Bernard Gallagher.

The Burma Road

When it opened, the West Course was found to be long and hard, tough enough for it to be dubbed the Burma Road. Its length is not so fearsome today but the name has stuck and twice a year television audiences get to see it in fine condition, hosting the PGA Championship in the spring and the World Matchplay in the fall. Recent adjustments to the course by Ernie Els (who lives on the estate) have pushed the overall length up from just over 7,000 yards/ 6,400 m to more than 7,300 yards/6,675 m. Visitors playing it from the yellow tees still find it quite long enough at over 6,700 yards/6,125 m.

Length is not everything, however, and some of the best holes are modest on paper. The delightful 154-yard/141-m 2nd, for instance, is played from a high tee across a road to an elusive ledge green. The 6th, 7th, and 8th are each among the shorter par 4s, but their greens are notoriously hard to locate. The short 14th is played uphill to a multi-level green, the hill being steep enough to deceive the eye, and club selection further complicated if there is a wind. Similarly, the 16th regularly sets problems for the professionals under tournament conditions.

A new tee has been found for the 17th, stretching it to a monstrous—and treacherous—610 yards/558 m. It is all too easy to drive out of bounds on the left, so the natural reaction is to err to the right, increasing the length of the hole and very probably resulting in a clinging lie, or even finishing behind a tree. Nor is the green easy to find, on high ground, the fairway constantly curving. The Els-modified 18th is now a particularly strong finishing hole.

▶ In addition to the PGA Championship and World Matchplay, the West Course has hosted the Ryder Cup (1953) and the Canada Cup (1956), when Ben Hogan made one of his all-too-rare visits to the U.K., winning the tournament with Sam Snead as partner.

CARD OF THE COURSE

Hole	Distance (yards)	Par
1	473	5
2	154	3
3	465	4
4	552	5
5	212	3
6	418	4
7	396	4
8	401	4
9	452	4
Out	3,523	36
10	184	3
11	416	4
12	531	5
13	470	4
14	179	3
15	490	4
16	383	4
17	610	5
18	538	5
In	3,801	37
Total	7,324	73

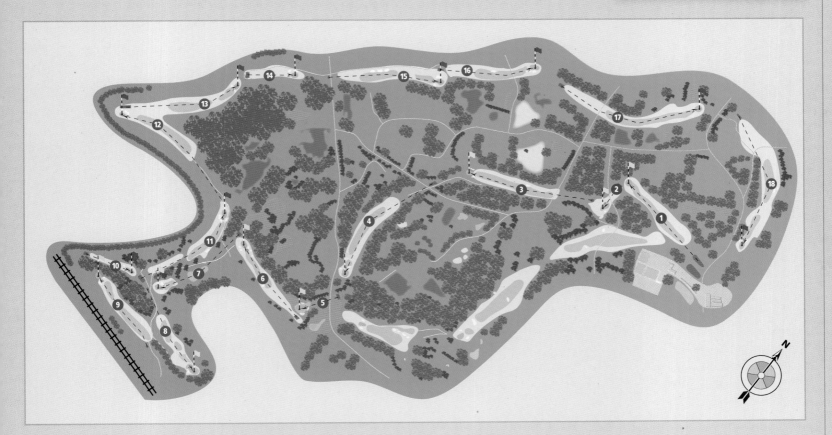

Woodhall Spa

Woodhall Spa

Hotchkin Course, Woodhall Spa, Lincolnshire, England

Of all Britain's great courses the Hotchkin Course at Woodhall Spa must be the least known—for the very simple reason that it lies in a remote corner of the country, not really on the way to or from anywhere. Despite its inviting title, Woodhall Spa is little more than a charming village, but it has had a golf course since 1890.

The club had rather a troubled history, and the local landowner, Stafford Vere Hotchkin, repeatedly came to the rescue, first by writing off the club's rent arrears and in 1919 by buying the club. After a succession of moves and different course layouts, the club was lucky enough to possess, by this time, a fine Harry Colt course laid out on a rare tract of sandy heath. But Hotchkin was not merely a financial benefactor, he was also a more than competent golfer and a course designer himself. Between 1919 and his death in 1953 he made a large number of refinements to the design, turning the course into one of England's most demanding. Hotchkin's son Neil continued to run the club after his father's death, which ensured that the design was not tampered with and Hotchkin's ethos maintained. In 1995 he sold the course to the English Golf Union, who made their headquarters there, bringing in Donald Steel to build a second—and utterly different—course (the Bracken), while keeping Hotchkin's course in the manner of which he would have approved.

RIGHT *The bunkering at Woodhall Spa is among the most formidable in Britain. It is deep, steep-faced, and prolific. This is the 5th green, surrounded by sand.*

▶ One of Hotchkin's principles of golf course design was: "The best results are obtained by making a course conform to the natural surroundings that already exist, so that it will not look artificial and fail to blend with the landscape." Woodhall Spa is a shining example.

▶ Because of its location Woodhall Spa has staged few professional tournaments, but it has featured prominently in the amateur calendar, hosting such tournaments as the English Amateur, Brabazon Trophy, St. Andrews Trophy, and Ladies' British Open Amateur.

N

▶ During a club match in 1982 a member holed the 12th in one—as, then, did his opponent, for the half!

CARD OF THE COURSE

Hole	Distance (yards)	Par	Hole	Distance (yards)	Par
1	361	4	10	338	4
2	442	4	11	437	4
3	415	4	12	172	3
4	414	4	13	451	4
5	148	3	14	521	5
6	526	5	15	321	4
7	470	4	16	395	4
8	209	3	17	336	4
9	584	5	18	540	5
Out	3,569	36	In	3,511	37
			Total	7,080	73

England's most frightening bunkers?

Until you have played Woodhall Spa it is difficult to imagine just how ferocious its bunkers are. It is a moot point whether Ganton or Woodhall Spa has the most savage bunkering in England. Ganton's are more visible and perhaps more frightening to the eye. Woodhall Spa's bunkers are deeper—sinister trenches very often topped off with eyebrows of heather—and sometimes invisible. A bunker may be as deep as the height of a man. In some cases these are set tight against elevated greens and you may have to raise the ball 10 feet/3 m vertically to gain the safety of the putting surface. The strange thing is that Ganton and Woodhall Spa are such lovely courses that, however roughly they may treat you, you still enjoy the experience immensely.

Woodhall Spa charms you from the outset, with a delicate, short two-shot hole to get play under way. You could be lulled into a false sense of security, but on the 2nd hole the course bares its teeth, with the deepest of bunkers threatening the drive of all lengths of hitters, and the green has a narrow entrance. And if a bunker does not get you the heather most surely will. It may look lovely, but a rash shot out of it may result in a broken wrist.

What makes Woodhall Spa so enticing is the wonderful variety of the holes, with no two the same. There are great long two-shotters, but it may be the collection of par 3s (only three of them) that remain in the memory longest.

Woodhall Spa

IN TUNE WITH NATURE

The Hotchkin Course occupies a valuable piece of heathland, a habitat that is disappearing all too quickly in Britain. It has, therefore, been designated as a Site of Special Scientific Interest. The National Golf Centre works in partnership with Natural England to manage the land to help preserve its biodiversity. It is an ongoing project and will, in time, restore more of the original heathland, removing plants and trees that are not natural to the heath. At the same time, long-lost bunkers and other features from the earlier courses are being discovered and brought back into action.

RIGHT *There is a timeless quality to golf at Woodhall Spa, a sense of getting away from it all, and this old ruined tower recalls an age long before golf.*

Celtic Manor

Twenty Ten Course, Celtic Manor Resort, Newport, Wales

The golf courses at Celtic Manor, host to the Ryder Cup in 2010, are contemporary in every way, but the ground over which they run is steeped in ancient history. They overlook the remains of the Roman town of Caerleon and, running from it, the Via Julia was an important communication route connecting this Welsh outpost to the Roman settlements in England. Its remains cross the Celtic Manor estate.

In the 5th century the lands were acquired by the Bishops of Llandaff and in the 17th century a manor house was built for the local high sheriff. But the estate as it now is first took shape in the 1860s when the enormously prosperous industrialist, Thomas Powell, had Coldra House built for his son. Subsequently the house became a maternity hospital. It closed in 1975 and was in danger of falling into ruin until a wealthy businessman, Sir Terry Matthews, bought it in 1981, restoring it for use initially as a small luxury hotel. Since then the story has been one of considerable expansion. The hotel can now accommodate almost 2,000 conference delegates and in 1995 golf arrived on the scene in the shape of the Roman Road Course, which, as its name suggests, keeps close company with the Via Julia.

The Roman Road Course was designed by one of the legends of golf course design, Robert Trent Jones, who in his 70-year career built over 300 courses, including the Ryder Cup venue, Valderrama, in Spain, and made alterations to a further 150. Jones returned to Celtic Manor to build a short course, Coldra Woods, and later to team up with his son, Robert Jr., to lay out the enormously long Wentwood Hills Course—an extraordinary mix of alpine holes and others that might have been lifted bodily from Florida, with the obligatory lakes to the fore in the lowland section.

Bold decisions

Matthews was ambitious for his resort. He wanted to attract the biggest stars in the game to play there and he set out to bring the Ryder Cup to Wales for the first time. His problem was that none of his existing courses could accommodate such a tournament. Roman Road was not tough enough and Wentwood Hills was spectator-unfriendly, with an exhausting hill climb required on the back nine. Drastic measures were needed, and Matthews was not afraid to take bold decisions.

The boldest decision was to abandon the Wentwood Hills Course, considered the jewel in the crown of the resort. It has not been wasted, for the upland holes have been incorporated in a new course designed by Colin Montgomerie, and nine of the low-lying holes have been retained as part of the course specifically designed to attract the Ryder Cup, lying entirely in the Usk Valley. Matthews's brave move was successful, and the Ryder Cup matches will be played in Wales for the first time in 2010, on this course now known as the Twenty Ten.

As might be expected, it is a heroic course playing to almost 7,500 yards/ 6,858 m from the back tees. For those matches that make it to the par-5 18th hole—one of three par 5s over 600 yards/549 m—there remains a death-or-glory gamble on whether to try to reach the green in two across a green-front lake. Roman gladiators would have understood the pressures; Ryder Cup spectators will relish the contest.

▶ Thomas Powell, founder of the Powell-Duffryn Company and the world's first millionaire, employed 13,500 workers in his coal business, 11,600 of them working underground.

LEFT *The tranquillity of the Usk Valley will become a cauldron of high emotion when the Ryder Cup matches are played at Celtic Manor. This is the 14th.*

CARD OF THE COURSE

Hole	Distance (yards)	Par
1	465	4
2	610	5
3	189	3
4	461	4
5	457	4
6	452	4
7	213	3
8	439	4
9	666	5
Out	3,952	36
10	210	3
11	562	5
12	458	4
13	189	3
14	413	4
15	377	4
16	508	4
17	211	3
18	613	5
In	3,541	35
Total	7,493	71

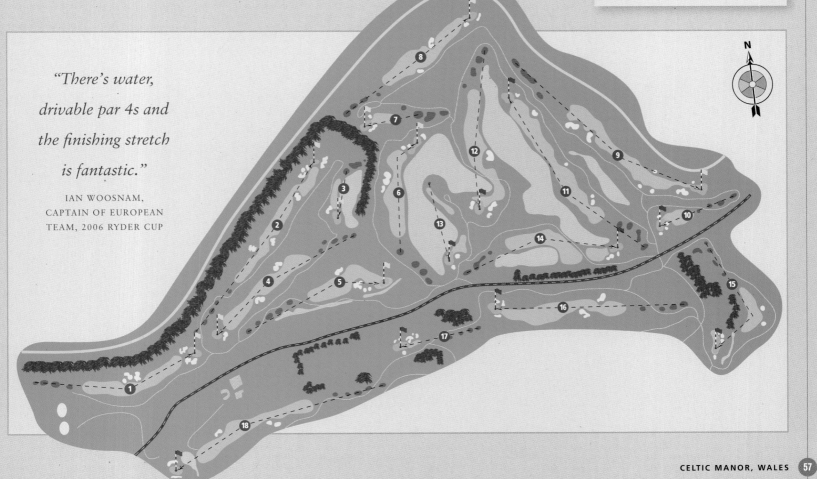

"There's water, drivable par 4s and the finishing stretch is fantastic."

IAN WOOSNAM,
CAPTAIN OF EUROPEAN
TEAM, 2006 RYDER CUP

Pennard

Pennard Golf Club, Southgate, Swansea, West Glamorgan, Wales

Pennard might seem an odd bedfellow for the many longer championship tests in this book, but it claims its place on merit. It is wonderfully scenic, full of character, quirky, and, most of all, enormous fun. What is more, it is a links course yet it is not on a level with the beach but high on the cliffs of the Gower Peninsula overlooking Oxwich Bay.

The club has been in existence since 1896, but it was not until 1908 that James Braid was first called in to lay out an 18-hole course. He returned to make amendments and improvements in 1911, 1920, and 1931. C. K. Cotton and Donald Steel have made significant alterations since then, but the bulk of the course remains Braid's work. Braid's genius was in locating so many very playable holes on such a humpy-bumpy site, nor was he afraid of the unorthodox, which is why the individual holes remain firmly in the mind long after the round is over.

There is never a dull moment on the course, simply because the ground on which it was built has so much movement to it. Even the 1st hole, striking inland away from the sea, is uplifting, with its crinkled fairway down which a long drive is required to get a view of the pin. And the 2nd, the shortest of short holes, is no pushover.

Between church and state

One of Pennard's finest stretches begins on the 6th, which overlooks the ruins of 12th-century Pennard Castle. The 7th, many people's favorite hole, threads a course between the castle and the ruins of a 13th-century church. Heady stuff! Both have brilliantly sited greens. They are followed by another pair of good two-shotters, the 9th being somewhat demanding with its left-turning route countered by its right-leaning fairway.

A par-5, the 10th involves a welcoming downhill drive but a stream crosses the fairway where long hitters would prefer it did not, and there is an uphill approach to the green, made harder by the presence of very visible bunkers. The short 11th is not a Braid hole, but one found by C. K. Cotton in 1965. It is played across a valley to a narrow shelf-green and there are no marks for coming up short. Another

excellent short hole comes at the 13th, again played across a valley to a hilltop green, and there is a lovely view of the castle on its sandy hill to be had from it.

Braid's favorite hole was the 14th, with its drive along a very bouncy fairway and an approach played so steeply uphill that it is like pitching into the sky. Incidentally, in Braid's era there was far less rough than there is today, being instead treacherous exposed sand. Cattle and sheep keep the rough grass in check nowadays. The most spectacular hole is yet to come. It is the 16th, with its magical green position right on the edge of the cliffs overlooking the sea. Incomparable!

▶ One-time Pennard professional Gus Faulkner, father of future British Open champion Max Faulkner, was given permission to shoot rabbits on the course—before 10 a.m.

▶ In the January 1928 edition of *Golf Illustrated*, Sir Ernest Holderness cited the 13th (Castle) as one of the finest holes in Britain.

▶ The distinguished golfer, Vicki Thomas, was a member of Pennard. She played in no fewer than six British Curtis Cup teams.

LEFT *For many, their favorite hole at Pennard is the 7th. What makes Pennard such fun is that the ground has so much character, with never a dull moment.*

CARD OF THE COURSE

Hole	Distance (yards)	Par	Hole	Distance (yards)	Par
1	449	4	10	492	5
2	145	3	11	180	3
3	365	4	12	298	4
4	517	5	13	196	3
5	165	3	14	368	4
6	400	4	15	165	3
7	351	4	16	493	5
8	357	4	17	488	5
9	437	4	18	399	4
Out	3,186	35	In	3,079	36
			Total	6,265	71

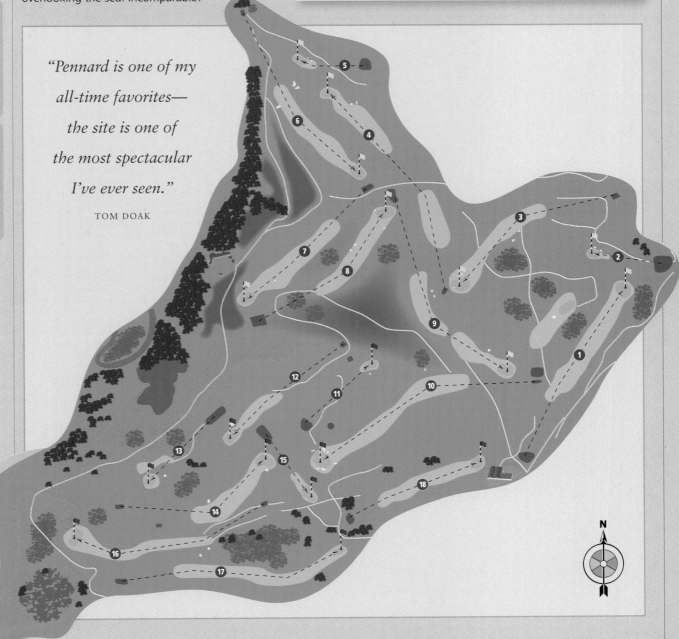

"Pennard is one of my all-time favorites— the site is one of the most spectacular I've ever seen."

TOM DOAK

Royal County Down

Royal County Down Golf Club, Newcastle, County Down, Northern Ireland

On the coast of Dundrum Bay, backed by the Mourne Mountains, 18 holes weave purposefully through dunes and gorse to create, in the words of Tom Watson, "a pure links." For over 100 years, Old Tom Morris's routing has changed little, and as such there is a sense that the course has always been here, quietly tucked away in this beautifully unassuming place.

Don't be mistaken in assuming that the age and tradition of the course have left it obsolete in today's game. Though quite capable of hosting major tournaments, Royal County Down has opted to avoid these events, fearing that the course and indigenous wildlife would suffer from trampling spectators and media villages—the Senior British Open and Walker Cup are the biggest events of recent times. It is especially impressive, therefore, that many great players have made the pilgrimage to this wonderful course simply to experience it. Famously, Tiger Woods has chosen these holes to sharpen his links skills before a British Open.

A perfect nine?

The front nine is commonly regarded as the best front nine in golf (not to say that the back nine is shabby). A great starting hole, the par-5 1st is reachable in two, but one must carry the ball long down the left-hand side to take advantage of the sloping fairway, which bounds the ball forward toward the green. As poor drives are punished, with dunes on both sides and the beach on the right, this hole sets the precedent that control is a necessity. Another somewhat daunting feature during the round is that of playing tee shots over dunes, blind or semi-blind.

After the first couple of drives, which play in the same direction over intimidating hills, when guests reach the 4th tee members often allow them to set up with driver aiming over the dune before pointing out that this is a par 3 played in the opposite direction! Looking in the correct direction from this elevated tee, one is blessed by a gorgeous view of the mountains and sea, but the player can also see the countless challenges ahead. After a carry over gorse bushes, nine brutish bunkers surround a green with large drop-offs to both sides and the back.

Possibly the best hole on the back nine is the 13th. Bunkers plague the dogleg on the right-hand side, and a decent hit down the left is rewarded with lengthy run on the mounds of the firm fairway. If the drive is too short, sight of the green is blocked by the gorse-banked dune on the dogleg. The broad, sloping green is nestled among dunes to create its own amphitheater, backed by swathes of lilac heather. The strength of holes like this, coupled with picturesque scenery and legendary hospitality, have led Royal County Down to a consistent ranking as one of the world's Top 10 courses.

LEFT *Slieve Donard, the highest of the Mourne Mountains, overlooks Dundrum Bay and the historic Royal County Down links. This is the excellent 3rd hole, viewed from behind the green.*

▶ In 1933, in the Irish Open Amateur Championship, Eric Fiddian recorded two holes-in-one in the final, yet still lost.

CARD OF THE COURSE

Hole	Distance (yards)	Par
1	539	5
2	444	4
3	477	4
4	213	3
5	440	4
6	398	4
7	145	3
8	430	4
9	486	4
Out	3,572	35
10	197	3
11	440	4
12	527	5
13	444	4
14	212	3
15	467	4
16	337	4
17	435	4
18	550	5
In	3,609	36
Total	7,181	71

BELOW *The bunkers at Royal County Down are serious, both in expanse and depth. Many are topped off by eyebrows of heather or clinging rough grass. These threaten the drive at the 8th.*

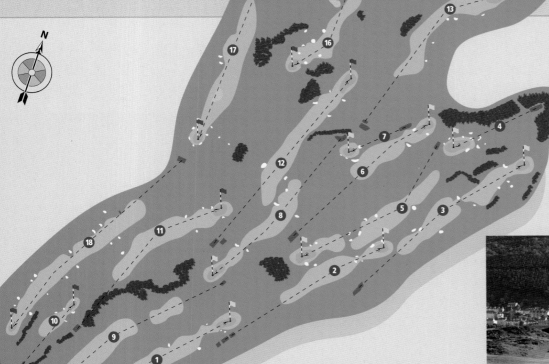

"For visual splendor and golf on a heroic scale, there is nothing better."

DONALD STEEL, *CLASSIC GOLF LINKS OF GREAT BRITAIN AND IRELAND*

Royal Portrush

Dunluce Links, Royal Portrush Golf Club, County Antrim, Northern Ireland

The Dunluce course at Portrush is the only course outside Great Britain to have staged the British Open, which it did once, in 1951, with the dapper Max Faulkner emerging victorious. There is little doubt that the course could still examine the world's best, but the infrastructure of this beautiful corner of Northern Ireland simply could not cope with the huge numbers of visitors, golfers, spectators, and the media that a modern British Open brings.

Royal Portrush is an old club, founded as the County Club in 1888, but its two fine courses (the other being the Valley course) owe their distinction to Harry Colt, who rebuilt and re-routed Old Tom Morris's original course in 1932. What Colt did was golf architecture at its simplest. He noted the parallel lines of sand dunes and routed the holes along the defining valleys between them. His genius, however, was to choose the optimum locations for tees and greens. Indeed, these greens are some of the most testing to find in top-class links golf, despite their having a mere handful of bunkers

guarding them. As a result of Colt's cunning use of the shapes of the dunes, none of the par 4s and 5s from the 2nd to the 16th is straight. They all bend one way or another. Dunluce Links is, then, one of the most demanding driving courses in British golf.

A mounting sense of expectation

Even before you reach the course anticipation is eager, the twisting road running along the magnificent rocky coast of County Antrim, past the Giant's Causeway and the ruins of

RIGHT *Colt took full advantage of the nature of the ground at Portrush to create brilliantly sited (and defended) greens, such as the 13th. The Dunluce needs, therefore, fewer bunkers than most other comparable courses.*

Dunluce Castle. Suddenly, round a bend, you espy the courses for the first time, and the sight is thrilling. Even the most experienced links golfer cannot fail to be excited by the tumbling nature of the ground and the broad seascape.

The course, too, builds over the first few holes, until on the 5th tee you stand overlooking a distant fairway angled away to the right towards a green located on the very edge of the Atlantic Ocean. Visually, it is a stunning hole, but already the screw is being turned. That hole had no need of bunkers, nor do two of the best short holes, the 6th and 14th. A full carry over inhospitable low ground is required to reach the plateau green of the 6th, the hole that carries the name of its architect, Harry Colt.

Calamity is the name of the 14th, probably the most famous hole at Portrush. It is an appropriate name if you come up short or, worse, down in the abyss on the right—woe betide those plagued by a slice. This hole is perhaps as near as you can get to a dogleg par 3! You have to aim left and allow the ground in front of the green to feed the ball to the right. A good, traditional ground-game shot is what is required here, and at a little over 200 yards/183 m a sound technique is demanded. Foozling does not work at Portrush!

▶ The Senior British Open Championship was held at Royal Portrush in 1995. It was won by Brian Barnes, the son-in-law of Max Faulkner, winner of the British Open on the same course in 1951.

▶ Inspired by a new putter, Max Faulkner led the field after the second round and was flamboyantly signing autographs "Open Champion 1951." Despite tempting fate so extravagantly, he did indeed go on to win.

CARD OF THE COURSE

Hole	Distance (yards)	Par	Hole	Distance (yards)	Par
1	392	4	10	478	5
2	505	5	11	170	3
3	155	3	12	392	4
4	457	4	13	386	4
5	384	4	14	210	3
6	189	3	15	365	4
7	431	4	16	428	4
8	384	4	17	548	5
9	475	5	18	469	4
Out	3,372	36	In	3,446	36
			Total	6,818	72

"Portrush is flying golf— one longs to take off after the ball."

PATRIC DICKINSON,
A ROUND OF GOLF COURSES

Ballybunion

The Old Course, Ballybunion, County Kerry, Republic of Ireland

A round of golf on the Old Course at Ballybunion is a unique experience. None other than Tom Watson would agree. He was very much responsible for alerting the world to the existence of this extraordinary place, which was largely unknown outside Ireland when he first visited in 1981. Now acknowledged as one of the world's greatest courses, many a star golfer has made the pilgrimage to play it.

Ballybunion is a long-established club, founded in 1893 in the far west of Ireland on a stretch of quite incomparable dunes overlooking the Atlantic Ocean. There are many golf courses in the west of Ireland set on dunes overlooking the Atlantic, but what sets Ballybunion apart is the way the course is routed over, through, across, and along the dunes. So the golfer is asked to play a huge catalog of different shots throughout the round to adapt to the constantly changing topography.

BELOW *The full might, majesty, dominion, and power of Ballybunion, as portrayed by the conjunction of the wonderfully sited 10th green and beyond it the magical 11th fairway.*

COASTAL EROSION

It is the stuff of nightmares—seeing your course washed away by the unstoppable power of the sea. The venerable Olympic Club in San Francisco lost a number of holes to the Pacific Ocean some years ago. Ballybunion, too, faced the prospect of losing some of its finest holes to the Atlantic Ocean in the 1970s. An appeal was launched, and that was when Ballybunion found that it had friends, generous ones, all over the world. With the threat of global warming raising sea levels, erosion is on many clubs' agendas throughout the world.

Natural hazards

The Old Course excites golfers of all abilities. The round starts ominously, for there is a graveyard awaiting the merest slice from the 1st tee, and from here to the corner of the dogleg on the 6th the course slides into gear rather as an Irish morning slowly gathers momentum. At this point the adrenaline kicks in, with a delicious pitch up to a green on top of the dunes, the first of a series of greens that seriously tests every department of the approach game. This hole has no need of a bunker and, once away from the opening (inland) holes, there are remarkably few bunkers on the course as a whole. Such is the brilliance of the green sites that grassy swales and fall-aways protect the holes even more strongly than sand would.

Indeed, one of the finest holes on the course—one of the world's great holes—has no bunker, either. It is the unforgettable 11th, a gorgeous hole tumbling down through the sand hills alongside the Atlantic with a green cleverly defended by encircling dunes. There are great holes still to come, but it was the short 8th that particularly appealed to Watson on his first visit, with an all-or-nothing shot to a tiny green and desperate recovery work required should the tee shot fail to hold the putting surface.

Ballybunion boasts back-to-back par 3s on the inward half, the 14th and 15th. Like every hole here, they were dictated naturally by the exciting land forms, and the 15th is a great short hole, played to a marvelous green backed by the Atlantic Ocean. Then the excellent 16th and 17th both make excursions to the oceanside. Ballybunion should be on every golfer's must-play list.

▶ Ballybunion was enlarged into an 18-hole course in 1926. The "designer" was a Mr. Smyth. His layout was so good that when Tom Simpson was engaged to upgrade it in 1937 he suggested only three minor changes.

▶ Ballybunion is so far from any major population center that it has hosted the Irish Open only once, in 2000. Sweden's Patrik Sjöland emerged victorious after opening rounds of 64 and 65.

CARD OF THE COURSE

Hole	Distance (yards)	Par
1	392	4
2	445	4
3	220	3
4	498	5
5	508	5
6	364	4
7	423	4
8	153	3
9	454	4
Out	3,457	36
10	359	4
11	449	4
12	192	3
13	484	5
14	131	3
15	216	3
16	490	5
17	385	4
18	379	4
In	3,085	35
Total	6,542	71

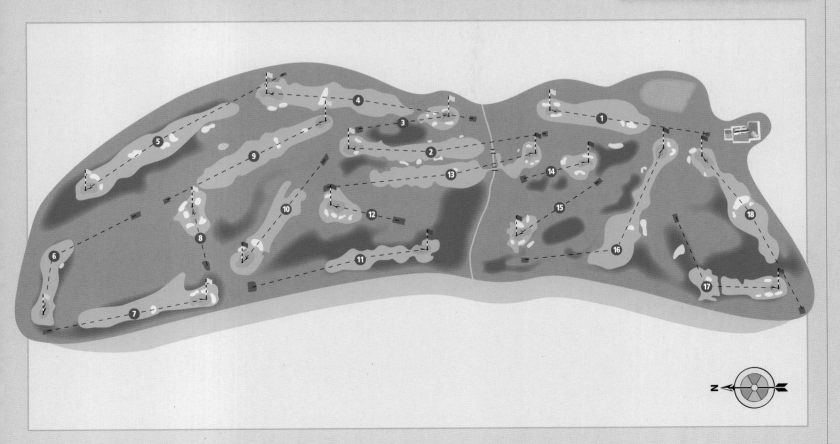

FINEST PIECE OF LINKSLAND

In the late 1960s the decision was taken to purchase further duneland to the south of the existing links. By 1980 sufficient funds had been raised to consider building a second course, and Robert Trent Jones was approached. He wrote, "I was given both a once-in-a-lifetime opportunity and a terrifying challenge . . . the property I had to work with is perhaps the finest piece of linksland in the world." In 1984 the Cashen Course was completed, but it is proving to be controversial. Jones made spectacular use of the site, but the course is too hard for higher-handicap players. That said, the Cashen possesses a fabulous collection of green sites, and Ballybunion as a whole offers a wonderful test of approach work.

RIGHT *Tom Watson rated the 11th "one of the toughest holes in the world . . . a small target with not a lot of room to miss right or left."*

The K Club

The K Club

The K Club, Straffan, County Kildare, Republic of Ireland

With Irish golf going from strength to strength in recent years, the K Club was a fitting venue for the 2006 Ryder Cup. Roared on by hoards of supporters, the golf was often inspired, not least Scott Verplank's hole-in-one on the 14th. But it was Europe who came to the fore, eventually equaling the record-winning margin of 18½ to 9½. The K Club will be remembered for these emotional scenes for many years to come.

Although most of the golf played at the K Club is medal or resort play, the course seems particularly suited to matchplay events. The majority of matches finish on the 16th and 17th holes and the Arnold Palmer design is strong at this point. It should be added that for professional tournaments the holes are played in a different order from the day-to-day routing. So what is normally the 7th plays as the 16th during events such as the Ryder Cup. Interestingly, on such occasions the length is reduced from a possible 600 yards/549 m to something around 570 yards/521 m or less in order to encourage players to go for the green in two, requiring a daring shot across the River Liffey. The 17th, too, is a treacherous, riverside hole calling for strong nerves, particularly on the approach shot, while the 18th is a par 5 that must be reckoned as a two-shot hole for the professionals, with a demanding approach to be played over a lake.

Palmer's cavalier style

Arnold Palmer's playing style was exciting to watch. He never ducked a challenge and he was not afraid of taking risks. Many holes at the K Club work on the risk-and-reward basis, and this makes for particularly fascinating golf in matchplay. Throughout the course, forward thinking and accurate execution will be rewarded with better lines to greens and shorter carries over trouble. But there are also holes requiring a little less finesse and a bit more Arnold Palmer! "Arnold's Pick" is the name of the 4th, and this par 5 can be played cautiously as a three-shot hole, but there is a suitably aggressive option as well. Requiring a hefty carry over a bunker-strewn hill, the Palmer line is fraught with danger, but is rewarded with a shot at the well-bunkered green.

With hole after hole of lush grass, clear waters, and mature trees, it is difficult to believe that the course was completed only in 1991. The fertile soils of Kildare produce the notably lush grass that has also made the county so popular for racehorse breeders. The famous Irish rain is obviously a contributory factor to this fertility, and the River Liffey and the many ponds and lakes on the course provide great fishing for the guests of the 5-star resort, and many a golfing hazard. In fact, given the perfect conditions and the rich history of the Kildare gentry who can trace their history back over 1,500 years, it is almost surprising that the K Club was not created earlier.

With tournament play of the highest caliber, bolstered by a second Palmer course in a more links style that also hosts European Tour events, it is clear that the K Club is making up for lost time.

▶ Colin Montgomerie led out the singles matches in 2006, maintaining his unbeaten record of eight straight Ryder Cup singles. The Europeans followed his example, dominating the singles and winning a third consecutive victory.

LEFT *Played as the 8th hole in the Ryder Cup, this treacherous short hole is the 17th for normal play, the River Liffey collecting many a golf ball every single day.*

CARD OF THE COURSE

Hole	Distance (yards)	Par
1	418	4
2	413	4
3	170	3
4	568	5
5	440	4
6	478	4
7	430	4
8	173	3
9	461	4
Out	3,551	35
10	584	5
11	415	4
12	182	3
13	428	4
14	213	3
15	446	4
16	570	5
17	424	4
18	537	5
In	3,799	37
Total	7,350	72

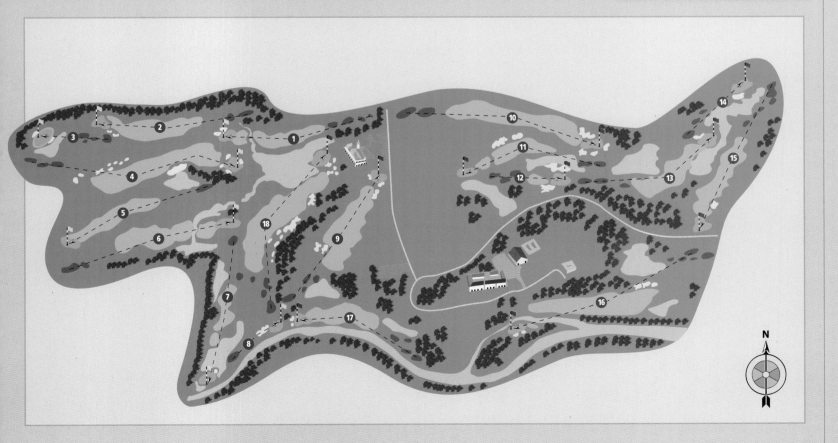

Lahinch

Lahinch

Old Course, Lahinch Golf Club, County Clare, Republic of Ireland

Lahinch! Now there's a place to set the romantic golfer's heart racing. Locals think of Lahinch as the Irish St. Andrews, and they have a point. This town simply exists for golf—that is untrue, of course, but it feels as if it does. And Old Tom Morris came all the way here from St. Andrews more than 100 years ago to develop its earliest course into what might be described as its first proper course.

Erosion of parts of the course and the desire by the members for something even better brought Alister MacKenzie to the town in 1927 to give the course a revamp, which turned out to be a very substantially new course, with only a few holes retained—but what classics they have proved to be. It was one of MacKenzie's very few forays into links golf, although he loved the medium, always citing the Old Course at St. Andrews as the model for all principles of golf design.

Alas, MacKenzie's course did not survive intact. Erosion again damaged parts of the course and lesser replacements were constructed. It was still a good course, but it was no longer in the very top flight. In 1999 the club decided to remedy the situation, and this time it was Martin Hawtree who was given the responsibility of putting Lahinch once again alongside Portmarnock and Ballybunion at the pinnacle of links golf in the Republic. He succeeded impressively.

Lahinch is blessed with such fabulous dunes that any course laid out on them would be at least good, and, given the pedigree of the architects who have worked here, it is no surprise that it is exceptionally good. There are many world-class holes, and the 3rd, 6th, 7th, 9th, 10th, 14th, 15th, and 17th can hold their heads up among the strongest par 4s anywhere. Furthermore, that 7th is one of two Hawtree holes, along with the 11th, which have opened up stunning seascapes lost for many years. And, for good measure, the 13th is one of the most delightful short par 4s imaginable—drivable perhaps, but with any number of ways of making you feel foolish if you do not succeed.

Klondyke and the Dell

Yet it is for two particularly anachronistic holes, the 4th and 5th, that Lahinch is perhaps best known. The former is known as Klondyke after the giant sand hill of that name that interrupts the fairway most of the way to the green. Those hoping for an eagle must play their second shot blind over it. It is not any easier to try to go round it. To make matters even worse, the green is hard up against a grassy bank beyond which is out of bounds. That eagle-seeking second shot must be hit absolutely spot-on.

If that were not enough, the 5th, Dell, is a short hole played entirely blind across a high sand dune to a sunken green on the far side. It has been left unaltered from Tom Morris's course, a charming reminder of days gone by. And if that were not enough, the tee shot on the final hole is played by crossing over both the 4th and 5th holes!

▶ Lahinch's weather forecasting is tried and tested: members observe the local goats that roam freely on the dunes. If they are out on the course, the weather will be fine. If they are up by the clubhouse, you may expect a downpour.

LEFT *Lahinch enjoys linksland of real character—humps and bumps all over the place. The crisp seaside turf makes the playing of all manner of shots a genuine pleasure.*

CARD OF THE COURSE

Hole	Distance (yards)	Par
1	381	4
2	534	5
3	446	4
4	475	5
5	154	3
6	424	4
7	411	4
8	166	3
9	400	4
Out	3,391	36
10	441	4
11	170	3
12	577	5
13	279	4
14	461	4
15	466	4
16	195	3
17	436	4
18	534	5
In	3,559	37
Total	6,950	72

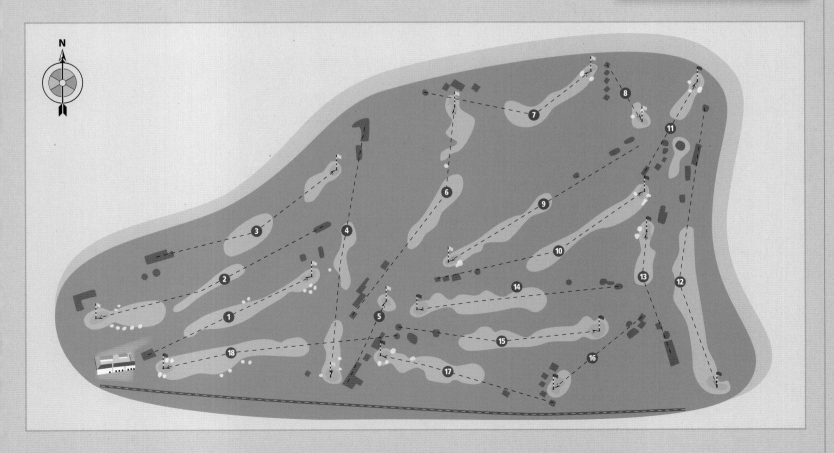

Old Head

Old Head Golf Links, Kinsale, County Cork, Republic of Ireland

If you suffer from vertigo or are strapped for cash think twice about visiting Old Head. It stands high above the Atlantic Ocean, with sheer cliffs plunging straight down into the pounding waves, and it boasts one of the highest green fees in Europe. Nevertheless, Old Head is a course no golfer should pass up an opportunity to play.

Old Head is a historic place, recorded in a map of AD 100 by the Egyptian mathematician Ptolemy. The Eirinn clan settled there in 900 BC, giving their name to Ireland. In 1915 the British liner *Lusitania* was torpedoed just off the headland by a German submarine, with the loss of over 1,000 lives. That incident was partly responsible for the United States entering World War I.

The atmosphere is set right from the outset when you approach the club through the ruins of a 12th-century tower. You will come across the remains of 17th- and 19th-century lighthouses as you play the 7th. But that will do for history, for what bowls the visitor over is the breathtaking setting. And because there is only just room enough for 18 holes on the headland every inch of ground is used, giving no fewer than nine holes clinging to the edge of the cliffs.

Brothers John and Patrick O'Connor bought this land in 1989, and it took four years to overcome objections before construction could commence, with the course finally opening in 1997. A raft of wise heads was engaged to design the course: Ron Kirby (who had been part of the Nicklaus design team), Paddy Merrigan (a Cork-based architect), Eddie Hackett (the talented and prolific Irish architect), Joe Carr (Ireland's greatest amateur player), and Liam Higgins (professional at Waterville).

Their biggest requirement was restraint—not of budget, but of exuberance, for the wind blows hard here almost every day, so greens could not be heavily contoured and fairways needed to be generously wide. Even so, it is a rare day when a four-ball manages to get round the course without losing boxfuls of golf balls to the Atlantic.

RIGHT *The wicked 4th fairway, clinging to the clifftop as it makes its ever-narrowing way to the distant green, itself perched right on the edge above the Atlantic.*

▶ Old Head was designed to be played at widely differing lengths, according to the golfer's ability. Consequently there are at least six separate teeing grounds on every hole.

▶ Kinsale has a reputation as the food capital of Ireland and hosts an international food festival each October.

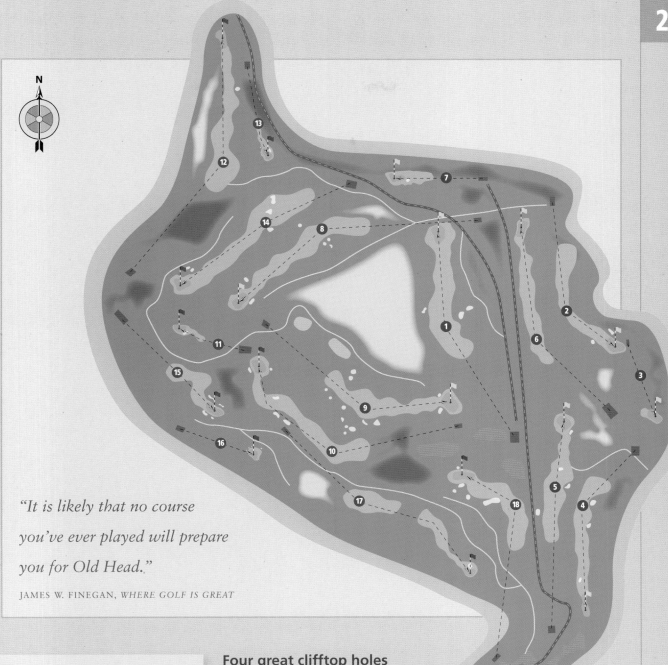

"It is likely that no course you've ever played will prepare you for Old Head."

JAMES W. FINEGAN, *WHERE GOLF IS GREAT*

CARD OF THE COURSE

Hole	Distance (yards)	Par	Hole	Distance (yards)	Par
1	446	4	10	518	5
2	406	4	11	198	3
3	178	3	12	564	5
4	427	4	13	258	3
5	430	4	14	452	4
6	495	5	15	342	4
7	192	3	16	190	3
8	549	5	17	632	5
9	475	4	18	460	4
Out	3,598	36	In	3,614	36
			Total	7,212	72

Four great clifftop holes

Iron out any rustiness in the swing early, for you will need perfect execution (and steady nerves) to survive the 4th, a dogleg played from a clifftop tee to a narrow fairway threatened by cliffs on the left all the way to a green raised up and perched directly on the cliff's edge, overlooked by the lighthouse of 1853 vintage, a constant reminder of the dangerous nature of these treacherous waters. You will be required to drive across a corner of the cliffs on the par-5 12th, and, once again, the green clings perilously to the edge of the cliffs—no place for a left-handed slicer! That is true also of the 13th, a long par 3 with yet another wonderfully sited green on high ground with the now almost obligatory drop to perdition on the left.

Finally in these world-class holes there is the 17th, another par 5, this time falling to a green set at the end of a long descent with the ocean, on this occasion, a constant threat on the right.

▶▶▶ Courses 28–46

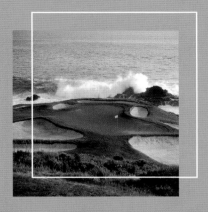

▶▶▶ North America

Is there a greater golfing nation than the United States? The answer has to be no. It has produced more world-class golfers, and has more golf clubs and courses, than any other country, and the number and variety of its golf resorts is amazing. Through its huge buying power it could change the whole nature of golf, yet it readily embraces the traditional: Merion, Shinnecock Hills, Augusta National—great courses and, importantly, great clubs.

In most respects Canada is similar, except that its golfing season is curtailed by the severity of its winter. However, Canada can claim to have beaten the United States to forming a properly constituted golf club, Montreal Golf Club (later Royal) having been founded in 1873.

A word of caution: unlike in most of the rest of the world, where a visitor can often turn up, pay a green fee, and play almost any course, in North America many clubs are strictly private—the only visitors allowed being members' guests. However, the good news is that public-access courses are plentiful, and resort courses include some of the finest in the world.

Augusta

Augusta National Golf Club, Georgia, U.S.A.

Tennis at Wimbledon or Flushing Meadow, motor racing at Le Mans or Indianapolis, racing at Longchamp or Churchill Downs, golf at St. Andrews or . . . ? Most people, even those who have little knowledge of golf, would probably answer, "Augusta National." Its modern-day fame comes from its hosting of the Masters, the first major of the professional golfing year, and the only major held annually on the same course. But that fame would not have arisen had it not been for one Robert Tyre Jones, or Bobby or Bob, depending on which side of the Atlantic you come from.

Jones was the greatest amateur golfer of all time, winning five U.S. Amateur titles and one Amateur Championship in Britain. But he was also good enough to take on and beat the best professionals of the day (the 1920s) taking the U.S. Open on four occasions and the British Open on three. Having won the Amateur and Open Championships of America and Britain in the same year, 1930, he retired from competitive golf, much to the relief of the rest of them!

BELOW *Catch your drive perfectly and you can take advantage of this downslope to reduce the playing length of the 10th hole significantly. The raised green is not one to miss.*

Jones's unlikely design partner

When Jones came to establish his ideal golf course, on which he and his wealthy friends might play, he had some novel ideas about how it might be set up, making the best players feel seriously tested while somehow allowing the high-handicapper to get round in 100 or so without feeling like abandoning golf for good. And it was a pure accident that led Jones to find the ideal architect to help him realize this concept. In 1929 Jones had been knocked out of the U.S. Amateur Championship unexpectedly early. That year the event was held at Pebble Beach, California, so he took the

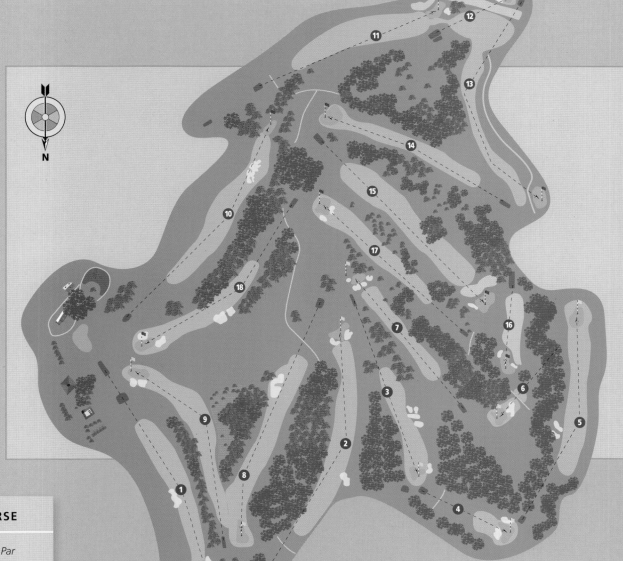

CARD OF THE COURSE

Hole	Distance (yards)	Par
1	435	4
2	575	5
3	350	4
4	205	3
5	455	4
6	180	3
7	410	4
8	570	5
9	460	4
Out	3,640	36
10	495	4
11	490	4
12	155	3
13	510	5
14	440	4
15	500	5
16	170	3
17	425	4
18	465	4
In	3,650	36
Total	7,290	72

opportunity to play nearby Cypress Point and Pasatiempo, both courses designed by Alister MacKenzie, a Leeds physician turned golf course architect—one of the very best in fact. Jones knew immediately that he had found the right man for the job.

Although today's course is little altered from the original (a new 16th hole and revisions to the bunkering) it is set up for the Masters in a manner far removed from what Jones or MacKenzie could have anticipated. Quite simply, the greens are maintained at frighteningly fast speeds, and trees and rough have been planted where previously there were neither. It provides a spectacle for television and it prevents scores becoming ridiculously low, but no high-handicapper would survive a hole, let alone 18!

Yet it remains a fabulous (and fabulously beautiful) course. How often we viewers are on tenterhooks as the leaders pass through the treacherous Amen Corner (11th, 12th, and 13th holes) with Rae's Creek awaiting just the tiniest slipup. Will they risk all and try to get on the 13th and 15th greens in two? And there are—to us—impossible putts on the 16th and 17th greens. Or how about that slick, downhill 8-footer on the last green that must go in or we are into a play-off? The Masters is always dramatic.

▶ Augusta is ablaze with azaleas during the Masters. Before it was a golf course, this was a nursery, Fruitlands, owned by a Belgian horticulturalist, Baron Berckmans, who popularized the azalea in America.

▶ When Tiger Woods won the 2001 Masters he became the first player to hold all four majors at the same time (having won the U.S. Open, British Open and USPGA the previous year). He was 65 under par for the four tournaments.

Augusta

A COVETED INVITATION

The Masters is unique among the majors for having an invited field of under 100 competitors of whom a number will be amateurs. The spectators, too, are a select group, tickets being guarded jealously by those lucky enough to have them, for they are not available for public sale, and any spectator behaving in an inappropriate or unsporting manner will have their ticket confiscated in what is effectively a life ban. Consequently the same patrons return year after year, their collective experience adding to their generous support for every player, giving the Masters' galleries a deserved reputation for knowledgeable and considerate support. In this, of course, they are upholding the traditions for sportsmanship embodied by Bob Jones.

The 13th (below), 16th (main picture), and 12th (top right) are favorite holes with Masters' spectators, for each hole witnesses great drama every day: an unlikely birdie or eagle, perhaps, or an undesired skirmish with the water and a rapid tumble down the leader board.

Bethpage

Bethpage

Black Course, Bethpage State Park, New York, U.S.A.

Bethpage Black was the first truly public golf facility to host the U.S. Open. True, Pebble Beach and Pinehurst are open to the public, but they are very expensive resort courses. As competitors in the 2002 U.S. Open can testify, it is a fearsome course—long, demanding, and punishing. Hardly surprisingly, the man who had the best answers to the questions posed was Tiger Woods. So successful was the 2002 U.S. Open that it has already been scheduled to host the 2009 event—a remarkably swift return.

Golf owes a huge debt of gratitude to one Robert Moses. He was the Commissioner of New York's State Parks in the dark years of the Great Depression. What was so remarkable about him was that he had the vision, as well as the political know-how (or sheer willpower, perhaps), to get three brand new golf courses of the highest class constructed in Bethpage State Park in the 1930s. Additionally he had an existing one on the site upgraded, and, for the record, a fifth course was added in the 1950s, all for the benefit of metropolitan golfers who could not afford (or did not have the required connections) to be members of a private club. So marvelous were these courses that they were soon being enjoyed for a modest green fee by many members of wealthy (but architecturally inferior) clubs.

Moses had the wisdom to employ the formidable Albert Warren Tillinghast as his architect of choice. Tillinghast did not moderate his design thoughts just because this was a public facility.

Sandy wastes

Tillinghast was given free run of a vast tract of sandy woodland with enough change of level to afford him plenty of natural sites for the greens. He plotted a route through the trees, felled no more than he had to, and liberally sprinkled the whole thing with formidable bunkers of huge proportions. So the course is narrow, calling for arrow-like shots to pierce the gaps in the trees and howitzer-like trajectories to find the few benign bits of fairway not otherwise occupied by sandy wastelands.

A glance at the card is sufficient to reveal that the strength of the course comes in its long two-shot holes, particularly over the back nine, with perhaps the 15th the most difficult hole on the course. Tillinghast's short holes are invariably demanding, and those at Bethpage Black do not disappoint, with the heavily bunkered 17th giving no respite on what is an exhausting home run. Oddly enough the weakest hole may be the last, even after Rees Jones lengthened it for the 2002 U.S. Open.

Interestingly, one of the best holes at Bethpage is the 4th, a par 5 of only 517 yards/ 473 m, surely easily reached in two shots by today's powerful players. But that is to ignore the difficulty of the drive, which is influenced by a bunker on the left of the fairway. Quite simply, if the green is to be reached in two, the drive must clear this on the most precise line imaginable. To balance that drive, Tillinghast calls for something similar on the next hole, but this time placing the compulsory bunker carry on the right of the fairway. He never lets up—which is why Tiger Woods with his superior powers of concentration was always likely to come out on top.

LEFT *This aerial view of the 4th hole shows well the huge scale of the architecture at Bethpage Black. Bunkering of this kind is very much a Tillinghast trademark.*

▶ The Red Course, famous for its tough opening hole, is a par-70 championship course of 7,366 yards/6,735 m. It shared with the Blue Course the hosting of the 1936 USGA Public Links Championship and hosts annually the Long Island Open.

▶ The name Bethpage has Biblical origins: "And when they drew nigh unto Jerusalem, and were come to Bethphage, unto the mount of Olives, then sent Jesus two disciples . . ."
St. Matthew 21.1
Bethphage means place of figs.

CARD OF THE COURSE

Hole	Distance (yards)	Par	Hole	Distance (yards)	Par
1	430	4	10	492	4
2	389	4	11	435	4
3	205	3	12	499	4
4	517	5	13	554	4
5	451	4	14	161	3
6	408	4	15	478	4
7	553	5	16	479	4
8	210	3	17	207	3
9	418	4	18	411	4
Out	3,581	36	In	3,716	35
			Total	7,297	71

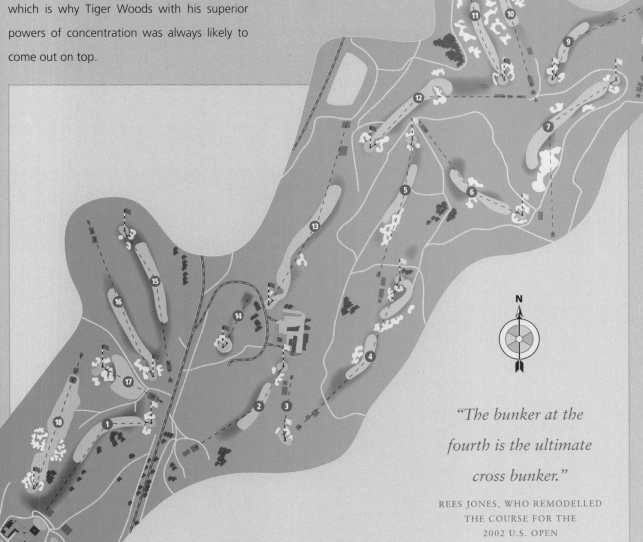

N

"The bunker at the fourth is the ultimate cross bunker."

REES JONES, WHO REMODELLED
THE COURSE FOR THE
2002 U.S. OPEN

Kapalua

Plantation Course, Kapalua Resort, Maui, Hawaii, U.S.A.

You could be forgiven for thinking that the Plantation Course at Kapalua is something of a monster, boasting as it does the longest hole on the U.S. PGA Tour. The 18th hole measures a mind-boggling 663 yards/606 m, yet it is regularly reached in two shots by today's mighty hitters. It does not bear thinking about! In fact the course is anything but a monster. The Plantation Course is a thing of rare beauty.

Kapalua Resort already boasted two Arnold Palmer-designed tracks, the Village and Bay courses, when the fledgling design team of Ben Crenshaw and Bill Coore were approached to build a third course over an upland site offering magnificent vistas and enough character in the landform to excite these two perfectionist craftsmen. They do not bludgeon courses out of the earth with mighty earthmovers and vast quantities of dynamite. They handcraft them. Their later work at Sand Hills (Nebraska), Friars Head (New York), Cuscowilla (Georgia), and Bandon Trails (Oregon) has been recognized by knowledgeable golfers and the golfing press as being world-class. The Plantation Course, only their second full 18-hole design, opened in 1991, has proved its merit each year since

1999 as the venue for the Mercedes-Benz Championship, which opens the Tour year in January, bringing together the winners of each of the previous season's tournaments.

Wind factor

Glance at the card of the course and you'll be forgiven for thinking that it is littered with misprints. Take the 1st, for instance, an apparently unreachable par 4 of 520 yards/475 m. Yet the architects routed the course so that this hole takes full advantage of a following wind, so the hole turns out to be perfectly reachable. In contrast, the 13th is a par 4 of a mere 407 yards/372 m, yet it turns out to be the most difficult hole on the course. Why? Because it plays directly

RIGHT *The 18th hole on the Plantation Course at Kapalua, the longest hole on the U.S. Tour, yet entirely in keeping with the glorious scenery that forms its backdrop.*

▶ Arnold Palmer's Bay Course offers an alternative to those not quite up to the challenge of the Plantation Course's considerable length. Although measuring 6,600 yards/6,035 m from the back tees there are only two par 4s in excess of 400 yards/366 m.

▶ The Plantation Course is unusual in having only three short holes, but they are among the most difficult on the course. Aiming straight at the pin will bring disaster. With wind a constant factor, they require you to drift or shape the ball into the green.

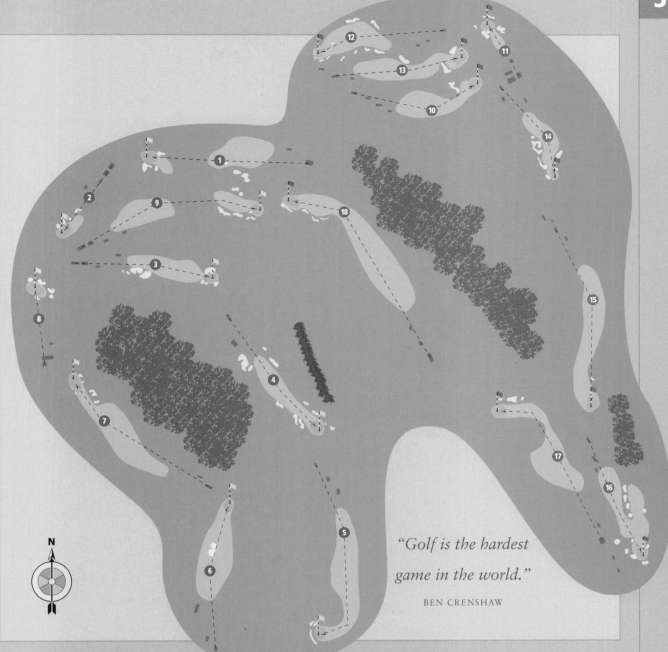

N

"*Golf is the hardest game in the world.*"

BEN CRENSHAW

CARD OF THE COURSE

Hole	Distance (yards)	Par	Hole	Distance (yards)	Par
1	520	4	10	354	4
2	218	3	11	164	3
3	380	4	12	420	4
4	382	4	13	407	4
5	532	5	14	305	4
6	398	4	15	555	5
7	516	4	16	365	4
8	203	3	17	508	4
9	521	5	18	663	5
Out	3,670	36	In	3,741	37
			Total	7,411	73

into the wind and even the world's best professionals only manage an average drive on this hole of 232 yards/212 m. Compare this with the downhill, downwind 18th on which they drive an average of 356 yards/326 m.

In a way, such statistics distort the true values of the course. These are no circus-trick holes, but thought-provoking, beautifully crafted gems that respond to thoughtful play. The 6th is a good example. Its fairway is wonderfully wide and inviting, but to have the easiest access to the green you must take the most daring line off the tee, to the right, risking perishing down the cliffs on that side, yet using the wind from the right to coax the ball on to the fairway.

The 6th is followed by another simple but strategic hole, with a wide fairway, requiring you to hold the ball on the left-to-right slope to gain the best line into the green. And, traditionalists that they are, Coore and Crenshaw constructed the approach to the green in such a way as to encourage the old-fashioned bump-and-run shot. Here the golf is as inspiring as the magnificent views.

Kiawah Island

Ocean Course, Kiawah Island Golf Resort, South Carolina, U.S.A.

Never has a name rung so true as "The Ocean Course," for the Atlantic Ocean is in view on every single hole. Ten holes are directly on the coast, the greatest number of seaside holes on any course in the northern hemisphere, and the other eight play parallel to them. This remarkable feature not only provides some of the most scenic golf imaginable, but also makes the course massively affected by the wind. Interestingly, as with the 17th at Sawgrass, this trademark was not intended by the designer Pete Dye, who had planned to sit the course behind the dunes until his wife Alice suggested raising the course in order to provide the stunning sea views.

The unbelievable beauty of the course disguises its brutal difficulty. Dye made use of the natural environment, with dunes and tall grasses devouring poor shots. The most distinctive design feature is that different shot options are always available. Many holes reward daring carries, but players are never forced to take these lines. From the tee and fairway, players must pick a shot to suit their ability and the conditions.

The wide range of options makes for innovative golf, and it is also mandatory on a course so affected by the wind. It has been estimated that wind changes can alter club selection by up to eight clubs, so there needs to be a route for every strength and direction of wind.

Extensive lakes and vast tracts of sandy waste await the inaccurate shot, making this a fine matchplay course but the very devil on which to keep a medal card going.

LEFT *Like the 17th at Sawgrass, Dye wondered if the par-3 17th was dramatic enough, so he added an enormous lake to carry!*

RIGHT *The sand areas are not considered hazards so you may ground your club. This is the par-4 9th hole.*

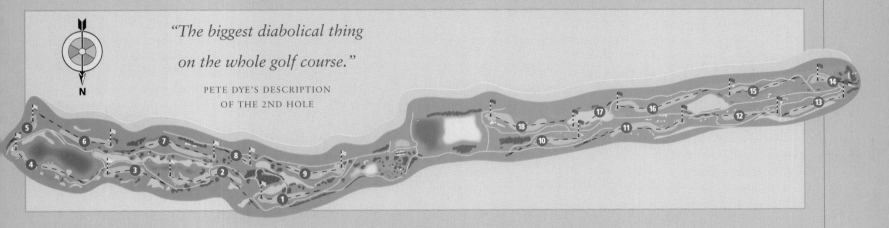

"The biggest diabolical thing on the whole golf course."

PETE DYE'S DESCRIPTION
OF THE 2ND HOLE

Creative challenges

The par-5 2nd hole is a good reflection of the course. From the tee, players will be struck by the epic view toward the ocean. But they will also be faced with golfing dilemmas in choosing the correct angle from the tee to cross the marshland that spells golfing disaster if you come up short. A safe shot plays out right for the less bold. If the drive was overly cautious, the second shot must be laid up short of another marsh, 110 yards/101 m in front of the green. Good players should be able to get around the green in two, but that is not the end of the story, as the green is a difficult raised shelf, rolling away into a deep bunker. After a gentle opening hole, the 2nd can be a real nemesis, and even the professionals rack up big scores here. In the 1991 Ryder Cup, Seve Ballesteros won the 2nd with a double-bogey to Wayne Levi's 8!

Like a true links, the options for shot-making are endless, and the longer holes tend to offer a route in on the ground, as well as an airborne approach. You are continually challenged to think hard and pick the right shot. With the design so demanding of creative golf it is no surprise that the Ryder Cup was such a success—the PGA Championship in 2012 should be a real treat.

CARD OF THE COURSE

Hole	Distance (yards)	Par	Hole	Distance (yards)	Par
1	395	4	10	439	4
2	543	5	11	562	5
3	390	4	12	466	4
4	453	4	13	404	4
5	207	3	14	194	3
6	455	4	15	421	4
7	527	5	16	579	5
8	197	3	17	221	3
9	464	4	18	439	4
Out	3,631	36	In	3,725	36
			Total	7,356	72

Merion

East Course, Ardmore, Pennsylvania, U.S.A.

"I love Merion. It is one of those old-time golf courses that doesn't have the length of some of the modern-day courses, but still stands the test. That's the mark of a great golf course to me." That was Jack Nicklaus's opinion of Merion East, one of two distinctive courses at this great club in the outskirts of Philadelphia. It held the record for being the shortest course in modern times to host the U.S. Open, which it last did in 1981. Happily, Merion has been reinstated on the U.S. Open roster and will see the return of this great championship in 2013.

BELOW A ridge crosses the 9th green making the putting surface uphill at the front and back, but downhill in the middle, which Ben Crenshaw described as "very tough to read."

Merion's golfing beginnings lay, strangely enough, within the members of the Merion Cricket Club. They formed a golf section and laid out a nine-hole course in Haverford, but it soon proved too short and too restrictive for their ambitions. One of their young members, Hugh Wilson, had captained the golf team at Princeton, and in 1910 he was despatched to Britain for seven months to study the architecture of the best courses. Perhaps it is no surprise, then, that there is a feeling of both English heathland and Scottish links about Merion, and the bunkering is every bit as formidable as that on any of the British Open links.

An aura of perfection

The distinguished golf course designer Tom Doak maintains that Merion's East Course is probably the only course that any major golf architect would find it difficult, if not impossible, to improve. That is quite a tribute to Wilson, who had never designed anything before.

Key to survival at Merion is to avoid the bunkers. There are 128 of them and a third of those are encountered in the first three holes. Key to winning at Merion is to overcome the subtleties of the greens, once described by Herbert Warren Wind, the doyen of golf writers, as wonderfully

varied, "plateau greens, bench greens, crown greens, sunken greens, large greens, small greens, two-level greens, three-level greens, and greens that slope in a hundred different directions."

One of the most intimidating opening tee shots is encountered at Merion, not because the hole is any more fearsome than the other 17, but because the tee is located right next to a terrace under the awning of which members and their guests take their coffee, lunches, and teas. The consequences of a snap hook are unthinkable! It is, in fact, a fine hole, calling for precise placement of the tee shot to give access to the cleverly angled green.

There are only two par 5s at Merion, but length is largely irrelevant here, guile being of the essence. Take the par-4 11th, for instance. Most of us would have no difficulty steering our tee shot downhill to the nominated landing zone, but the pitch to the green is entirely over deep rough, a stream bounds the green to the right and behind, and the putting surface is small and firm. It was on this famous green that Bob Jones completed his "Impregnable Quardrilateral" in 1930 by winning the U.S. Amateur.

The finish from the 14th is memorable, with the 16th and 17th being played over the remains of an old quarry, and the drive at the 18th formidable, up and over a rock face.

HOGAN'S COURAGE

Ben Hogan played the 1950 U.S. Open at Merion in great pain, having been seriously injured in an automobile crash the previous year. On the 13th hole in the final round he said to his caddie that he could not go on. "I don't work for quitters. I'll see you on the 14th tee, Sir," was his caddie's reply. Hogan labored on, through terrible pain, and forced his way into a three-way play-off (over a further 18 holes) for the title, which he duly won.

CARD OF THE COURSE

Hole	Distance (yards)	Par
1	350	4
2	556	5
3	219	3
4	597	5
5	504	4
6	487	4
7	345	4
8	359	4
9	206	3
Out	3,623	36
10	325	4
11	367	4
12	403	4
13	120	3
14	438	4
15	411	4
16	430	4
17	246	3
18	505	4
In	3,245	34
Total	6,868	70

▶ When Bob Jones won the 1930 U.S. Amateur at Merion, he was never taken beyond the 14th hole. In the 36-hole final, his margin of victory over E. V. Homans was 8 and 7.

▶ Merion's flagsticks are topped not with flags but with wicker baskets, so that the golfer can get no indication of the strength or direction of the wind.

"Merion has an aura of perfection to it that all other courses lack."

TOM DOAK

Oakmont

Oakmont Country Club, Pennsylvania, U.S.A.

Oakmont is a family course, owing its whole concept and being to Henry Fownes and his son William. Henry was an exceedingly wealthy steel magnate who purchased a large plot of land near Pittsburgh in 1903 with the idea of creating a world-class golf course. William subsequently became one of America's best amateur golfers, winning the 1910 U.S. Amateur Championship and twice playing in the Walker Cup, and was also very influential within the political side of the game. Between them, they created something approaching a golfing behemoth, and had the clout to ensure that it was used for the most prestigious tournaments.

As first built, the course was long but not particularly difficult. It was William who beefed it up in the 1920s, making it so unforgiving that it has been called the toughest course in America. For starters he set about rebunkering the course. At one time there were 220; today about 175 remain. For these Fownes devised a venomous rake: it created golf-ball-sized furrows in the sand, which were drawn across the line of play to make escape almost impossible! And then there were the greens, quite unlike any others, a remarkable assortment of sizes and shapes and, in particular, slopes. To make them the most terrifying greens in the world he had them rolled with huge barrels of sand, insisting that absolutely no watering was done to them.

The greens were also cut phenomenally low—shaved—and with the deep, clinging rough grown in to narrow the fairways for a major tournament the course fully justified its macabre reputation. Today's professionals are used to tricked-up courses with lightning-fast greens, but, with the exception perhaps of Augusta, they rarely play courses with such contours to the greens.

Great design

Surprisingly, Oakmont is not grotesque. It is handsome (more so since the removal of a great many trees that had threatened to choke the course) and strategic, and it responds to thoughtful play. The 3rd hole, for instance, is famed for its Church Pew bunkers—deep sandy trenches separated by rows of treacherous grass ridges—but the greater interest is provided by the green, which is difficult to access, being raised up to repel anything but the truest of approach shots. Miss this green and that's when the scrambling starts.

A glance at the card might suggest that the 17th would be a pushover for today's powerful champions. Not so! It can be driven, but that involves successfully carrying a minefield of bunkers on the left (the direct line from the tee) and somehow managing to squeeze the ball on to the putting surface between another bunker and deceptive low ground to the left. The hole can be played conservatively, but it is dangerously tempting to attack and remarkably resistant to it. And that seems to sum up so much about Oakmont.

LEFT *The famous Church Pew bunkers separating the 3rd and 4th fairways. As can be seen from this photograph, the bunkers to the right of the fairway are hardly less intimidating!*

CARD OF THE COURSE

Hole	Distance (yards)	Par	Hole	Distance (yards)	Par
1	482	4	10	435	4
2	341	4	11	379	4
3	428	4	12	667	5
4	609	5	13	183	3
5	382	4	14	358	4
6	194	3	15	500	4
7	479	4	16	231	3
8	288	3	17	313	4
9	477	4	18	484	4
Out	3,680	35	In	3,550	35
			Total	7,230	70

▶ Describing Oakmont's one-time bunker rakes, Jimmy Demaret said, "You could have combed North Africa with those and Rommel wouldn't have got past Casablanca."

▶ In 1973 Johnny Miller scored an unbelievable 63 in the last round to win the U.S. Open. It is considered by many to be the greatest round of golf ever played.

Pebble Beach

Pebble Beach Golf Links, Pebble Beach, California, U.S.A.

Pebble Beach is universally regarded as one of the world's best public courses. It was chosen as the venue for the 100th U.S. Open in 2000, the fourth time it had hosted the Open, yet anybody can simply book a tee time and play on this historic stage. There are, of course, two snags: it is very expensive and you must book long in advance.

Pebble Beach opened in 1919 and ten years later became the first course west of the Mississippi to host the U.S. Amateur Championship. A young Jack Nicklaus capped an impressive amateur career here when he won the 1961 U.S. Amateur. The "Golden Bear" was again victorious when Pebble Beach staged its first U.S. Open in 1972. Despite coming second to Tom Watson in 1982, his affection for Pebble Beach never waned, and eventually he bade farewell to the U.S. Open here in 2000, an emotional Nicklaus poignantly sitting on the fence behind the 18th tee, surveying one of the best finishing holes in golf.

The par-5 18th requires nerves of steel, as the entire hole teeters on the edge of the Pacific. It really should be played as a three-shot hole, often with a 3-wood from the tee. In the 2000 U.S. Open, even the apparently infallible Tiger Woods, who would coast to victory by a margin of 15 shots, managed to pull his tee shot into the sea.

Tom Watson showed the perfect way to play the closing holes at Pebble Beach in the 1982 U.S. Open. With one of golf's most famous chip-ins, he made birdie from the rough on the par-3 17th to claim a one-shot lead over Nicklaus. Sensibly Watson hit a 3-wood for position from the 18th tee and laid up with his second shot in the fairway with a 7-iron to leave himself a short iron approach. Again he played safely, approaching the heart of the green as the pin was tucked in behind the front bunker. From there he finished in style, rolling the 20-ft/6-m putt into the center of the cup for a birdie, birdie finish.

Glorious coastal holes

Stunning holes are abundant here, and from the 4th there is a fabulous sequence of seven consecutive oceanside holes, including the amazing 7th— with wind blowing into your face and the ocean awaiting if you overhit your shot, the prospect from the tee is nerve-racking. The sequence from the 8th to the 10th is one of the greatest trios of consecutive par 4s in world golf. At the 8th, after an exciting drive, you play an awesome approach shot across a corner of the ocean to find the typically small and unreceptive green.

Throughout the round you are presented with daunting drives at undulating fairways, but it is the approach shots where ingenuity is called for. On one hole with wind behind, only a high fade will stop on the tiny green, but on the next you may be playing straight into the wind and having to hit a low punch shot. With a course designed for such inventive golf, and backed by breathtaking views, many golfers would share Jack Nicklaus's view that this is possibly the best course in the world. As Billy Andrade said, "It's the Holy Grail for us."

LEFT *One of the best-known, and most photographed, closing holes in golf, the 18th at Pebble Beach, hugging the Pacific Ocean for every one of its 543 yards/497 m.*

▶ In 2001 *Golf Digest* ranked Pebble Beach the No.1 course in America , the first time a public course achieved this position. It's a course that everyone wants to play, and it will cost you around $500 to do so.

▶ 17-Mile Drive, which passes through Pebble Beach, is a private toll road. The Pebble Beach Company owns the copyright on all photographic sites on this scenic route—and there are a lot of them!

CARD OF THE COURSE

Hole	Distance (yards)	Par
1	381	4
2	502	5
3	390	4
4	331	4
5	188	3
6	513	5
7	106	3
8	418	4
9	466	4
Out	3,295	36
10	446	4
11	380	4
12	202	3
13	399	4
14	573	5
15	397	4
16	403	4
17	178	3
18	543	5
In	3,521	36
Total	6,816	72

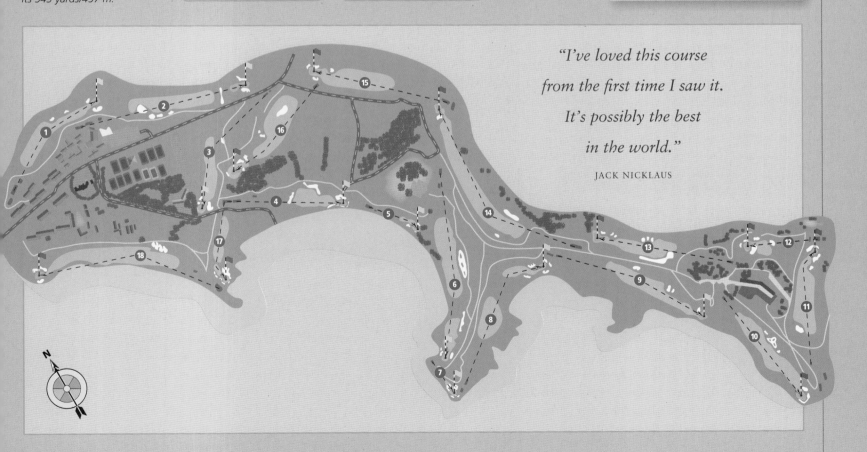

"I've loved this course from the first time I saw it. It's possibly the best in the world."

JACK NICKLAUS

Pebble Beach

AN IMPRESSIVE QUARTET

The world-famous Pebble Beach Golf Links is but one of four challenging courses at this luxury resort. Spyglass Hill, designed by Robert Trent Jones, is one of the hardest courses on the professional tour. It starts in links-like country beside the ocean before moving inland among woods. The Links at Spanish Bay is one of the few courses in which Tom Watson had a hand in the design (with Robert Trent Jones Jr. and Sandy Tatum). It pays homage to the great Scottish links. Less well-known is the charming Del Monte Golf Course, the oldest course (opened in 1897) in continuous use west of the Mississippi.

ABOVE *It is said that Robert Louis Stevenson walked this shore many times looking for inspiration for Treasure Island. This is the 9th tee.*

RIGHT *Bucking the trend that holes need to be outrageously long to be testing, the diminutive 7th is a mere 106 yards/97 m long. Its difficulties are plain to see.*

Pine Valley

Pine Valley Golf Club, Clementon, New Jersey, U.S.A.

Pine Valley has a reputation for being the hardest course in the world. Yes, the Ocean Course at Kiawah Island might play considerably harder from the back tees in a gale, and many a modern layout, with water on all 18 holes, could be tricked up to be almost unplayable. But, on a daily basis, Pine Valley is the hardest, simply because it asks the golfer to play total golf on every single shot, with the penalty for failure dire. What is so extraordinary about Pine Valley is that no one who has played it would begrudge it a single dropped stroke. It is a masterpiece.

It was a Pittsburgh hotelier, George Crump, a fine amateur player in his own right, who came up with the idea for this course. He had clear views about what he wanted to achieve and for some five years he lived on the site, directing construction. However, he was wise enough to consult others, including Walter Travis and Jerome Travers, two of America's leading amateur golfers in the early years of the 20th century, and the English architect Harry Colt. Quite how much each of them contributed may never be known, but Crump died in 1918 before the course was finished. Today's 12th to 15th holes were completed by Hugh Wilson, the genius of Merion, probably with advice and input from Hugh Alison, Colt's design partner.

Pine Valley today is rather different from the course that was completed in 1919, in that hundreds of thousands of trees have matured to add to the existing perils. Essentially there are tees, narrow strips of grass, which might be called fairways, swathes of sandy waste, and a dense forest—and fiendish greens.

BELOW *The shortest hole at Pine Valley, the 10th, is a wicked little hole. The target is tiny, and missing it is likely to call for miraculous powers of recovery.*

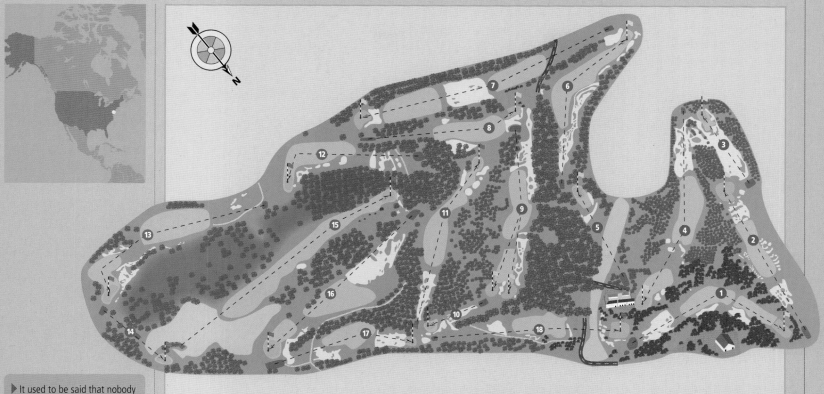

BELOW *The 5th hole remains extraordinarily demanding with 21st-century clubs and balls. What it must have been like with those of 1919 hardly bears thinking about.*

The ultimate in punitive golf

There are no weak holes at Pine Valley, but three in particular have world renown—the 5th, 7th, and 13th. The 5th is a brutal "short" hole—a full carry of around 230 yards/210 m over a lake and up a hill to a raised green isolated in the woodlands. It would be intimidating at half its length.

Most famous of all the holes is the 7th, a remarkable par 5 made infamous by Hell's Half Acre, a huge expanse of sand splitting the fairway between 285 yards/261 m and 385 yards/352 m from the tee. Get your drive wrong and you cannot clear it with your second. Get the drive right but mishit the second and you are still facing disaster. Get your first and second right and you are left with a devilish pitch to a green entirely surrounded by sand.

It is something similar on the 13th. You drive over a wilderness to an island fairway in the far distance. Then follows a terrifying shot, all carry, of 200 yards/183 m or more over scrub and sand to a green angled away to the left with no margin for error front, back, left, or right. Yet despite the difficulties of each hole there is amazing variety to the course, with welcome change of pace, particularly within the two-shot holes. Hard yes, but still we come back for more.

CARD OF THE COURSE

Hole	Distance (yards)	Par
1	421	4
2	368	4
3	198	3
4	451	4
5	235	3
6	387	4
7	636	5
8	326	4
9	459	4
Out	3,481	35
10	161	3
11	397	4
12	337	4
13	486	4
14	220	3
15	615	5
16	475	4
17	345	4
18	483	4
In	3,519	35
Total	7,000	70

Pinehurst

Pinehurst

Pinehurst No. 2, Pinehurst Resort, North Carolina, U.S.A.

Pinehurst No. 2 stands as a pinnacle of classic golf course design in the United States. Because any major changes to the course happened in its infancy and were overseen by its legendary architect, Donald Ross, the holes share a remarkable harmony.

Ross learned his trade from the best, with an apprenticeship under Old Tom Morris at St. Andrews, following a youth spent at Dornoch on Scotland's Sutherland coast. His career took him to the United States, where he was soon employed at Pinehurst. In 1907 Ross's signature course was completed. His affection for it was such that he built himself a house next to the 3rd green. The course evolved under his watchful eye. In 1934 the greens were converted from compressed sand (common in the southern states at that time) to grass, and in 1935 the layout was altered for the last time to roughly its present state.

"Fun golf"

Strange to say, No. 2 has no "signature holes" as such. It is the collection of all 18 holes that makes this a great course. Wide fairways and large greens reflect Ross's links influence, although here the fairways amble through tall pines. The fairway width requires players to target a particular side depending on where the pin is cut. "Turtle back" greens have always been a feature of the course, rolling away poor shots uncompromisingly. In the 1999 U.S. Open, the professionals demonstrated the difficulties, finding just 52 percent of the greens in regulation on the first day.

CARD OF THE COURSE

Hole	Distance (yards)	Par
1	405	4
2	472	4
3	384	4
4	568	5
5	476	4
6	224	3
7	407	4
8	467	4
9	190	3
Out	3,593	35
10	611	5
11	478	4
12	451	4
13	380	4
14	471	4
15	206	3
16	510	4
17	190	3
1	445	4
In	3,742	35
Total	7,335	70

ABOVE *The par 3s on No. 2 are perhaps less celebrated than the par 4s, but they are each handsome, requiring intelligent and subtle play to tame them. This is the 15th.*

LEFT *The daunting approach to the 5th green on Pinehurst No. 2, the putting surface raised up in typical Ross fashion, repelling all but the most truly struck of golf shots.*

Pinehurst has been the venue for a number of great tournaments, but it is the 1999 U.S. Open—one of the hardest-fought championships of all—for which it is best remembered. John Daly fell foul of Ross's design on the final day, as his putt from off the green on the 8th failed to climb the slope, rolling back to his feet. He whacked it away in frustration while it was still moving, eventually putting out for an 11. All the big names were in the hunt at the end, with Woods, Vijay Singh, and Phil Mickelson challenging. After precision golf all week, Payne Stewart needed a putt of 15 feet/5 m on the last to win. "When I looked up, it was about two feet from the hole and breaking right into the center of the cup," he recalled. Stewart was the first person in U.S. Open history to hole a sizable putt on the last to win. A few months later he died in a flying accident.

Woods sums up the attributes of this hundred-year-old design: "I play courses on tour and we all see it—miss the green, atomic lob wedge, hack it out of the rough. That for me is not fun golf. Fun golf is Pinehurst."

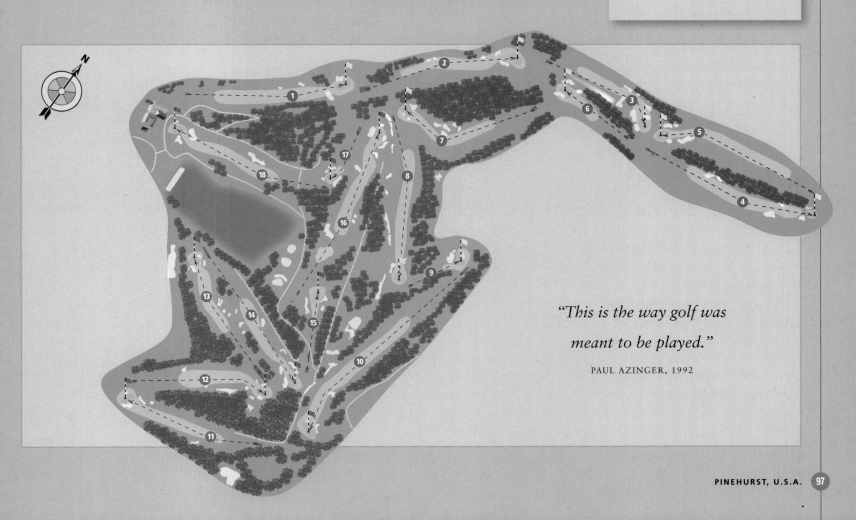

"This is the way golf was meant to be played."

PAUL AZINGER, 1992

Shinnecock Hills

Shinnecock Hills Golf Club, Southampton, Long Island, New York, U.S.A.

One of the United States' oldest championship courses, Shinnecock Hills was founded in the affluent Hamptons on Long Island back in 1891. By 1896 it was ready to host its first important championships, the U.S. Amateur and U.S. Open, both being held for only the second time. After taking its place at the top of the pecking order, Shinnecock merged into the background for nearly 100 years, its golf being entirely social.

ABOVE The routing of Shinnecock Hills brings the 9th and 18th holes back in parallel to deliciously sited greens on the slopes beneath the club's splendid clubhouse.

A new layout followed in 1916, but the club did not seek further public attention. The same happened when the building of a new highway on Long Island forced further changes in 1930–31, a layout ignored for further national championship play until 1986, when the golfing world at large was awakened to the magnificent course that had been hidden from public gaze for so long. The U.S. Open had returned and it was clear that this would not be a one-off affair—there were repeat visits in 1995 and 2004.

To create this long-concealed gem, the club called on William Flynn, an architect who had previously worked mostly in the Philadelphia area. He and his business partner Howard Toomey are now recognized as one of the most imaginative partnerships in what was a particularly creative era of American golf design, between the two World Wars. In fact Flynn retained two holes from the previous course (designed by Charles Blair Macdonald and Seth Raynor, another great partnership) but the rest was brand new.

A genuine links?

Shinnecock Hills has been described as the nearest America gets to a true links, as exemplified by Britain's ancient links. Is this so? The answer has to be "No" on two counts. First, there are "inland links" far from the sea, such as Sand Hills in Nebraska, which play more like the Old Course than Shinnecock ever can. Second, the sea is not really a factor in how play is made, how the shots must be shaped, as it is (if often indirectly) on a true links. And yet, in so many ways, Shinnecock reminds us of a links. Its wide spaces are windswept, and the direction of the wind is often hugely important in how the play of an individual hole might change from day to day, or hour to hour. And Shinnecock is far hillier than Dornoch, Royal Aberdeen and St. Andrews thrown together.

It would be invidious to single out any particular hole at Shinnecock because it is the collective strength of all 18 holes that makes this such an outstanding course. It might be by far the shortest of recent U.S. Open courses, but part of its strength is the way the course is maintained, with firm-and-fast conditioning demanding great skill in approach work allied to formidable rough—the sort of thing the R&A conjured up for the infamous 1999 British Open at Carnoustie. At Shinnecock that is normal!

This is, in golfing terms, a favored corner of Long Island, with the famous National Golf Links literally next door and the Jack Nicklaus/Tom Doak Sebonack adjoining that.

▶ Shinnecock's clubhouse, designed in 1892 by fashionable architect Stanford White (whose womanizing led to his murder in 1906), was the first purpose-built clubhouse in the United States and is still in use today.

CARD OF THE COURSE

Hole	Distance (yards)	Par
1	393	4
2	226	3
3	478	4
4	435	4
5	537	5
6	474	4
7	189	3
8	398	4
9	443	4
Out	3,573	35
10	412	4
11	158	3
12	468	4
13	370	4
14	443	4
15	403	4
16	540	5
17	179	3
18	450	4
In	3,423	35
Total	6,996	70

Torrey Pines

South Course, Torrey Pines, San Diego, California, U.S.A.

Named after the indigenous trees that dot the fairways, the two courses at Torrey Pines occupy a remarkable location, perched atop high cliffs that fall steeply into the Pacific Ocean. There are exceptional views from the courses. Both courses—North and South—are of high quality, and when the annual Buick Invitational is played, for the first two days play is divided between the two courses with one round played on each. For the weekend, however, all rounds are played on the South Course.

In 2001, Rees Jones renovated the South Course at a cost of $3.5 million, which saw the holes lengthened to a staggering 7,607 yards/6,956 m. At 483 yards/442 m, the 4th is a long, unforgiving par 4, with two bunkers lurking down the right fairway. But players' eyes are inevitably drawn left to the stunning view of pine trees marking the edge of land and the beginning of the Pacific. As with most of the tee shots, the fairway is actually played to at a slight angle, and this brings its own difficulties in finding the short grass from the tee. Tucked among the trees and protected by a large bunker, the heart-shaped green appears very small when approached by the long-iron or wood of most players.

Like so many great courses, the South Course also finishes well, with a decision-making par 5. Bunkers left and right narrow the fairway landing area, but a straight shot leaves the potential to attack the green in two. With a substantial water hazard in front of the left-hand side of the green, many players inevitably lay up. Undoubtedly, it is a dramatic finishing hole for the 2008 U.S. Open, the first major to be played here.

Tiger's winning streak

Though the length might be intimidating for most players, the longest course in regular PGA tournament play must seem fairly simple to Tiger Woods, who tamed the brutal course with a final-round 66 to win the Buick Invitational in 2007. In an awesome finale, Woods overcame his two-shot deficit in the first two holes and displayed the power and finesse necessary for success at Torrey Pines by lashing a 3-wood 265 yards/242 m to reach the par-5 9th, and rolling in the 25-foot/8-m eagle putt. His victory earned him his fifth Buick title; it was his seventh consecutive PGA win in 2007. He added an astonishing sixth Buick the following year.

Despite the more prestigious tournament pedigree of the South Course, many golfers prefer the slightly easier North Course. Occupying an even more scenic setting, the North Course is shorter, at 6,874 yards/6,286 m, and presents golfers with more tactical challenges of placement and planning as opposed to the sheer brute force of its southern neighbour. The combination of the two courses makes Torrey Pines one of the best and most spectacular municipals in the world.

▶ The city of San Diego owns these municipal courses, and anybody can line up and get a starting time. The only problem is that the wait starts from as early as 6 p.m. the night before!

LEFT *The 12th is the toughest hole on the South Course, a long par 4 with a tightly protected raised green. The view over the Pacific Ocean is incomparable.*

▶ Torrey Pines is only the second municipal course (after Bethpage Black) to host the U.S. Open. The USGA is demonstrably keen to spread its gospel ever wider.

CARD OF THE COURSE

Hole	Distance (yards)	Par	Hole	Distance (yards)	Par
1	452	4	10	405	4
2	387	4	11	221	3
3	198	3	12	504	4
4	483	4	13	541	5
5	453	4	14	435	4
6	560	5	15	477	4
7	462	4	16	227	3
8	176	3	17	442	4
9	613	5	18	571	5
Out	3,784	36	In	3,823	36
			Total	7,607	72

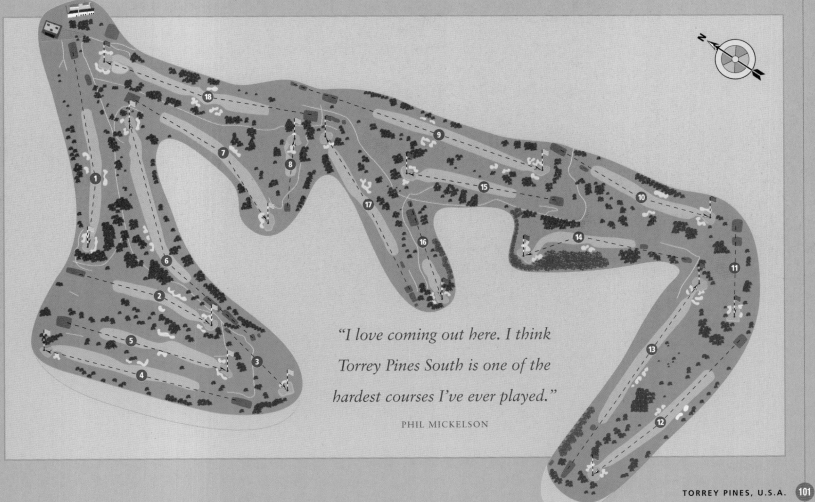

"I love coming out here. I think Torrey Pines South is one of the hardest courses I've ever played."
PHIL MICKELSON

TPC Sawgrass

Stadium Course, TPC Sawgrass, Ponte Vedra Beach, Florida, U.S.A.

When the two-year-old course hosted its first tournament, the Players Championship of 1982, the professionals were almost unanimous in their verdict: they hated it! Although the design had always aimed to be tough, clearly it was too much, and Pete Dye, the renowned U.S. golf course designer, modified the course slightly to soften the greens and change particularly brutal bunkers. The changes worked and the Players Championship has now become the unofficial fifth major.

The professionals' opinions were especially important at Sawgrass as TPC (Tournament Players Club) courses are owned by the PGA (Professional Golfers' Association) for the purpose of hosting tournaments. The course is respected by the professionals, as the clever design does not favor a specific type of player. Long hitters like Davis Love and Tiger Woods have won the Players Championship, but so have those relying on accuracy such as Hal Sutton, Justin Leonard, and Tom Kite. Adam Scott won at the age of 23; the following year Fred Funk won aged 48.

The island green

The PGA ownership is reflected in the design, in that the course was created for tournament golf. Huge amounts of earth were removed from the site and used to create spectator mounds surrounding the fairways and greens, the deep holes left from excavation being filled with water, creating plentiful lakes. Such is the fame of the island-green 17th, one of golf's most feared short holes, that an American sports channel devotes itself to showing uninterrupted coverage of the hole during the Players Championship. Interestingly, Dye never intended the 17th green to be surrounded by water. He was planning to make it a giant bunker until his wife suggested the island.

Water comes into play on most holes, notably on the brutal 18th. With a lake on the left of this tough dogleg, players are faced with a "bite off as much as you can chew" concept from the tee. If the drive is not perfectly placed you must lay up the approach, as an aggressive second shot, especially from the clingy rough, tends to be water bound.

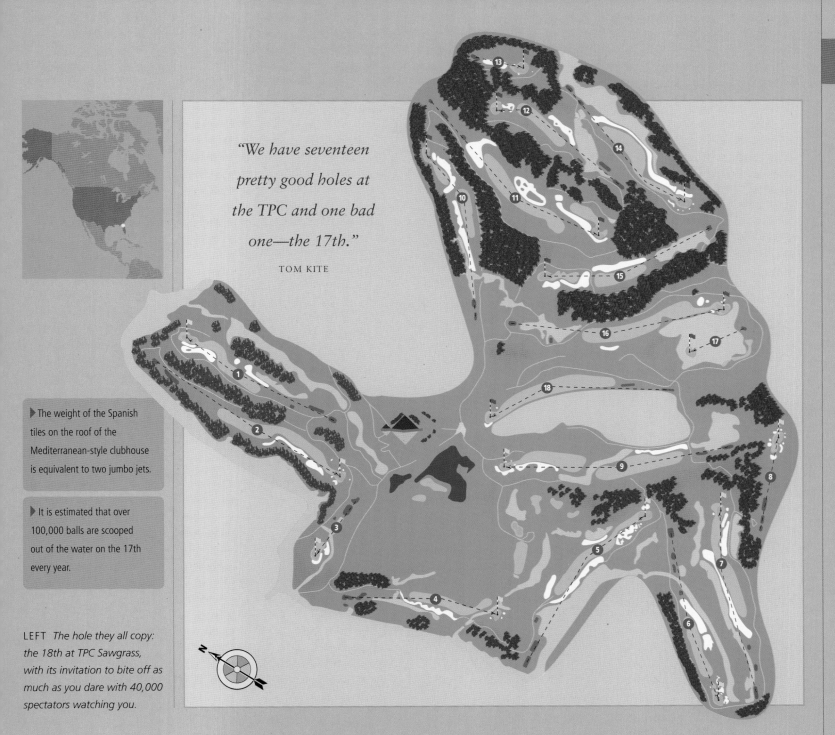

"We have seventeen pretty good holes at the TPC and one bad one—the 17th."

TOM KITE

▶ The weight of the Spanish tiles on the roof of the Mediterranean-style clubhouse is equivalent to two jumbo jets.

▶ It is estimated that over 100,000 balls are scooped out of the water on the 17th every year.

LEFT *The hole they all copy: the 18th at TPC Sawgrass, with its invitation to bite off as much as you dare with 40,000 spectators watching you.*

CARD OF THE COURSE

Hole	Distance (yards)	Par	Hole	Distance (yards)	Par
1	392	4	10	424	4
2	532	5	11	535	5
3	177	3	12	358	4
4	384	4	13	181	3
5	466	4	14	467	4
6	393	4	15	449	4
7	442	4	16	507	5
8	219	3	17	137	3
9	583	5	18	447	4
Out	3,588	36	In	3,505	36
			Total	7,093	72

You don't have to hold your breath for the course to kick in on the 17th. One of the best holes is the reachable par-5 2nd. With palm trees lining the fairway an accurate draw is required from the tee. The hole is deliberately kept at a realistic length so that it is hittable in two, but the second shot is played to one of Dye's trademark small greens, with penalizing rough and pot bunkers offering ample protection.

Recent alterations to the course have emphasized the "hard and fast" style of the design. The result of this is that a wayward shot now has even more chance of running away into trouble, which has been increased through the addition of 200 newly planted trees. The length of the course has changed little since it was first built, only about 200 yards/183 m having been added in nearly 30 years. The emphasis, then, is on creating exciting golf through reachable distances— refreshing in an era when too many other courses are put on steroids for tour events! The biggest change is a new clubhouse in the "stately home" style.

TPC Sawgrass

ABOVE AND RIGHT *The 17th hole has acquired a notoriety all of its own. On the opening day of the Players Championship in 1984 no fewer than 64 balls were hit into the water under blustery conditions. The stroke average was 3.79, making it the hardest par 3 in Tour history to that date.*

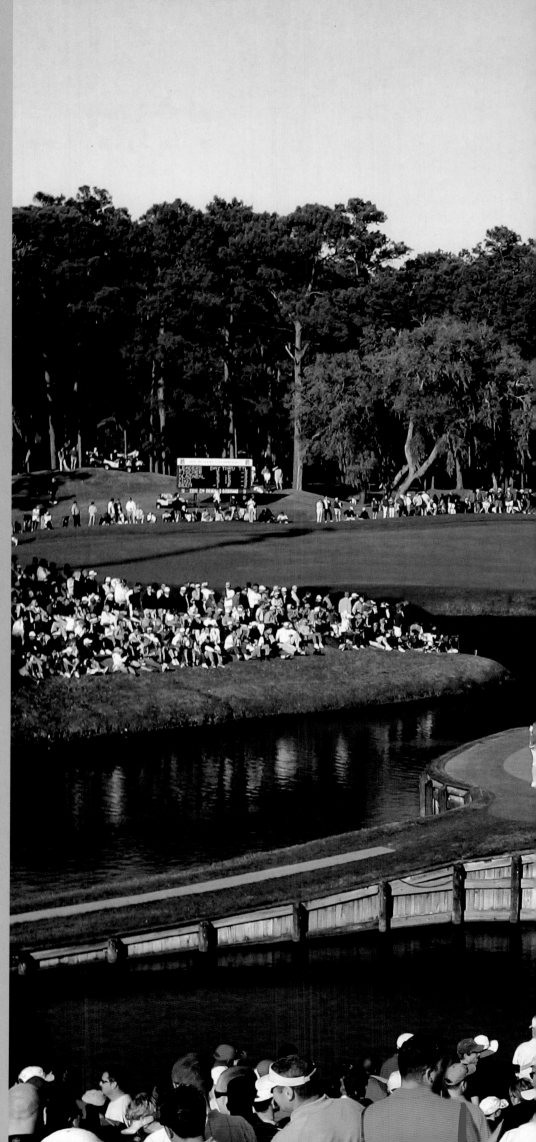

TPC Scottsdale

Stadium Course, TPC Scottsdale, Arizona, U.S.A.

Exhilarating golf is abundant when the Tour comes to Scottsdale for the FBR (formerly Phoenix) Open, with the quality of the course playing its part along with the 500,000 fans who make this golf's largest spectator event. The permanent earth galleries around the greens remind one that this is a TPC and, like Sawgrass, it was designed to host PGA events.

Scottsdale has seen many memorable moments, including the famous double-eagle described on the right, Tiger Woods's more conventional hole-in-one on the signature par-3 16th, and Mark Calcavecchia's record 28-under-par tournament total in the 2001 Phoenix Open. Evidently the Weiskopf/Morrish design—commissioned to test the best in Phoenix Open week while allowing fee-paying amateurs who play it the rest of the year a none-too-humbling experience—brings the best out of golfers. It is hard to believe that Scottsdale was one of the first collaborations between the former Open champion Tom Weiskopf and architect Jay Morrish, because the course flows so well. But, then again, this was one of the best design teams of its era.

DOUBLE EAGLE

One of the most memorable shots of tournament golf was played at Scottsdale. On the par-4 17th, Andrew Magee decided to take the water and bunkers out of play by attempting to drive the green. Forgetting to check that the match ahead had left the green, he successfully drove the green, whereupon his ball struck the putter of a surprised Tom Byrum, who was lining up his putt. Byrum was even more surprised to see Magee's ball deflected straight into the hole. It is the only double-eagle scored on a par 4 in PGA Tour history.

RIGHT *With its green grass and plentiful water TPC Scottsdale is reminiscent of an oasis. It is popular with the professionals, who appreciate its fairness.*

Fairway and sand

Like all the great desert courses, Scottsdale takes advantage of the natural defense offered by the desert scrub, while the contrasting colors of fairway and sand always make for a picturesque setting. However, the course is not as natural as it may seem. The barren land was far too flat for a golf course and much earthmoving had to take place, with the eventual creation of the six water hazards that refresh and nourish the lush grass.

The front nine, slightly more difficult than the more water-based back nine, relies heavily on the desert and severe bunkering for protection. There are 72 bunkers on the course and from the tee of the short 4th it seems as if all of them are protecting the three-tiered green. Needless to say, accuracy is crucial here, as it is throughout—although the greens are generally large, the tiers and slopes are unforgiving to mediocre approaches.

Despite its length—7,216 yards/6,598 m from the back tees—the course seems to play shorter as there are no real carries over the desert from the tee. Big hitters will almost certainly have a go at the par-5 15th. With water down the left, a good drive is essential, leaving the enormous temptation to go for the island green in two. This is obviously a great spot for spectators, but the most popular hole with the fans is always the 16th. With the hole viewed from above by tall galleries of cheering fans there is the feeling of gladiators in an arena who play to the small area of green in a sea of desert.

Scottsdale is clearly one of the best courses in the world to watch the drama of "stadium golf."

▶ Mark Calcavecchia's total of 256 in the 2001 Phoenix Open was one stroke better than the PGA tournament record set in 1955. Calcavecchia said of his tap-in for the record that he "just flinched it into the hole. All I could think about was, don't blow this one, you dummy."

CARD OF THE COURSE

Hole	Distance (yards)	Par
1	410	4
2	416	4
3	554	5
4	175	3
5	453	4
6	436	4
7	215	3
8	470	4
9	464	4
Out	3,593	35
10	403	4
11	469	4
12	195	3
13	595	5
14	477	4
15	552	5
16	162	3
17	332	4
18	438	4
In	3,623	36
Total	7,216	71

Valhalla

Valhalla Golf Club, Louisville, Kentucky, U.S.A.

When Tiger Woods walked purposefully toward the first tee of the 2000 U.S. PGA Championship at Valhalla, he stopped and winked at a commanding-looking old man in the crowd, joking: "You're awfully well dressed to be sitting out here!" The man was Dwight Gahm, founder of Valhalla. Gahm had dreamed of creating a major championship course, not to make a profit but to give something back to the game. He bought a 486-acre/197-ha plot of rolling land and commissioned golf's great champion, Jack Nicklaus, to design the course. Nicklaus described the land as "a golf designer's dream because there is a variety of terrain, vegetation and water to work with." After considering 40 possible routings, the course was finally completed in 1986.

The quality of the course was instantly recognized and Valhalla was chosen to host the 1996 and 2000 PGA Championships. Valhalla is refreshingly original, made up of two very different nines. The front nine is reminiscent of a heathland course, with wide, sloping fairways confined by mounds of thick Kentucky bluegrass. The inward nine is built on higher, tree-covered terrain and plays more like a traditional parkland course. The difficulty of the course is consistent through both nines.

Heathland meets parkland

One of the more unusual holes on the course is the 7th, featuring a double fairway. The safer route is to the right, but you cannot reach the green in two. You can from the left-hand fairway but the drive is tough, with serious rough awaiting if the fairway is missed.

Summing up the challenges is the par-5 10th. The tee shot must be aimed center right, as anything too far right will find a new fairway bunker, while anything left is blocked by trees. Even after a good drive most will lay up, as the hole plays a serious 590 yards/539 m from the back. The dangers around the green include a large slope behind the hole so that long shots will run away, a tough bunker short, and the thick rough that accompanies every hole. The green itself has two distinct levels, and you must find the correct tier to avoid three-putting.

The signature hole is the 13th, the shortest par 4 on the course but just as testing as the long holes. Most players take an iron from the tee for safety as the landing area is riddled with bunkers. You have to be on the fairway to have a chance of finding the small green perched on a bed of rocks almost totally surrounded by water.

Valhalla is now owned by the PGA of America. The PGA has always wanted to own a number of select courses from which to run major championships, and Gahm realized that Valhalla would be guaranteed tournament golf if he sold it to them. So far it has proved a perfect venue, inspiring wonderful golf watched by thousands of spectators seated in the natural amphitheaters around the greens. As promised, Gahm chose not to make a profit out of the game; he sold the course for exactly what he had paid. His reward came with the realization of a dream – with Valhalla hosting the 2008 Ryder Cup and thereby taking a seat at the great hall of golfing mythology.

▶ In Norse mythology, Valhalla is the great hall where the souls of dead warriors feast and rejoice with the gods.

LEFT *Although Jack Nicklaus was one of the most powerful players of his era, he has always made room for the short two-shot hole in his designs. This is the 13th.*

CARD OF THE COURSE

Hole	Distance (yards)	Par
1	450	4
2	535	5
3	210	3
4	375	4
5	465	4
6	495	4
7	600	5
8	190	3
9	420	4
Out	3,740	36
10	590	5
11	210	3
12	470	4
13	350	4
14	215	3
15	440	4
16	510	4
17	475	4
18	545	5
In	3,805	36
Total	7,545	72

"That's as good as it gets."

TIGER WOODS, AFTER WINNING
THE 2000 U.S. PGA CHAMPIONSHIP
AT VALHALLA

Whistling Straits

Straits Course, Whistling Straits, Kohler, Wisconsin, U.S.A.

With so much competition, it is rare that a new course is credited with the honor of hosting a major, and rarer still that this major turns out to be one of the most dramatic tournaments in years! The Straits Course was only six years old when its quality was recognized with the 86th U.S. PGA Championship. After benign conditions for the first three days, the wind picked up on the Sunday and the players felt the full force of the design. Like any great links, the Straits is open to the elements, and with wind rushing off Lake Michigan, the course reared its head. Played at 7,536 yards/6,891 m, this was the longest course in major championship history, and the scores showed it. After a dramatic play-off, Vijay Singh claimed his third major, and found his way into the record books for the highest ever final round by a PGA champion—with a 76!

Whistling Straits is an extraordinary place, built around the Village of Kohler, a community created by the wealthy Kohler family. This quaint garden village plays host to a vast resort. Four exceptional courses head the Kohler experience, each the creation of Pete Dye, commonly regarded as the most inventive course architect of the last fifty years. The two older courses, the Meadow Valleys and River courses, collectively known as Blackwolf Run, track through an ancient glacial valley and make good use of the natural slopes and water features. They have hosted the U.S. Women's Open and World Championship of Golf and have both received the coveted five stars from *Golf Digest*.

RIGHT *Dye littered the Straits Course with bunkers, as on a Scottish links where the wind—and sheltering sheep—exposed natural sand scrapes. Such bunkers are much in evidence on the 3rd and 4th holes.*

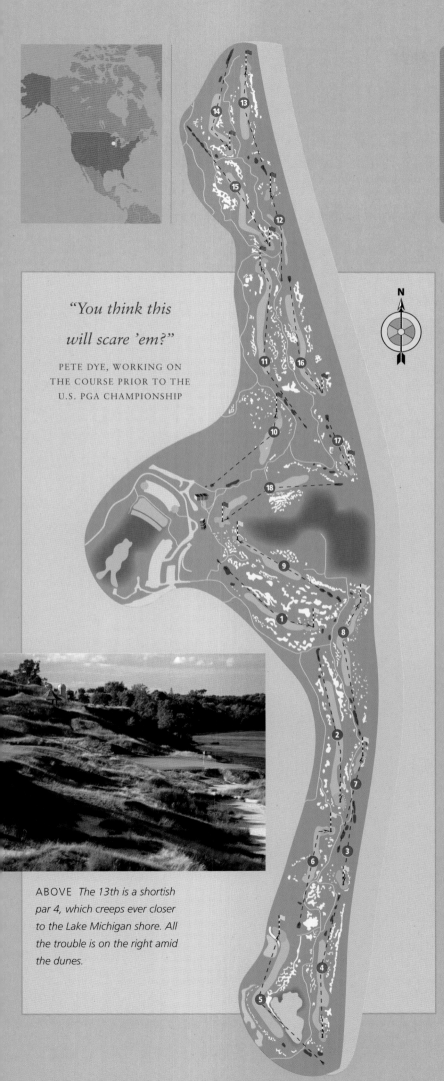

CARD OF THE COURSE

Hole	Distance (yards)	Par	Hole	Distance (yards)	Par
1	405	4	10	389	4
2	592	5	11	619	5
3	183	3	12	166	3
4	455	4	13	403	4
5	584	5	14	372	4
6	391	4	15	465	4
7	214	3	16	535	5
8	462	4	17	223	3
9	415	4	18	489	4
Out	3,701	36	In	3,661	36
			Total	7,362	72

"You think this will scare 'em?"

PETE DYE, WORKING ON
THE COURSE PRIOR TO THE
U.S. PGA CHAMPIONSHIP

ABOVE *The 13th is a shortish par 4, which creeps ever closer to the Lake Michigan shore. All the trouble is on the right amid the dunes.*

On the shores of Lake Michigan

With 36 superb inland holes established in Kohler's American Club Resort, the plumbing magnate acquired an abandoned army base on the shoreline of Lake Michigan, 9 miles/14 km from his village, and requested the help of Pete Dye to create a traditional links. Having completed massive earthmoving operations in the past, Dye was unperturbed by the drearily flat land, and began the lengthy process of creating the dunes and character of a true links. The result was Whistling Straits, two courses of exceptional charm. Located just inland from the lake, the Irish Course features beautifully mounded fairways surrounded by wispy rough. Incorporated into the traditional links style are four streams to give the course a pleasing variety, with water hazards more associated with parkland.

Most acclaimed of all is the Straits Course. Though the holes may be intimidating, the clever design, including eight waterfront holes, makes this a magnificent place. The 4th hole, named Glory, is truly spectacular, a daunting par 4, with a fairway that kicks left toward the dunes on the edge of Lake Michigan. A long iron is needed to approach the raised green, which sits above devastating bunkers backed by a perfect view of the lake. The 17th is known as Pinched Nerve, which accurately describes one of Dye's most intimidating par 3s of all—and he has designed some very tough ones indeed.

This visually stunning course is creatively designed for interesting golf, but do not pay too much attention to your score—nobody plays to handicap here!

Winged Foot

West Course, Winged Foot Golf Club, Mamaroneck, New York, U.S.A.

The winged foot is the emblem of the New York Athletic Club, a group of whose members founded the golf club of the same name in 1923. Given that Winged Foot is one of New York's premier clubs, located just off the I-95 New England Thruway, and no more than half an hour from central Manhattan, you might expect the place to be noisy, bustling, and full to the brim with golfers on every hole. Nothing could be further from the truth.

For a start, Winged Foot has two courses: the West, which is the championship course, and the East, which is pretty much its equal. The clubhouse is palatial, and the members know how to relax on a golf course. And yet they do not dawdle on the round. The club expects matches to take no longer than four hours, even in tournaments.

Both courses were laid out by Alfred Tillinghast, an architect of considerable lasting fame in the United States, with Baltusrol, Baltimore, and Bethpage State Park sharing with Winged Foot the honor of hosting U.S. Open Championships. The founding members wanted "a man-sized course," and they got it. What "Tilly" had to work with was largely flat parkland—not, you might think, the most promising canvas. But surely the sign of a great architect is to be able to produce a great course despite the lack of helpful topography, and here he produced two great courses.

RIGHT *Tillinghast's short holes are a study in themselves, so often imaginatively created from unpromising terrain. The 10th at Winged Foot West is one of his absolute best*

Tillinghast's masterly greens

"If it has not got anything about it that might make it respectable, it has got to have quality knocked into it until it can hold its head up in polite society," was Tillinghast's philosophy, and the quality he knocked into Winged Foot was particularly on and around the greens. They are nearly all raised up above the generally flat fairways, mischievously contoured and punishingly bunkered. Fortunately Tillinghast's design blueprints survive (he worked in minute detail) and to their credit the club has been able to restore the greens to their original size and contours.

Even from the members' tees Winged Foot West is long. Unless you can drive a good distance you will find yourself banging away with wooden-club approaches and if you are not devilishly straight you must surely tangle with the defensive bunkers or lack the control necessary to get the ball close to the pin on these tough greens. And when there is a shorter par 4, such as the 6th, the entrance to the green is incredibly narrow, with the putting surface seriously canted and hidden behind a right-hand protective bunker.

There are moments of respite on the short holes, but, again, only if you can find a way past the narrow entrances and guardian bunkers. Each of the greens is raised sufficiently to reject the shot that is not quite good enough. One of those short holes, the 10th, is world class, played across a valley to a plateau green loyally attended by punitive bunkers. A bewildering putting surface awaits if you do make it safely on to the green. Such is the genius of Tillinghast, whose courses should be on every golfer's wishlist!

▶ During the 2006 U.S. Open the 1st and 18th were the joint most difficult holes against par, both averaging 4.471. The only hole to have an average score below par was the par-5 5th, which averaged 4.654.

▶ Winged Foot may look natural to the eye, but it was actually created by blasting 7,200 tons of rock and felling 7,800 trees. It took a workforce of 200, with 60 teams of horses and 19 tractors, to complete the task.

CARD OF THE COURSE

Hole	Distance (yards)	Par
1	450	4
2	453	4
3	216	3
4	469	4
5	515	5
6	321	4
7	162	3
8	475	4
9	514	4
Out	3,575	35
10	188	3
11	396	4
12	640	5
13	214	3
14	458	4
15	416	4
16	478	4
17	449	4
18	450	4
In	3,689	35
Total	7,264	70

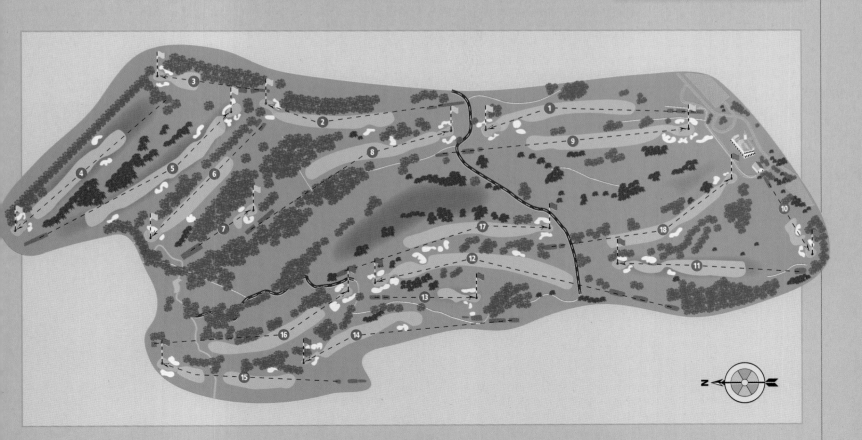

Banff Springs

Stanley Thompson 18, Fairmont Banff Springs Hotel, Banff, Alberta, Canada

Early golf courses simply evolved. Golfers found a route through whatever natural obstacles they found where they had chosen to play. There was minimal earthmoving. The emergence of the earliest course architects, such as Old Tom Morris, toward the end of the 19th century was accompanied by earthmoving on a very small scale—as much as a couple of men with shovels or possibly with a horse and scraper could move. Enter the steam shovel. It could hardly move mountains, but it could shift a large amount of dirt in a day. Throw in dynamite and almost anything became possible, or it did if you had a huge budget.

The enormous Banff Springs Hotel belonged to the Canadian Pacific Railway (CPR). It was the jewel in their crown, standing proudly overlooking the Spray and Bow Rivers surrounded by the stunning scenery of the Rocky Mountains. It had had a golf course of sorts since 1911, but it hardly matched up to the rest of the facilities on offer at this world-class hotel. The CPR had money and they also had railroad trucks, trainloads of them. They had seen what Canadian architect Stanley Thompson had achieved at their rival railroad Canadian National's resort at Jasper Park, so they hired Thompson themselves.

LUCKY ACCIDENT

Banff's most famous hole, the 4th, Devil's Cauldron, was not part of Thompson's original plan. He had no intention of using this area of the extensive property. However, during the winter of 1927, when heavy snows and bitter temperatures had halted construction work, an avalanche created a new glacial lake. When Thompson returned to Banff he spotted the lake and its potential as the basis for a world-class short hole immediately.

The world's most expensive golf course

It took Thompson and his team two years to build the Banff course, and when it opened in 1929 it was said to be the most expensive course ever built. The great thing about the course is that you would never guess that Thompson had spent so much money and moved so many thousands of tons of earth, for it all looks so natural. And what the unsuspecting eye might not notice is that a lot of Thompson's creativity went into ensuring that manufactured features, such as bunkers, raised greens, and mounds, were perfectly scaled to the grandeur of the surrounding forests and mountains. As a result of such empathy, the course is not overwhelmed by the scenery.

In recent years a new clubhouse has been erected and the original order of playing the holes abandoned. So the course now starts with a hole that throws the golfer straight into the forests. The next two holes turn to face Mount Rundle. Thompson needed dynamite to blast away enough room to build the 3rd fairway. Further dynamite was required to clear the site for the 4th green, but it was well worth it, for the 4th is a world-class short hole (so good that *Golf Magazine* ranks it in the top four in the world), calling for a drop-shot down over a glacial lake to find a well-bunkered green on the far side. After three more holes in the forests the course emerges for a sequence of beautiful holes alongside the Bow River.

Thompson's original opening hole is now the 15th, and many an experienced golfer has stood on that tee and been knocked off their game by the sight ahead, with the sparkling Spray River far below and the tree-lined and bunker-strewn fairway uncomfortably distant on its far side.

▶ Because it is too remote from major centers of population Banff Springs has never hosted an important professional tournament.

▶ Banff Springs is in the middle of a vast national park. Deer are frequently found on the course, and bears are occasional visitors.

LEFT AND BELOW
Wonderful golf in an exquisite setting. Stanley Thompson's course at Banff Springs is exceptional—the 4th hole is, quite simply, one of the greatest holes in golf.

CARD OF THE COURSE

Hole	Distance (yards)	Par
1	415	4
2	180	3
3	535	5
4	200	3
5	430	4
6	380	4
7	610	5
8	160	3
9	510	5
Out	3,420	36
10	225	3
11	425	4
12	450	4
13	230	3
14	445	4
15	480	4
16	420	4
17	385	4
18	585	5
In	3,645	35
Total	7,065	71

"It's out of this world."

BOBBY LOCKE, THE GREAT SOUTH AFRICAN GOLFER

Highlands Links

Highlands Links Golf Course, Ingonish Beach, Cape Breton, Nova Scotia, Canada

This extraordinarily beautiful golf course had its origins in the aftermath of the Great Depression. The Canadian government wanted to kick-start tourism on this stretch of the Atlantic coast and having observed how successful Stanley Thompson's courses at Jasper Park and Banff Springs had been in boosting the fortunes of both resorts, it seemed sensible to see what he could do at Cape Breton. He would have nothing like the extravagant budget available to him at Banff, but the site had such enormous potential that Thompson leaped at the chance.

Thompson's masters wanted a course that made the most of the sea shore. Thompson, on the other hand, felt that there were, indeed, good holes there, but that an even better course could be made by taking the course inland through the woods and hills of the beautiful Clyburn River valley. Thompson got his way and plenty of manpower to create his course. We can only be thankful that those charged with setting up this course listened to sense and that those who now conserve it do so with understanding.

ABOVE The fabulous, and inviting, view from the 6th tee, calling for a long and accurate drive to find the far-distant fairway on this excellent hole.

Enjoy the views

The first six holes keep close company with the Atlantic, giving magnificent seascapes from the higher ground. In fact the opening hole climbs sufficiently to make it a bogey 5 for most of us, but the reward is a long, helpful descent on the 2nd. Already it is apparent that these are some of the bumpiest fairways to be found on a golf course. It is not entirely accidental, for Thompson was a great admirer of Scottish links golf and he used the natural contours of the

BELOW *Stanley Thompson's genius was not only to route a course to make the most of gorgeous views such as this, the 15th, but to create great holes to indulge them.*

land tellingly—when he could. He also helped to create them artificially, by burying piles of stones and rocks and covering them with grass. This may sound crude, but Thompson was an artist.

Continuing along the coastal stretch of the course, two short holes frame a tempting, but treacherous, short two-shot hole, before the final hole in this section—the first-rate par-5 6th, which is particularly exciting from the championship tee with its 220-yard/201-m carry diagonally over water simply to find the fairway. A walk over the Clyburn River takes us up into the woods for the next par 5, which tumbles down, corkscrewing as it goes to a delightful green at the bottom of the hill. It is a superb hole technically, but even if it were an average hole it would still be ravishing, so glorious is the scenery. So it goes on, fascinating hole after fascinating hole, and so good is it that we forgive Thompson for giving us a long walk, almost a route march from the 12th green to the 13th tee, for it is a lovely walk in its own right.

There is, still to come, a truly breathtaking hole—the 15th. In golfing terms it's a wonderfully stimulating par 5, tempting all of us to have a crack at the green in two, downhill through a jumble of humps, bumps, and sidehill lies. Yet this is played out against the backdrop of the Atlantic Ocean, restored to us after our woodland playground, with the fairway perfectly aligned on Whale Island. Had the fairway and green been a few feet to either side this would have been a good hole. Placed where it is it really does take your breath away.

CARD OF THE COURSE

Hole	Distance (yards)	Par
1	405	4
2	447	4
3	160	3
4	324	4
5	164	3
6	537	5
7	570	5
8	319	4
9	336	4
Out	3,262	36
10	145	3
11	512	5
12	240	3
13	435	4
14	398	4
15	540	5
16	460	5
17	190	3
18	410	4
In	3,330	36
Total	6,592	72

▶ The holes at Highlands Links all have fanciful names with Scottish connections. The short 10th, for instance, is called Cuddy's Lugs, because the bunkers either side of the green reminded Thompson of a donkey's ears.

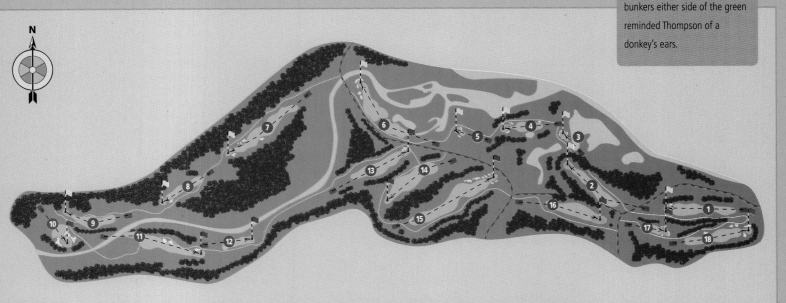

St. George's

St. George's

St. George's Golf and Country Club, Etobicoke, Ontario, Canada

Stanley Thompson must have known he was on to something good when he was given 2,000 acres/809 ha of rolling hills and meandering rivers from which to plan a course in the new Humber Valley Village. Built in the 1920s, this planned community was designed to resemble an English village, and required a fitting golf course to attract people to the area. With such an enormous expanse of land at his disposal, Thompson was able to decide upon an almost perfect stretch of golfing terrain.

Tall trees, rivers, and an undulating landscape all helped to capture the essence of the best English parkland courses, complementing the feel of the village. Although the course has been altered and toughened slightly over the years, the original charm remains.

A picturesque view from the elevated 1st tee gets the round off to a pleasant start. The tree-lined fairway, climbing up toward a raised green, makes for an appealing target with 3-wood in hand. The green is protected by deep, creatively shaped bunkers, the first in a sequence of interesting sand traps. Another good view is rewarded from the 2nd tee, but this time it is of an intimidating carry over

a gorge cutting diagonally through the hole. The longer the drive, the straighter the angle of the green for the approach, and at 466 yards/426 m many will be hitting a long club at a green angled away to the right.

An interesting feature at St. George's is that the fairways are rarely mowed in a straight line, instead bulging and narrowing to accentuate the holes. On the par-5 9th, for example, the fairway opens wide to accommodate shorter tee shots, while those looking to take too much distance from the tee will find the target is narrowed by two daunting bunkers pinching into the fairway from both sides. The same applies for the second shot, when a layup

is played to a relatively large portion of short grass, but the fairway gets tighter toward the green, so one thinks twice about attempting to get on in two.

Tough finish

A formidable finishing stretch begins on the 14th, a long par 4 with a river in play down the right-hand side, which eventually cuts across the front of the green. Many players will have to play this as a three-shot hole rather than chance the river with a long iron. Holes 17 and 18 used to be par 5s, and the accommodating bulges of the fairways are similar to the set-up of the 9th. The difficulty is that, as they are now par 4s, one must take on the tighter, longer lines previously designed for someone trying to get on under regulation. Despite the tough finish, a feeling of relaxation prevails on the short walk to the traditional clubhouse, the gentle hills, weaving fairways, and tranquil river making St. George's a delightful course in true English style.

CARD OF THE COURSE

Hole	Distance (yards)	Par	Hole	Distance (yards)	Par
1	370	4	10	377	4
2	466	4	11	528	5
3	198	3	12	399	4
4	474	5	13	213	3
5	432	4	14	466	4
6	201	3	15	570	5
7	446	4	16	203	3
8	223	3	17	470	4
9	538	5	18	451	4
Out	3,348	35	In	3,677	36
			Total	7,025	71

▶ After U.S. golfer Art Wall had won the 1960 Canadian Open with a score of 19-under, Stanley Thompson's protégé and friend, Robbie Robinson, was brought in to toughen up the course. He remodeled five of the holes, including the 4th (pictured left).

LEFT *At 474 yards/433 m the 4th is short for a par 5, but it is tightly bunkered on the approach to the green and trees constrict the fairway on both sides.*

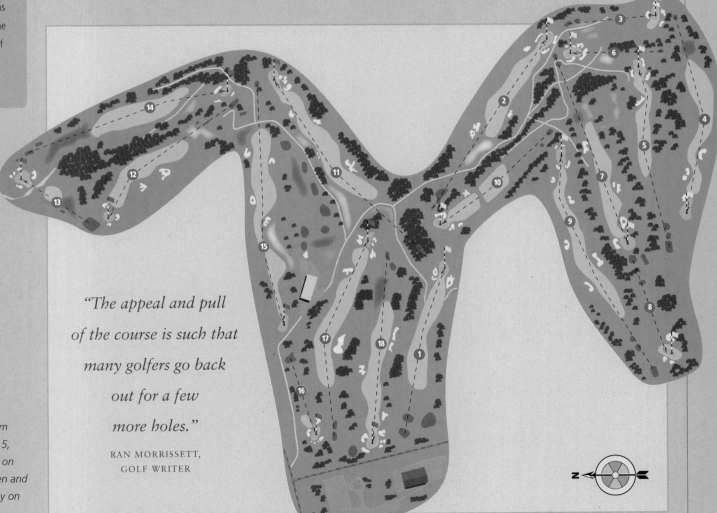

"The appeal and pull of the course is such that many golfers go back out for a few more holes."

RAN MORRISSETT,
GOLF WRITER

▶▶▶ Courses 47–56

Caribbean, Central & South America

Golf first came to South America toward the end of the 19th century, when British engineers traveled to Argentina and Brazil to build railroads and set up factories. As in many other parts of the world, the British (and the Scots in particular) were the evangelists for the game. Early courses were established close to the major centers of population and, inevitably, they were somewhat exclusive. Climate, geography, political unrest, and demography have been factors in keeping down the growth of golf since then, although the achievements of Roberto de Vicenzo and Angel Cabrera emphasize that there is no shortage of talent.

Engineering techniques learned in the Far East during World War II and the Vietnam War were put to use to enable golf courses to be built in the hot and steamy jungles close to the Equator. The development of grass strains capable of providing viable putting surfaces has made it possible to create golf courses of an international standard in Central America and the Caribbean. With the expansion of Mexico's tourist industry has come a raft of high-class, big-name resort courses.

Mid Ocean

Mid Ocean Golf Club, Tucker Town, Bermuda

The combination of the Bermudan pace of life, its climate, and the wonderful oceanscapes of Tucker Town would be sufficient enticement for most of us to be happy lazing over a cocktail or two all day, rather than exerting ourselves on a game of golf. And Mid Ocean's golf course is not dissimilar to a dozen and a half cocktails: lovely to look at, enchanting to play, one hole slipping down ever so easily after another, but with the power to create a horribly sore head when the score is added up.

The architect of our sore heads was none other than Charles Blair Macdonald. Somehow he escaped attention in the North American section of this book, but he designed the first 18-hole golf course in the United States (in Chicago) and also one of the most influential courses, architecturally—the National Golf Links of America on Long Island. In Bermuda he was invited to come out of semi-retirement by a steamship line, Furness Withy—its money, the site it had available, and the lure of the climate. Macdonald decided where the course could best be routed (where the grass grew best, along the valley floors), drew up his plans and departed, leaving construction to his business partner Seth Raynor. He

knew it was in safe hands and declared, "I can assure my golfing friends, a more fascinating, more picturesque course than the Mid Ocean will not be found in a pilgrimage around the world. There is nothing commonplace about it."

That was in 1921, and no one dissented from Macdonald's opinion. Mid Ocean had a glorious start to its life. Sadly, by the end of World War II, Furness Withy was in financial straits and decided to dispose of its golf club. A London banker gathered together a group of friends and business associates to purchase the course and turn it into a members' club, which they did in 1951. Happily, the club has gone from strength to strength ever since.

RIGHT *The risk of going for glory is very evident in this view of the 5th hole. It is also plainly visible that the challenge cannot be entirely ducked.*

A touch of old Scotland

Macdonald was not afraid of taking well-known Scottish holes as models and reworking their playing characteristics into his courses. So there are holes at Mid Ocean that remind the traveled golfer of St. Andrews, North Berwick, or Prestwick. There is even a Biarritz, modeled on a now long-disappeared hole in the French resort. They are not replicas, but they take sound design principles and use them to advantage. Perhaps the best of the lot, however, is the 5th—Cape. Its principle is one of risk and reward. The more you bite off with the drive the better shape you are in for the second shot—but only if you get it absolutely right. Otherwise the egg thrown on the face is in direct proportion to the inability to resist greed. On this occasion a mangrove swamp awaits with a basketful of eggs.

▶ Changes were made over the years that radically altered the nature of the course, particularly the bunkering. Recently the club has done much to restore Macdonald's vision of strategic golf while keeping the course playable by all skill levels.

HEROIC CHALLENGE

The 5th at Mid Ocean is the archetypal "Cape" hole. The term comes from the placing of the green on a peninsula with trouble both sides of it and through the back. However, most of the best examples also feature a drive over trouble of some sort, on which you bite off as much of the carry as you dare—the risk being a lost ball in treacherous rough or water, the reward being a better position from which to attack the green. The 18th holes at TPC Sawgrass and Ganton are fine examples, the former with water, the latter without.

CARD OF THE COURSE

Hole	Distance (yards)	Par
1	418	4
2	471	4
3	167	3
4	330	4
5	433	4
6	360	4
7	164	3
8	349	4
9	406	4
Out	3,098	34
10	404	4
11	487	5
12	482	4
13	238	3
14	357	4
15	504	5
16	376	4
17	199	3
18	521	5
In	3,568	36
Total	6,666	70

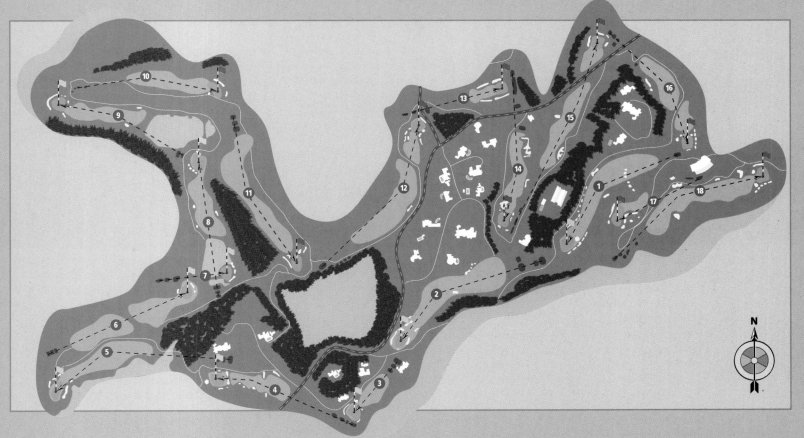

Tryall

Tryall

The Tryall Club, Montego Bay, Jamaica

On arrival in Jamaica it takes about ten minutes, and maybe the odd local beer or rum, to fully succumb to the relaxed attitude indigenous to the islands. The Tryall Club is the perfect setting in which to enjoy this laid-back environment, with the former sugar plantation turned luxury hotel complex adjacent to the palm-swept coastline. As you would expect, the weather plays a huge role in the appeal of the club, but the site affords more than endless sun, as there are also strong winds from the sea. Texan architect Ralph Plummer designed the course to take full advantage of these.

Although the course was fairly short when it was opened in 1958, and is just 6,722 yards/6,146 m at its maximum today, the strength of design and trademark sloping greens, not to mention the constant winds, have meant that the course has never been demolished by the professionals over the years. Because of these challenges, trajectory and control have always been more important than length.

BELOW *As is often the case, a hole can look so much simpler and less intimidating when viewed from behind. This is the signature 4th hole.*

HEADY DAYS

With the American and European tours joining forces with other tours, professional tournament golf is now a year-round, worldwide affair. It was not always so, and there was room in the calendar for extra events. Such an event was the Johnnie Walker World Championship, which brought famous players to Tryall for a bit of end-of-season sun and fun, and a lot of cash! Fred Couples was the last winner in 1995.

Despite its formidable record, Tryall is actually very playable for the average golfer. Unlike a tough British or U.S. Open course, golfers are not simply battered off the course by head-high rough and astronomic yardages. The whole round is wonderfully enjoyable, and it's easy to be beguiled by the plantation legacy, lush scenery, and ocean views only to find that the wind and challenging short game have stolen shots from you.

The hole that designed itself

Tryall's signature hole is the 4th, built when an area of land adjacent to the sea was purchased. The hole simply designed itself. With the Caribbean Sea down the left, the Flint River in front and the tricky prevailing wind blowing from the sea, tee shots do not come more dramatic than this. Even if you manage a decent shot, the work is not over: many players will fall foul of the sloping green to walk off with a bogey.

Despite several other memorable tee shots, Tryall's greatest interest must surely lie in the quality of its approach shots. Anything too safe will result in three putts on these tough greens, so you must take on the challenging pin positions and be creative in using the slopes and borrows around the greens that roll the ball satisfyingly on to the putting surface. It helps to have the benefit of a little local knowledge from the excellent caddies.

▶ As first built Tryall was somewhat shorter at just under 6,400 yards/5,852 m, with water affecting only two holes, but much of the original remains intact.

▶ During the 1990s Tryall was home to the Johnnie Walker World Championship whose winners included Fred Couples (twice), Nick Faldo, Larry Mize, and Ernie Els.

CARD OF THE COURSE

Hole	Distance (yards)	Par
1	373	4
2	193	3
3	521	5
4	175	3
5	367	4
6	510	4
7	434	4
8	482	4
9	404	4
Out	3,459	35
10	170	3
11	500	5
12	213	3
13	373	4
14	450	4
15	445	4
16	429	4
17	391	4
18	342	4
In	3,313	35
Total	6,772	70

RIGHT *Played into the prevailing wind from an elevated tee, the 15th is one of the toughest, and most dramatic, two-shot holes at Tryall.*

Casa de Campo

Teeth of the Dog Course, Casa de Campo Golf Club, La Romana, Dominican Republic

Golf grew up by the sea: first in Scotland, later in England and Ireland. It was inevitable that as golf spread throughout the world many of the game's finest courses were constructed along the shores of the great oceans and seas. Those early British courses played *near* the sea. Many of their successors play *over* it, few more compellingly so than the Teeth of the Dog Course at Casa de Campo.

The name of the course refers to the native coral—*dientes del perro*—which was crushed and used to build peninsula tees out into the Caribbean and for the low retaining walls preventing the precious land from returning to the sea—until the passing of an occasional hurricane, that is. It was not the only innovative practice employed in the construction of the course, the fairways and greens being neither seeded nor turfed, but planted by hand with individual tufts of grass. But then, this was never going to be an ordinary course.

It was one of the early courses of Pete Dye, arguably the most inventive of those course designers working in the last quarter of the 20th century. He had already displayed vision and creativity far beyond his thus-far limited experience at Harbour Town in South Carolina. At La Romana he was given a blank canvas, and he took himself up in a helicopter to explore every inch of this huge resort until he found a stretch of promising coastline. He delivered more than his wealthy patron could have hoped for, unquestionably the Caribbean's finest golfing challenge. Dye has been back twice more to create two further imaginative courses at this extraordinary resort, which is more a way of life than somewhere to spend a vacation.

RIGHT *The 5th is the first of Teeth of the Dog's compulsory carries over the sea. It may not be long, but the penalty for inaccuracy is obvious!*

Entrancing ocean holes

It would be wrong to ignore the inland holes, for they are testing enough, two of the first four holes being modeled on famous originals at Prestwick and Pinehurst and a third being a tribute to Charles Blair Macdonald, one of the most influential of all golden-age American golf designers. The first skirmish with the sea is made at the short 5th, an all-or-nothing par 3 from a promontory tee to a green set out into the sea. There are similar short holes at the 7th and 16th, and yet in no way is there a sense of blind repetition of a good idea. Dye was too individual a character to resort to that.

Spectacular though these holes are, and lasting though they are in the mind, it is probably the two-shot holes beginning with a drive over the water that are the stars of the show. The 8th is just such an example, where you are asked to bite off as much as you can chew from the tee, but very likely tempted to try just too much. There are mirror-images at the 15th and 17th, too, part of a stirring back nine. All three courses are fascinating, but it is Teeth of the Dog that captures the heart of the golfer as well as the soul of La Romana.

RIGHT *With the sea on your left on the way out, your right coming in, if you cannot play straight you might as well give up! This is the 16th.*

▶ The newest of the Pete Dye courses, the Dye Fore Course, measures an astonishing 7,770 yards/7,105 m from the back tees.

▶ Even the fairway soil on the Teeth of the Dog Course is unconventional, being a blend of sand, dirt, and a by-product of sugar refining, *cachaza*.

CARD OF THE COURSE

Hole	Distance (yards)	Par
1	401	4
2	378	4
3	545	5
4	327	4
5	155	3
6	449	4
7	225	3
8	417	4
9	505	5
Out	3,402	36
10	377	4
11	540	5
12	445	4
13	175	3
14	505	5
15	384	4
16	185	3
17	435	4
18	440	4
In	3,486	36
Total	6,888	72

"Pete Dye discovered a natural violence at Casa de Campo well suited to his creative expression."

ANDRE-JEAN LAFAURIE,
GOLF WRITER

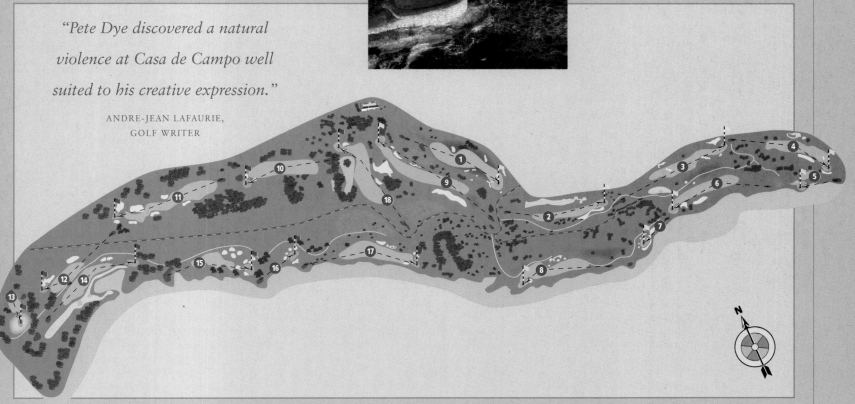

BACK TO COLUMBUS

The Dominican Republic has a long European history, dating back to December 1492 when Christopher Columbus first landed on the island. It can claim the first cathedral and university in the Americas. At the Casa de Campo resort in 1976 it was decided to try to build a replica European settlement using the techniques of the late 15th century—Altos de Chavón. It is now an artists' paradise with studios, a design school, and archaeological museum, with a wealthy cultural foundation to support it all. There is even a copy of a Greek open-air theater. For golfers the best place to view all this is from the Dye Fore Course, which roams inland from the resort, overlooking the artists' village and much else, for this is a long course—7,770 yards/7,105 m from the back tees.

RIGHT *It all looks so simple on the 7th hole when the sun is up on a calm day. The island of Hispaniola on which the course is located provides a buffer between the Atlantic Ocean and the Caribbean Sea. When the wind gets up Teeth of the Dog is a tough course.*

Mahogany Run

Mahogany Run Golf Course, St. Thomas, U.S. Virgin Islands

Mahogany Run markets itself as "Home of the Devil's Triangle," three extraordinary holes played along the edge of precipitous cliffs high above the crashing waves of the Caribbean. But it is much more than just three spectacular holes. It is amazingly compact and wonderfully varied, running up hill and down dale through tropical rainforest, before and after bursting out to the cliff's edge.

The uncle-and-nephew team of George and Tom Fazio were commissioned by the brothers Jim and Robert Armour to lay out the course in the late 1970s, and it opened for play in 1980. The steep hills and plunging valleys, and the modest acreage, restricted the course routing and ensured that it is tight. Accurate, thoughtful play, therefore, is of far greater value than unrestrained power hitting. Fortunately it is not a long course, even from the back plates.

This is the only course on St. Thomas, and, given the geography of the island, is likely to remain so! On such a site the scorecard tells only part of the story, for on some holes hills, up or down, add or subtract much distance from the player's point of view, and going for glory can readily end in a lost ball, for this is seriously dense rainforest. And there are a number of significant doglegs calling for placement above all else, such as the first three holes. Water is used sparingly—apart from the sea, that is—although it is used tellingly on the 1st, 10th, and 15th. The short holes—five of them—are just that, and most of the two-shot holes are under 400 yards/366 m, some of them significantly so.

RIGHT *The Devil's Triangle is extreme golf, as is shown in this picture of the 14th with its narrow green perched on the edge of a precipice.*

▶ Iguanas and pelicans are among the spectators at Mahogany Run, and fresh mangoes may drop from the trees as you walk along the fairways.

▶ According to Mahogany Run's website, "Golfers who play all three without a penalty stroke are awarded a special 'I Survived the Devil's Triangle' certificate."

ABOVE RIGHT *On a hole such as the 13th, the bunkers are there to help you—to prevent the ball bounding away forever.*

CARD OF THE COURSE

Hole	Distance (yards)	Par	Hole	Distance (yards)	Par
1	414	4	10	363	4
2	355	4	11	153	3
3	519	5	12	351	4
4	133	3	13	327	4
5	355	4	14	159	3
6	376	4	15	564	5
7	305	4	16	146	3
8	148	3	17	415	4
9	415	4	18	510	5
Out	3,020	35	In	2,988	35
			Total	6,008	70

The Devil's Triangle

The 13th is one of the drive-and-pitch par 4s, apparently nothing much according to the card. But that does not take into account the sea, for the narrow fairway runs down steeply toward a tiny green perched on the end of the land, high above the deep blue waters. The Devil's Triangle has arrived. Nerves are frayed, and seemingly simple shots, such as a wedge approach, are suddenly twice as demanding. It is a marvelous spot for a green.

Next in the Triangle is the longest of the short holes, a mere short-iron, but in a wind the ball may have to be played out over the sea to be brought back in on the wind to find the putting green. Again a cool head is required. Whatever the state of play of the match the views are to be savored. The Devil's Triangle finishes with an uncharacteristically long par 5. Few will risk trying to get home in two shots, because a sizable pond fronts the green and out-of-bounds lies just behind the putting surface. Beautiful, but unforgiving!

Cabo del Sol

Cabo del Sol

Ocean Course, Cabo del Sol Golf Club, Baja California, Mexico

Baja California, with its enviable climate (350 days of sun per year), was bound to catch on as a vacation resort at some point. As far as the Mexicans were concerned it might as well have been another country, for apart from a tiny strip of continuous land at the very north of the peninsula it is separated from the mainland by the many hundreds of miles of the Sea of Cortes.

The Americans and Canadians solved its accessibility problems by flying in, which they now do in considerable numbers, in the early days to fish or whale-watch. It was inevitable that they would want to play golf, too, and the two contrasting courses at Cabo del Sol provided a very potent seed from which further developments are arising.

To confirm to the traveling public that Cabo del Sol is a top-of-the-range resort, two of the great names of golf course design were commissioned to lay out courses—Jack Nicklaus and Tom Weiskopf. Nicklaus was unquestionably the greatest golfer of his era (many would say of all time) and a master player at demolishing a golf course, but his own-design courses are more generous to the average

player than you might expect. He took to heart the adverse criticisms of his early designs, as "too hard and made for Nicklaus." Weiskopf, on the other hand, had one of the most elegant swings of all time and a formidable technique, yet did not perhaps achieve as many major results as were once forecast. His golf courses, however, are frequently far more thought-provoking than those of some of the more prolific winners among his contemporaries.

BELOW *The 17th hole, played across the beach even from the very front tees, is beautifully routed to align with the distant peaks.*

CARD OF THE COURSE

Hole	Distance (yards)	Par
1	436	4
2	574	5
3	327	4
4	555	5
5	458	4
6	190	3
7	207	3
8	438	4
9	469	4
Out	3,654	36
10	436	4
11	352	4
12	515	5
13	213	3
14	366	4
15	530	5
16	429	4
17	178	3
18	430	4
In	3,449	36
Total	7,103	72

▶ Although golf tourism is relatively new to this part of Mexico, tourists of another kind colonized the area in the 1730s: the Spanish, who established a presidio in San José del Cabo. Nor are modern tourists only golfers—fishing is big here, too.

ABOVE RIGHT *The 13th, the only inland par 3 on the Ocean Course, is a fine hole, played downhill to a green defended by bunkers, cacti, and scrub.*

Desert and ocean

Cabo boasts two completely different styles of course. Weiskopf's Desert Course was built inland, a rugged course (admittedly with fine ocean views) that asks the golfer contemporary questions of length, accuracy, and finesse. Nicklaus's Ocean Course is in many ways gentler, although there are compulsory carries over the Pacific on the 5th and 7th, 17th, and 18th holes. Yet, to the competent player, water carries are hardly intimidating. What the good player might enjoy more is the challenge of the approach shots to the 5th and 16th, whose greens are deceptively set up on the very edge of the ocean and therefore call into question the golfer's trust in his or her yardage and commitment to the shot. Psychological golf can be such fun!

Vista Vallarta

Nicklaus Course, Vista Vallarta Club de Golf, Puerto Vallarta, Mexico

Hardly had the Nicklaus Course opened than it played host to a star-studded field of famous professionals, who assembled there to contest the World Cup of Golf of 2002. In fact it is one of two courses at Vista Vallarta, both opened in 2001. They could hardly be more different, yet they sit side by side. Jack Nicklaus was given the higher ground on which to build his course, so it offers extensive views into the mountains of the Sierra Madre as well as distant oceanscapes of the Bay of Banderas. For his course, Tom Weiskopf was allocated a patch of unadulterated jungle, with deep ravines and fast-flowing streams.

Played from the back tees, the Nicklaus course stretches to more than the 7,000 yards/6,400 m that nowadays seem to be mandatory for any course aspiring to hold professional tournaments. Nevertheless, the World Cup winners, Shigeki Maruyama and Toshi Izawa of Japan, tore the course up in recording a record low score for the tournament of 36 under par. Lesser mortals are offered tees giving course lengths of 6,595 yards/6,030m or 6,031 yards/5,515 m but, because of the hilliness of the site, the course generally plays longer than the yardage might indicate. Nicklaus and his team used the topography to considerable effect, and there are some cleverly sited greens. Generously wide fairways offer room from the tee, so the emphasis is mostly on well-thought-out approach work.

RIGHT *The scenery at Vista Vallarta is exhilarating, contrasting with the altogether gentler nature of Jack Nicklaus's course.*

Sloping lies

The hilliness of the course is evident immediately, with the opening tee shot played to a fairway that slopes significantly from left to right, leaving the ball beneath the feet for the second shot as you attempt to get to the right part of a two-level green. Nicklaus is not a lover of uphill holes, but here he had no option, and the 2nd climbs noticeably. You climb again on the par-5 3rd, a true three-shotter with the third shot very likely played blind to the green. The views make the climbing worthwhile.

There is plenty of variety in the challenges Nicklaus sets, perhaps the most remarkable being the 10th hole, a par 5 with a choice of fairways to aim at from the tee. The safe option is to take the left-hand route, but big hitters could easily drive too far and finish in a creek cutting across the fairway. They will more likely aspire to making the far longer carry to the right-hand patch of fairway, from which it may be possible to get home in two, but only if allowance is made for the left-to-right slope of the fairway in front of the green.

Nicklaus saved one of the best holes for last, a par 4 played from an elevated tee with a long carry to find the fairway. Position is of paramount importance here, for the green is tucked away round a corner to the left and the putting surface rises considerably toward the back left. It is hot and humid here, but, after a refreshing drink, you are bound to want to try the very different but equally fascinating Weiskopf course.

▶ During the 2002 World Cup Phil Mickelson drove the green at the par-4 13th hole, making a treacherous carry over trees, giving him the opportunity to hole out for an eagle two.

BELOW *Phil Mickelson displaying his legendary recovery skills during the 2002 World Cup.*

CARD OF THE COURSE

Hole	Distance (yards)	Par
1	401	4
2	429	4
3	550	5
4	381	4
5	213	3
6	452	4
7	426	4
8	534	5
9	182	3
Out	3,568	36
10	536	5
11	394	4
12	580	5
13	340	4
14	440	4
15	177	3
16	423	4
17	170	3
18	445	4
In	3,505	36
Total	7,073	72

Papagayo

Papagayo

Arnold Palmer Course, Four Seasons Golf Club Costa Rica, Peninsula Papagayo, Guanacaste, Costa Rica

With views of the Pacific Ocean on 14 holes, one might assume that this is a seaside course, but it is in fact built in a tropical forest. The course is stunning, backed by forests and the ocean, played to a soundtrack of hugely diverse wildlife. Efforts to protect this ecology, combined with the difficult terrain, have resulted in a spread-out course with huge distances between some of the greens and tees, so it is essential to use a buggy.

As with all resort courses, the real challenge lies in making it playable for golfers of all standards. Arnold Palmer's design team has made a great blueprint for others to follow, especially in such difficult surroundings. Successful use of multiple tees is an important feature, but the greatest asset is the design of the holes themselves, many of them providing alternative routes to the green according to the level of a golfer's competence. On the 4th, for example, a par 5 with a slight dogleg left, long hitters can try to carry the fairway bunkers 270 yards/247 m away to shorten their approach. But there is interest for shorter hitters, too, as they must negotiate bunkers on their own route.

It is enjoyable to play a course with such variety. All too many courses use excessive distance as their main defense, but this course is far more inventive. The holes twist and turn through the tall trees, with slopes coming into play, so players must choose their angles carefully and really plan their way around.

Palmer used the land he was given, rather than forcing it into something unnatural. A strong nerve is called for, especially on the short 7th, which requires a breathtaking carry over a gaping valley. Even though it is only a short iron to the green, most players take one more club than they might from the middle of a fairway.

In Palmer's footsteps

Confidence is important on the long par-4 13th, with an obligatory carry over a lake from the tee before playing uphill to the large green. These longer holes are rare, though, and it is the shorter holes that really capture the essence of the course, allowing players to "go for broke" the way Palmer always did.

At least three of the par 4s are theoretically drivable, and this always creates exciting golf—one or two players out of a competent fourball will usually take on the shot. One such hole is the 3rd, which measures 367 yards/336 m if you follow the dogleg but via the direct line is far shorter and, given the prevailing wind, makes the green reachable from the tee. With trouble in the form of a tree and bunkers, the safe shot is down the fairway with a lofted wood. But it is almost a slur on the style of the great man to take that option!

And what could be more essential Palmer than the 18th, with its all-or-nothing shot across a lake in an attempt to make one last eagle?

LEFT *The short 17th at Papagayo is interestingly bunkered through the back of the green, and it readily illustrates the charm of golf in this glorious location.*

CARD OF THE COURSE

Hole	Distance (yards)	Par	Hole	Distance (yards)	Par
1	543	5	10	433	4
2	174	3	11	207	3
3	367	4	12	601	5
4	538	5	13	468	4
5	215	3	14	383	4
6	446	4	15	350	4
7	133	3	16	305	4
8	390	4	17	163	3
9	522	5	18	550	5
Out	3,328	36	In	3,460	36
			Total	6,788	72

▶ From the beginning Papagayo has set out to be different from other clubs. There is no dress code. The emphasis is on sheer enjoyment. And they boldly state that they "will also offer free golf for kids on Sundays." Green fees, too, are refreshingly inexpensive.

▶ The holes have names in Spanish, the short 2nd being Tiburon (Shark). The shark's fin is a strip of fairway enclosing a bunker, while the shark's mouth is where the most testing pin position is. The 3rd is named, most appropriately, Buena Vista (Beautiful View).

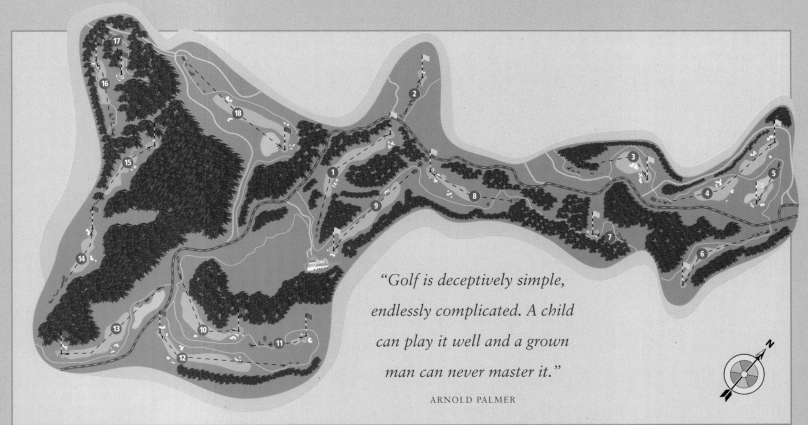

"*Golf is deceptively simple, endlessly complicated. A child can play it well and a grown man can never master it.*"

ARNOLD PALMER

The Jockey Club

The Jockey Club, San Isidro, Buenos Aires, Argentina

At the 2007 U.S. Open, the world found out that Argentinian golf is seriously underrated as Angel Cabrera stormed to victory; the same goes for Argentinian golf courses. Few would consider this country for a golfing break, but the region is home to some fine courses, the best being the Jockey Club.

Founded in 1882 for the polo-playing social elite, the club decided to add golf to its activities in the 1920s. Wisely, they hired Alister MacKenzie (who already had Royal Melbourne and Cyprus Point in his portfolio) to design two courses on an area of land they had purchased. MacKenzie accepted, pleased to escape from the depression engulfing the United States where he was then living, but he soon found himself staring at a grimly flat landscape. His solution was to create the signature features of both courses: the countless artificial mounds that adorn both fairways and greens. MacKenzie adored St. Andrews, and he recaptured much of its spirit on

this very dissimilar terrain. It is often said that golf course architects should be judged by their work on unpromising land. MacKenzie robustly proves that contention here.

The Blue Course is the shorter of the two, and accuracy is called for to navigate its tight fairways. In a final salute to St. Andrews, the 9th and 18th greens are joined together to create a stunning double green, divided by one of the many substantial mounds. Though both courses are similar, it is the longer Red Course that has seen tournament action, including the 2001 Argentine Open, won by none other than Angel Cabrera.

RIGHT *The extraordinary mounds surrounding the 16th green are closely shaven to give multiple options for a recovery shot.*

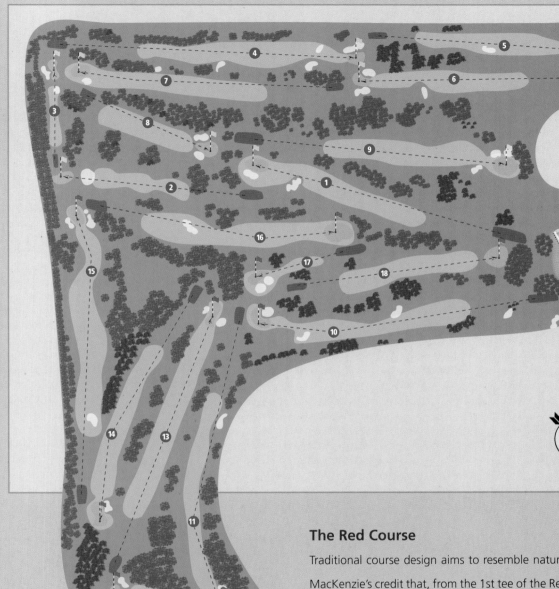

▶ In 2005 Kevin Stadler won the Argentine Open (in its centenary year) at the Jockey Club. His father, Craig, having triumphed in 1992, they became the only father/son winners in the tournament's history.

The Red Course

Traditional course design aims to resemble nature, and it is to MacKenzie's credit that, from the 1st tee of the Red Course, the mounds sweeping the fairway look entirely natural. It is also apparent that these mounds are a major strategic feature, many easily as tall as a golfer, and there will rarely be a flat lie or straight fairway roll. That is not to say that the course is needlessly penalizing. MacKenzie designed courses to be enjoyable to play, and this becomes evident on the 2nd. At just 350 yards/320 m, this is far from the slog of too much modern design, but the hole must be played with skill as the green is mountainous. Creativity is called for, with the design urging players to dream up running shots and long-range putts in true links spirit. The undulations provide such a thorough test that it was even debated whether the course needed bunkers at all.

Today the Jockey Club represents something of an oasis. When you walk down the bunkerless 18th, backed by the thumping of thoroughbred hooves from the adjacent polo field and racecourse, it is hard not to be smitten with the traditional atmosphere. This charming course has something different to offer than the more distance-orientated modern game. Argentina truly is an underrated golfing destination.

CARD OF THE COURSE

Hole	Distance (yards)	Par	Hole	Distance (yards)	Par
1	425	4	10	470	4
2	350	4	11	506	5
3	148	3	12	175	3
4	490	5	13	444	4
5	340	4	14	390	4
6	355	4	15	511	5
7	425	4	16	401	4
8	208	3	17	170	3
9	415	4	18	354	4
Out	3,156	35	In	3,421	36
			Total	6,577	71

Ilha de Comandatuba

Comandatuba Ocean Course, Ilha de Comandatuba, Una, Bahia, Brazil

Brazil's reputation is more one of stunning beaches than of stunning golf courses, but the Hotel Transamérica Ilha de Comandatuba resort shows the two need not be independent of each other. Cut off from the mainland by a river, the resort is considered an island, and 13 miles/21 km of private beach skirt the hotel. Sitting between the sea and the mangrove swamp is an eye-catching golf course, the creation of American architect Dan Blankenship, who has crafted the unusual character of the land he was given to work with into a highly original design.

The Ocean Course plays five of its holes along the sea, features 12 lakes on nine of the holes, and incorporates the retreating beach in the style of a desert. Vast expanses of sand surround the fairways, eliminating the need for rough, and as the sand is so compact it is eminently playable—a far more appealing prospect than endless rough, given that the majority of golfers here are on vacation. Nature, in the form of coconut trees and forest vegetation, provides a perfect backdrop to the lush fairway grass and contrasting sand dunes, and from this tropical foliage emerge countless exotic birds, capuchin monkeys, foxes, and anteaters to add to the unique environment of the course. The use of Bermuda grass for fairways and a dwarf Bermuda for greens helps present the course well, despite the climate.

Multiple choice

Given the extraordinary location, the hole design is suitably idiosyncratic, as fairways balloon around lakes and sand, giving the golfer several options on each shot. Scoring well requires golfers to be decisive in judging the correct line for their skill. On the par-5 12th, you are even confronted with parallel fairways (though they eventually merge into one). Short hitters are advised to drive down the right-hand fairway, but they risk running out of room from the more forward tees. Big hitters may be tempted to try for the left-hand fairway, leaving a better approach shot, but a mighty carry is required over the sand that surrounds the entire hole and cuts in front of the green.

Another par 5, the 5th, offers a choice of ways to drown! At some point most golfers are going to be tempted to shorten the route to the green—probably with dire results. The whole golfing experience is hugely enjoyable, with the monstrous 18th, played along the coastline, offering a picturesque finale to the round—though those prone to slicing could easily end up on the beach, racing toward the water.

▶ The hotel built Brazil's biggest private airport to cater to its guests who, in addition to the golf and luxury spa, can take surfing and circus lessons and go deep-sea fishing for giant blue marlin on Charlotte Bank.

RIGHT An aerial view of Isla Comandatuba reveals just how much sand has been incorporated into the course.

LEFT Somewhere out there is a fairway—reaching it from the back tee calls for a sure technique and steady nerve.

CARD OF THE COURSE

Hole	Distance (yards)	Par
1	412	4
2	192	3
3	408	4
4	367	4
5	596	5
6	162	3
7	397	3
8	432	4
9	511	5
Out	3,477	36
10	379	4
11	416	4
12	518	5
13	217	3
14	399	4
15	480	4
16	293	4
17	187	3
18	562	5
In	3,451	36
Total	6,928	72

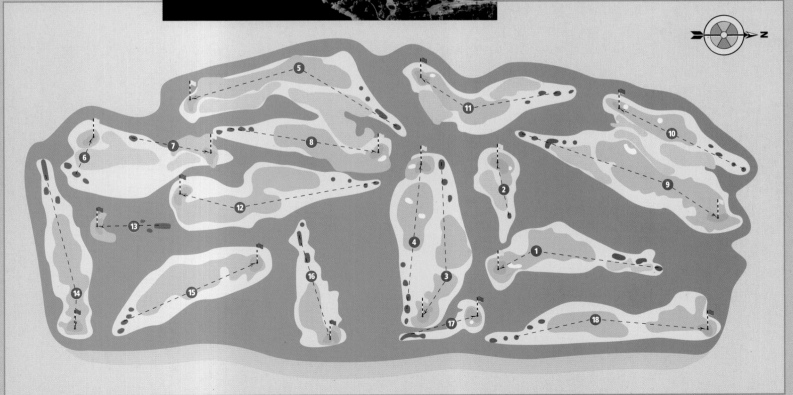

La Dehesa

Club de Golf La Dehesa, Santiago, Chile

Chile is without doubt one of the most geographically diverse countries in the world. Huge parts of the land are uninhabitable, as the country is dominated by the vast Andes mountain range. Much of the land is under permanent snow, yet the country also features inhospitable desert, with certain areas having never recorded rainfall! Stretching its entire length along the Pacific, Chile's coastline is almost as long as the width of the United States. There are also areas of dense forest and the Chilean Lake District—and premium wine-growing country—to the south. In this great melting pot of terrains, Santiago has emerged with the best of all these features, and it is here, under the backdrop of the snowcapped Andes, that La Dehesa Golf Club rests.

The course itself is fairly traditional in design, although it is relatively modern by golf's historic standards. Created in 1964, the original five-hole layout has today been superseded, but it remains in existence as a children's course. On the main course, all skill levels are catered for, with numerous tee positions giving course lengths up to 7,048 yards/6,445 m.

The 520-yard/475-m 1st hole gives an impression of the difficulties to come, while allowing the player to make a positive start. A slight dogleg calls for a soft fade from the tee, with a cleverly placed bunker awaiting a nervous pull. Precedent is set that strong driving will be crucial, as trees will devour loose shots and block out approaches on the many doglegs. Given a strong drive, you might be tempted to attack, but a pond short of the green adds doubt so early in the round. Decision making is a factor on every hole, and a cautious approach is usually the most successful.

RIGHT *The course might look flat but there are plenty of features to keep you thinking. Stray off-line on the 7th and your route into the green will be blocked by the trees.*

▶ The 1998 Eisenhower Trophy was held at La Dehesa and nearby Los Leones, with Peter McEvoy captaining the Great Britain and Ireland side to victory.

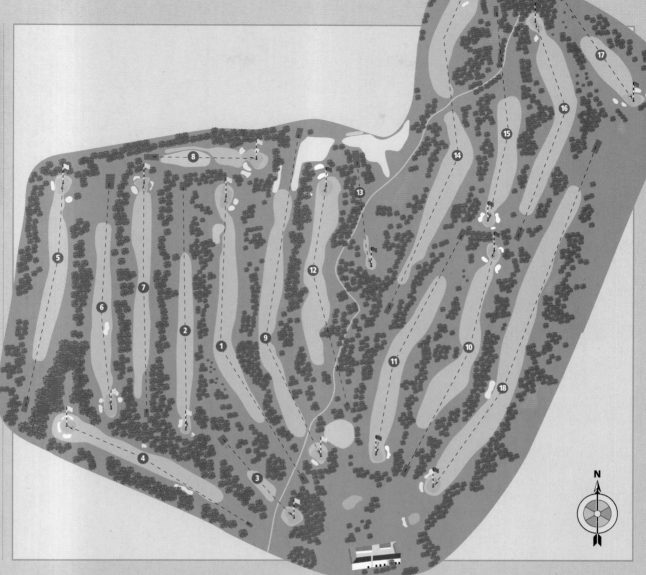

CARD OF THE COURSE

Hole	Distance (yards)	Par	Hole	Distance (yards)	Par
1	520	5	10	395	4
2	410	4	11	400	4
3	185	3	12	400	4
4	420	4	13	165	3
5	385	4	14	555	5
6	405	4	15	370	4
7	390	4	16	370	4
8	180	3	17	215	3
9	575	5	18	620	5
Out	3,470	36	In	3,490	36
			Total	6,960	72

Chile's longest hole

La Dehesa's best-known hole is the monstrous par-5 18th, Chile's longest hole, but it is actually rather tedious. Playing dead straight for 660 yards/603 m from the championship tees, it leaves no room for creativity and is an unfair reflection on the quality of the design on the rest of the course.

A far better example would be the par-5 9th, with a design reminiscent of the famous 13th at Augusta. A relatively easy tee shot to a wide, sloping fairway shows the architect's desire to get players into a positive position. Being well placed on the fairway calls for a decision on the approach shot because, as at Augusta, a river cuts in front of the green, leaving a long but feasible carry. Accuracy is important too, as a pond to the left of the green is well in range of a miscued shot from this distance.

Skillful design means that players are required to consider their best strategy, with choices over safety or aggression throughout the round. Atmosphere too is a huge selling point, demonstrated by the existence of the children's course. La Dehesa's affordable, encouraging approach to sport is all too rare at so many country clubs.

▶▶▶ Courses 57–81

▶▶▶ Continental Europe

Golf was introduced to many European countries by the British: to France in 1856 at Pau by retired soldiers, to Belgium in 1888 at Antwerp by English businessmen, and to Portugal in 1890 near Oporto by members of the port wine trade. As golf spread, clubs were formed where there were international communities, near the major cities and in and around the fashionable spas.

In the early years of the 20th century two British course designers, Tom Simpson and Harry Colt, were particularly active in Europe, but golf was an elite pastime and few courses were required. That was not the case in Germany, where golf enjoyed huge popularity before World War II, and a fine native designer, Bernhard von Limburger, emerged.

All changed with the coming of the jet airplane, cheap vacations, and the birth of golf tourism. Demand for resort golf in countries such as Portugal and Spain spawned a new generation of international and home-bred course designers as Europe's potential was tapped, while the fall of Communism in Eastern Europe has opened up a burgeoning golf industry there.

Murhof

Steiermärkischer Golfclub Murhof, Frohnleiten, Austria

As far as golf goes, Europe is full of surprises. Austrian golf is just such a revelation. There is mountain golf, such as at Seefeld and Innsbruck, and there is championship golf, such as the Jack Nicklaus-designed Gut Altentann. And there is charm—and rarely does a course have greater charm than Murhof.

The small market town of Frohnleiten is to be found in the fertile Mur Valley close to the old city of Graz. Its golf course was laid out in 1963 by the prolific German golf course designer Bernhard von Limburger. Alterations were made to the course between 1996 and 2000, during which time the course played host to three Ladies' Austrian Opens on the Ladies' European Tour. These have been followed by two tournaments on the men's European Challenge Tour.

Although the golf course does not adjoin the Mur River, it has a number of watery graves awaiting the inaccurate golfer. There is a pond to be avoided on the 2nd and 3rd holes and something approaching a lake threatening on the 6th and 14th holes. Although the course as a whole is not overwhelmingly long, there are several stiff two-shot holes and a couple of distinctly stout par 3s when played from the back plates.

Warm up first!

After a straightforward opener you are soon thrown into the serious business. While the 1st hole may be viewed as something of a preamble, the 2nd finds out who has warmed up properly and is striking the ball efficiently. A 223-yard/204-m short hole is not to be taken lightly even in these days of vastly improved club and ball performance. The pond should not really trouble you here—unless you have had rather too much Sachertorte, the aristocrat of Viennese

cakes, before setting out—but a bunker short and right of the green collects more than its fair share of ineffectual tee shots, while another bunker close by the green awaits the tugged ball. On the 3rd you will have to flirt with the pond if you hope to find the green in regulation on this substantial par 4.

At 469 yards/428 m, the 6th is a two-shot hole that challenges even the best players. In striving for length from the tee, the lake on the left becomes a serious factor, yet that is the better side of the fairway to be in order to get to the left-to-right angled green. Not for nothing is this considered the most difficult hole on the course.

For gamblers with the game for it, the 14th is a death-or-glory hole. It is a par 5 of 512 yards/468 m, nothing to speak of for today's big hitters, but the lake that threatened the 6th on the left now intimidates on the right. With the fairway curving all the time there is no soft option. You can play safely away from the trouble for a regulation five, but if you seek a birdie or eagle then you must be spot-on. Overall, though, golf at Murhof is not about blasting the ball prodigious distances. It is more about taking time to enjoy the beautiful surroundings. The score really does not matter!

▶ The course record of 62 is held by the young Austrian tour professional Markus Brier, while the ladies' course record of 64 was recorded by English golfer Samantha Head and New Zealander Lynette Brooky.

LEFT *Murhof's hardest hole, the 6th, appears benign when viewed against the backdrop of the mountains overlooking the verdant Mur Valley, but that is to ignore the threat of the lake.*

CARD OF THE COURSE

Hole	Distance (yards)	Par
1	392	4
2	223	3
3	460	4
4	146	3
5	443	4
6	469	4
7	489	5
8	354	4
9	519	5
Out	3,495	36
10	524	5
11	456	4
12	336	4
13	241	3
14	512	5
15	428	4
16	167	3
17	340	4
18	422	4
In	3,426	36
Total	6,921	72

Royal Belgium

Old Course, Royal Golf Club de Belgique, Tervuren, Brussels, Belgium

Belgium has produced few internationally famous golfers. As a result it tends to get overlooked when those lists of the finest golf courses in the world are compiled by the golfing press. There was a time when the Belgian Open was a regular fixture on the European Tour, but it seems to have fallen out of favor in recent years. No longer do the golfing journalists get to enjoy their mussels and chips washed down with lashings of Trappist beer.

While it is undoubtedly true that there are no world-class courses in Belgium, its list of Royal courses is impressive, and, were any golfer to visit Belgium for business or pleasure, it would be wise to leave a little spare time for golf. It was for this precise purpose that King Leopold II decided to promote golf in Belgium in the first decade of the 20th century, so that diplomats and businessmen might be able to conduct their meetings over a round of golf in idyllic settings. Leopold II was not a golfer, but his son Leopold III played in the Belgian Amateur Championship at Royal Zoute, and in so doing became the only reigning monarch to have played in a national championship.

THE ROYAL CLUBS

The Belgian Royal family has allowed the Royal prefix to be used at nine clubs: Royal Antwerp, Royal Belgium, Royal Golf Club des Fagnes, Royal Hainault, Royal Latem, Royal Ostend, Royal Sart-Tilman, Royal Waterloo, and Royal Zoute. Of these, Royal Zoute is a fine championship links and frequent Belgian Open venue. Royal Antwerp is a forest design by Tom Simpson, who also laid out the expansive Royal Sart-Tilman near Liège and the upland Royal GC des Fagnes in the hills above Spa.

RIGHT *The elegance and ambience of the course and clubhouse of Royal Belgium is evident from this photograph of the 2nd hole, a strong 420-yard/384-m par 4.*

Royal hunting park

King Leopold seems to have had a pretty good idea of what was required for outstanding golf courses and at Tervuren he donated a royal hunting park plus a collection of magnificent trees from his nearby Royal Arboretum to make possible the creation of the Royal Club of Belgium. There is no record in the club's archives of who designed the original course but it is thought that it was, if not designed, at least "inspired" by Seymour Dunn, who laid out several courses in Europe and was known as "the architect of the kings." The course was then rebuilt by Tom Simpson in 1928 and in 1990 underwent a 10-year modernizing program under the direction of Martin Hawtree.

What is certain is that this is a thought-provoking course in an idyllic setting. It is not a long course, with few par 4s over 400 yards/366 m in length, yet it is a gloriously strategic course, with the rolling ground used to maximum effect and many a dogleg cleverly set up to ask questions of golfers of all abilities. In a way the course is summed up by such gems as the 9th, a mere bagatelle of 336 yards/307 m. Its curling, downhill fairway directs unthinking drives into its many bunkers, and the green is, again, tightly bunkered, the putting surface narrowing toward the rear.

For good measure, the hole plays back to one of the most beautiful clubhouses in world golf, the old manor house of Ravenstein (by which name the club is also known), which dates from 1748. In fact the estate as a whole is even more historic, having been established in 1460 by Louis the Good, Duke of Burgundy.

▶ The course record of 65 has stood since 1935, when it was set by the great Belgian player Flory van Donck. Van Donck won the Belgian Open 16 times between 1935 and 1968.

▶ The royal connection with the club continues to this day through King Albert II, who is President of Honor of the club, a title previously held by King Leopold III and King Baudouin.

CARD OF THE COURSE

Hole	Distance (yards)	Par
1	491	5
2	420	4
3	156	3
4	415	4
5	521	5
6	209	3
7	373	4
8	361	4
9	336	4
Out	3,282	36
10	349	4
11	417	4
12	194	3
13	522	5
14	330	4
15	446	4
16	336	4
17	419	4
18	305	4
In	3,318	36
Total	6,600	72

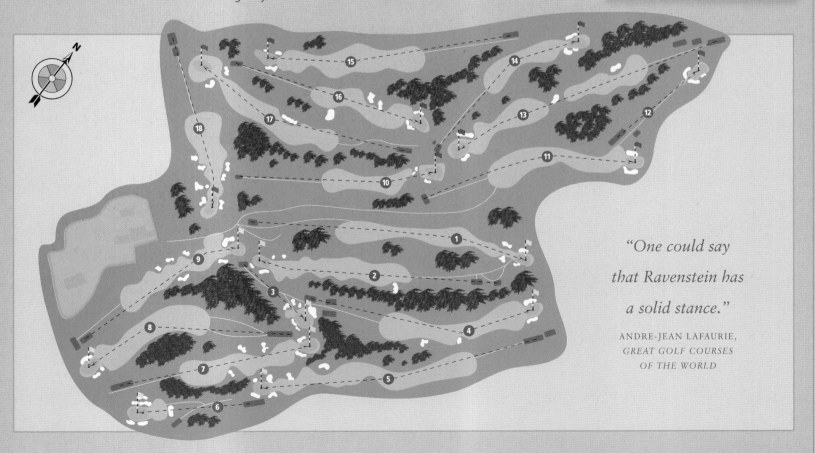

"One could say that Ravenstein has a solid stance."

ANDRE-JEAN LAFAURIE,
GREAT GOLF COURSES
OF THE WORLD

Rungsted

Rungsted Golf Club, near Copenhagen, Denmark

Copenhagen may be a charming capital city but it is not known for its golf. With the completion of the new Øresund bridge, Denmark's capital is within easy striking range of Sweden's finest course at Falsterbo. But taking the coast road north from Copenhagen, heading for the ferry to Sweden at Helsingør, soon brings you into the elegant suburbs, where the Copenhagen Golf Club has long been established with its pleasant parkland course. A few minutes on from there and you find Rungsted, for many years considered Denmark's leading course.

Rungsted is a parkland course on pleasantly undulating ground. Everything about it suggests an English-style course, as might be found around the belt of Surrey heathland. It is not, in fact, heathland, but were someone to say that Colt, Fowler, Simpson, or Abercromby had designed it no one would question it. It is in fact mostly the work of Major C. A.—Charles—MacKenzie, brother of the rather more famous Dr. Alister MacKenzie. Charles first became involved with golf course construction when he teamed up with Alister, working as his construction manager on site. The two gradually drifted apart, and Charles carried on on his own. Rungsted is probably Charles's finest work.

A tale of two (unequal) halves

The course is divided by the railroad track that runs north from Copenhagen. The clubhouse and the majority of holes are on one side of it, and these are generally the superior holes. Those on the other side of the bridge under the tracks are a little more cramped, lacking the length to provide a truly testing finish, although recent changes to these holes have improved the situation.

It is the expert routing of the holes on the clubhouse side that makes Rungsted so interesting to play, with plenty of change of pace and direction. From the 1st tee the challenge is immediately apparent, with the fairway angled to the left from the instinctive driving line. Somewhat shorter, the 2nd doglegs left with water on both sides of the fairway, and a ditch crosses in front of the 3rd green before continuing down the side of the putting surface. The most substantial of the two-shot holes follows, a well-bunkered hole with out-of-bounds threatening the pushed drive. Each of the following holes has plenty of character, the 5th climbing beyond a stream, the 7th also climbing, the 8th, 9th, and 10th all doglegged.

No two holes follow the same direction on the outward nine, but most of the back nine is played in parallel with the railroad. Strangely, it is not until the 11th that the first par 5 is encountered, but it is a lovely hole, climbing to an exposed and well-bunkered green. No score is safe, however, until the 17th hole has been negotiated—it is a treacherous, shortish par 4 requiring pin-point accuracy. There is always the chance of recovering a stroke on the eminently reachable par-5 final hole.

▶ Good golf in Denmark is not confined to Zealand. Jutland, for instance, has first-rate courses at Esjerg, Holstebro, and Silkeborg. If an opportunity ever presents itself to play Fano Golf Links on Fano Island, don't miss it. It may be short, but it is a genuine links—a rare thing in continental Europe.

LEFT *A well-bunkered par 5 with out-of-bounds running the length of the hole on the right completes the round at Rungsted. It offers a genuine birdie chance.*

CARD OF THE COURSE

Hole	Distance (yards)	Par
1	419	4
2	373	4
3	181	3
4	444	4
5	381	4
6	175	3
7	396	4
8	385	4
9	370	4
Out	3,124	34
10	396	4
11	484	5
12	321	4
13	323	4
14	357	4
15	116	3
16	516	5
17	391	4
18	481	5
In	3,385	38
Total	6,509	72

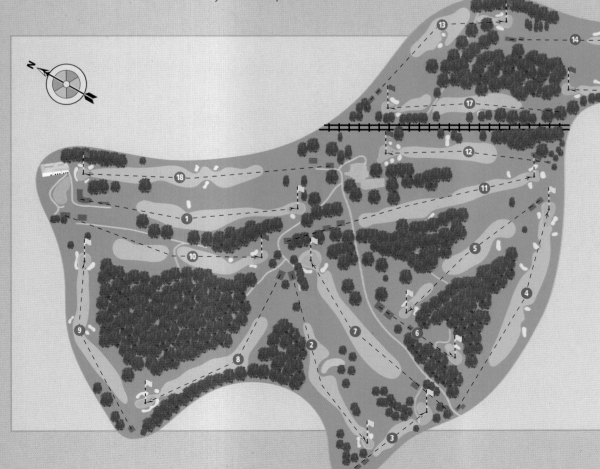

"I can't wait to come back."

TIGER WOODS, WHO EAGLED THE 18TH TO TIE AN INTERNATIONAL MATCH AT RUNGSTED IN 1999

Master

Master Course, Master Golf Club, Bodom, Espoo, Finland

With its harsh winter climate and dark winter days, Finland may not be the first place one would think of to be witnessing something of a golf explosion. But it is! Not only are the Finns playing golf in rapidly increasing numbers, but they also have the space on which to build their courses. Much of Finland is made up of forests and lakes, and Finnish golf course designers have become adept at maximizing the strategic potential of these natural features. The two courses of the Master Golf Club at Espoo are the work of Kosti Kuronen, and they make full use of the lakes, ponds, and forests of the estate of a former country home, not far from the main coast road from Helsinki.

The Forest Course is aptly named, for all but a few of the holes run through dense forest, giving great privacy to each hole. Wildlife abounds, and it is a delightful course—as long as you can hit straight. The 1st and 18th are out in more open country and significantly bunkered. Bunkers are largely unnecessary on the rest of the course because there are lots of small ponds on the site and they have been used tellingly by Kuronen, especially on the tough 17th.

Water, water everywhere

Ponds are also in abundance on the Master Course; trees, too. The course runs beside an expansive lake, and while you are never required to take on the lake as a strategic hazard, Kuronen has ensured that it is often visible through the trees, which can act as a ball saver for the wayward.

On the 1st hole there is a pond, but it should be of no concern to the competent player apart from its restricting

the length of the tee shot. It interrupts the fairway but does not threaten the green. The lake makes a first appearance on the 2nd and, again, it should not trouble a decent player, for it is beyond a row of trees to the right of the fairway. At this point it is a handsome backdrop. Similarly the 3rd keeps company with the lake, but it is at a safe distance, the slight climb to the green a welcome variation in this flat part of Finland. The 4th, 5th, and 6th occupy a promontory, yet they are woodland holes. We get enticing glimpses of the lake through the trees, but only a dreadful shot could find its waters.

The course heads inland for a lengthy run from the 7th to the 15th holes, albeit featuring a number of ponds and ditches. Of these holes the 8th and 9th are back-to-back par 5s, the former making demands of position and length off the tee, while the 9th is very much a second-shot hole, with water threatening over the last 80 yards/73 m or so. The 16th and 17th return to the lakeside in handsome fashion, while the final hole is theoretically drivable, as long as trees, bunkers, and a spot of water are avoided.

LEFT *The 16th hole on the Master Course is a solid par 3 over water, but of greater concern are the deceptive slopes on the putting surface.*

▶ The Finnish golfing season may be short (lasting as it does from April or May to September or October, depending on the weather) but it is quite possible to play for 24 hours a day during the summer.

CARD OF THE COURSE

Hole	Distance (yards)	Par
1	345	4
2	413	4
3	374	4
4	550	5
5	146	3
6	407	4
7	372	4
8	457	5
9	532	5
Out	3,596	38
10	414	4
11	351	4
12	397	4
13	440	4
14	194	3
15	513	5
16	186	3
17	422	4
18	292	4
In	3,209	35
Total	6,805	73

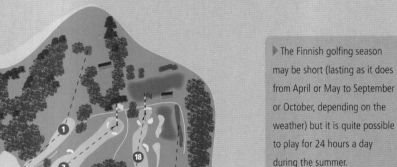

Le Golf National

L'Albatros Course, Le Golf National, Guyancourt, France

Built on flat land, nowhere near the sea, and with 353,000 cubic yards/270,000 cubic metres of artificial lakes, it may seem preposterous to liken Le Golf National to a Scottish links. But when the wind gusts over the dunes, through the ashen rough and straight into your face, the similarities become clear. In true links fashion, the course is open to the elements, but the design also features the lakes and stadium golf of an American TPC course. It is this mix of styles that creates the course's main defense, as one is called upon to be creative, playing links shots as well as target golf.

Popular French golf only really took off in the 1970s, when the economic potential of the game was realized. Courses sprang up all over the place, spearheaded by a new wave of course architects. The effects of this golfing revolution are apparent today, with a sudden influx of good French professionals. Le Golf National is probably the most important course to come out of this era, becoming the permanent home to the French Open Championship.

The course must have seemed somewhat of a gamble when it was proposed. Not only was the country new to the golfing buzz, but the land was also far too flat to fulfil the brief: to create France's first course capable of hosting regular tournaments. Two years later, after the transportation of 400 trucks of earth a day, the course was both undulating and teeming with bunkers and lakes, and plentiful spectator mounds.

RIGHT *In many respects this bleak, windswept site resembles a links, but what it cannot have is true links turf and genuine seaside sand dunes.*

▶ There is a shorter 18-hole course, L'Aigle, which has a distinctly Scottish feel to it, and a charming nine-hole course for training.

BELOW *The short 16th is one of several holes on the back nine with treacherous water carries.*

"All the shots you have to play offer multiple choices."

SEVE BALLESTEROS

CARD OF THE COURSE

Hole	Distance (yards)	Par	Hole	Distance (yards)	Par
1	415	4	10	377	4
2	202	3	11	191	3
3	530	5	12	437	4
4	439	4	13	410	4
5	404	4	14	552	5
6	377	4	15	421	4
7	443	4	16	175	3
8	207	3	17	470	4
9	563	5	18	514	5
Out	3,580	36	In	3,547	36
			Total	7,127	72

Scotland meets Florida

All these features are apparent from the 1st tee.

The fairway is narrowed by a large lake on the left, which also adds intimidation to the approach shot. Bunkers mark the right-hand edge of the fairway before the land turns to dunes. At 415 yards/379 m, position is more important than length, and a 3-wood down the right-hand side gives the best line at the enormously long green. From here there is great diversity in holes, but one must take early birdie chances, as the course gets consistently harder.

Looking down the fairway from the 15th tee, you really could be in Florida, with an expansive lake on the right dwarfing the playing surface. Inevitably most shots are played too cautiously down the left, but this leaves a long approach to a green almost surrounded by the vast lake. In the 1991 French Open, seven balls were lost in the lake by a three-ball!

On the opposite side of the lake, the 18th is almost a mirror image of the 15th. Water stretches all the way down the left side of this par 5. But the fairway is wide and, with a relatively easy approach over the water, it is possible to finish in style. Unlike Retief Goosen, who was five shots clear on the tee in 1997 and opted to lay up short of the water. He topped the ball into the water and finished with a seven to win by only three!

Les Bordes

Les Bordes, Saint Laurent-Nouan, France

When the sun rises above the Sologne forests and illuminates the rolling fairways and shimmering lakes, there are few places better to wake up than in the traditional Loire Valley cottages that provide accommodation at Les Bordes. The location is hard to beat, and the quality of golf is such that Les Bordes is consistently ranked as one of the finest and toughest courses in continental Europe.

Les Bordes, opened in 1986, was the brainchild of industrialist Baron Marcel Bich and his trading partner Yoshiaki Sakurai who, having made a fortune from their pen company Bic, decided to build a course in the grounds of the Baron's hunting lodge. For centuries, monarchs, politicians, and wealthy industrialists have chosen to live in the Loire region, for it combines idyllic tranquillity with easy access to Paris. Although the project might have seemed risky, as the area had no golfing history, these captains of industry knew their "dream course" could be carved out of this beautiful area.

A supreme lakeside challenge

Robert von Hagge was the Texan architect chosen to transform dream into reality. He drew on his experience of over 200 courses to create a stunning design that makes full use of the natural features of the land. Sologne's lakes protect 12 of the holes, while the forest and undulating mounds eat into the narrow fairways. Inventive bunkers are also common throughout the course. Indeed all these troubles await the golfer on the 1st hole. An intimidating carry over a lake makes for a daunting first tee shot, and

from there the fairway narrows and veers right, skirting the edge of the forest. Though the green is fairly large, it appears much smaller as it is almost surrounded by an enormous bunker. It's a tough opening hole, but a fair reflection of the challenges to come.

Baron Bich's favorite hole was reputedly the 7th. It epitomizes the marriage between design and landscape that makes Les Bordes so special. A solid tee shot is a must on this par 5, as water protects both sides of the landing zone. The fairway turns at right angles, and, given a perfect drive, the green is reachable in two. However, it calls for strong nerves as the second shot is played almost entirely over water. Even a layup requires a decent shot played to a severely angled fairway.

One of the few waterless holes, the 15th requires accuracy to avoid a long bunker on the right of the fairway. Following the picturesque holes that sweep through lakes and forests, the straight, dry 15th may appear to be somewhere to catch your breath. Far from it—the bunker provides enough difficulty from the tee, and the approach shot is played through seemingly endless undulations before the bunkerless green.

Although the course is extremely demanding, it is impossible not to enjoy the round. The whole experience is uplifting, from waking up in that charming cottage, playing the teasing course, being at one with nature, to enjoying the region's traditional food and wine. The dream course is reality!

LEFT The 7th is a wicked hole, almost turning back on itself. It is the sort of hole, making great use of water, that is now almost obligatory in resort golf.

CARD OF THE COURSE

Hole	Distance (yards)	Par
1	439	4
2	522	5
3	388	4
4	165	3
5	435	4
6	385	4
7	507	5
8	156	3
9	390	4
Out	3,387	36
10	512	5
11	399	4
12	413	4
13	185	3
14	558	5
15	437	4
16	215	3
17	454	4
18	447	4
In	3,620	36
Total	7,007	72

SOLOGNE BACKWATERS

Establishing a golf resort in the backwaters of the Sologne was a bold move. This was not typical golf course country—the Sologne was famous in France for its winged game, prized by gastronomes as the best in the country. Baron Bich chose his architect well, for Robert von Hagge was not afraid of felling forests or creating minor lakes to carve his course out of unpromising material. The course is noted for its bold gestures yet von Hagge succeeded in maintaining the Sologne country atmosphere.

Von Hagge went on to build up a distinguished portfolio of golf courses in France. He was part of the team at Le Golf National. Many cite his course at Seignosse in southwest France as one of his best. A membership at Royal Mougins, near Cannes, is much sought after by the ultra-wealthy who winter in the area.

BELOW *The course may be American-designed, but the clubhouse at Les Bordes retains the style and feel of a typical farmhouse of the Sologne.*

Morfontaine

Morfontaine

Morfontaine Golf Club, Senlis, France

Early golf in France was mostly played by Britons living there. The likes of Pau, Biarritz, and Dinard had their origins within British communities, and they were the main players. When, in the early 20th century, the French took up the game, it was mostly kept within a socially restricted group of wealthy and well-connected players. Chantilly, Fontainebleau, St. Cloud, and Morfontaine were examples of just such clubs, and to a large extent they have not changed. Unless you know the right people you will find it hard to get a game at Morfontaine. Those who are fortunate enough to make it happen will find a club and course with a very British feel to it—which is perhaps not surprising because the architect who laid it out, Tom Simpson (much of whose best surviving work is in France and Belgium) was British.

Morfontaine started out as a nine-hole course in 1910 and that course (good of its kind) is still in play. Simpson returned in 1927 to lay out the 18-hole course, which remains the club's pride and joy. The club has not hosted professional tournaments so the course has not needed unnecessary lengthening, with the exception of the 12th, which is now a par 5 of 620 yards/567 m. What the club did, in a recent revision of the course by Kyle Phillips (architect of Kingsbarns), was to move the green some 60 yards/55 m beyond where it used to be, so that it plays as a full three-shot hole just as it did in Simpson's day. In other respects Simpson would recognize Morfontaine were he to come back tomorrow.

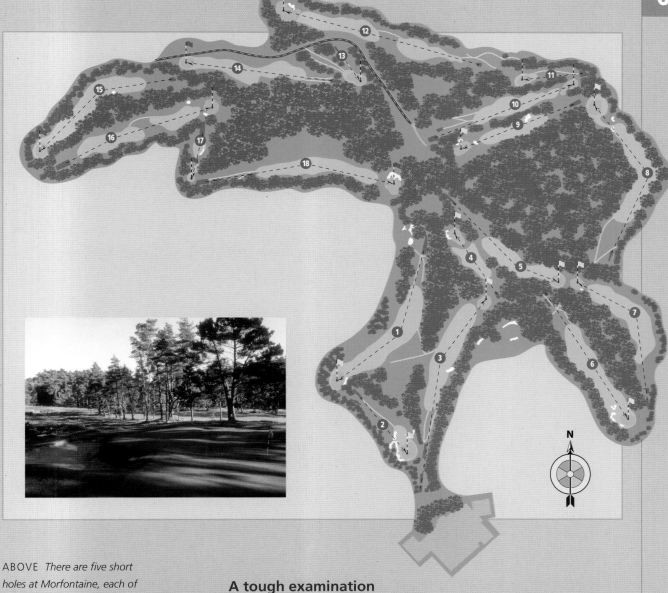

▶ Tom Simpson was quite a character. He is said to have attended meetings with potential clients dressed in beret and overcoat, shooting stick in hand, having been chauffeur driven to the meeting in his Rolls-Royce.

LEFT *One of the toughest holes at Morfontaine, the 16th. With its uphill fairway split by a band of heather it is demanding even as a bogey 5.*

ABOVE *There are five short holes at Morfontaine, each of them good. This one, the 11th, comes after a run of six consecutive two-shot holes.*

CARD OF THE COURSE

Hole	Distance (yards)	Par	Hole	Distance (yards)	Par
1	453	4	10	418	4
2	197	3	11	152	3
3	500	5	12	620	5
4	179	3	13	147	3
5	350	4	14	373	4
6	392	4	15	450	4
7	430	4	16	456	4
8	430	4	17	170	3
9	371	4	18	493	5
Out	3,302	35	In	3,279	35
			Total	6,581	70

A tough examination

The opening is serious: a long par 4, a by no means short par 3, and a par 5 that plays longer than its yardage as it runs uphill. After another short hole played across a valley, there is a sequence of six par 4s, with the 7th and 8th particularly noteworthy for the demands they make on shaping the shot from the tee. Morfontaine, as with so many of the courses of this age, asks many questions of the golfer's technique and mindset.

One of the more unusual holes is the 13th, a short hole of no great length, but with a somewhat disconcerting obstacle between the tee and the green— a tree. In truth, it is not difficult to clear it, but, just because it is there, many a thinned shot has been hit from this tee.

Morfontaine has another pair of stout holes still to come to test the ball-striking skills of even the finest players—the 15th and 16th. Both call for strong, well-shaped drives, followed by confident striking on the second shot, for incursions of heather interrupt both fairways short of the green. What is more, that 16th plays uphill, being a very strong par 4.

Contemporary golf course architects could do worse than make a point of studying the finer details of Morfontaine's classic design. It is timeless.

Club zur Vahr

Club zur Vahr, Garlstedt, Germany

The Club zur Vahr is an enormous sporting club based in the old German city of Bremen. It was established in 1905 and offered its members facilities for tennis, polo, hockey, and golf. In time it also came to embrace athletics, shooting, cricket, and rugby. On site in the city of Bremen there is a nine-hole golf course. During the 1960s the club began a search to find a suitable site for an 18-hole course. Their chosen spot was a dense wood some 20 minutes' drive northwest of the city. Their chosen architect was the great German, Bernhard von Limburger. He clearly understood that future generations would need much longer courses, and he built a course of prodigious length for its time (1966) of over 7,200 yards/6,584 m.

For a number of reasons the course has perhaps not attracted the wealth of tournaments its length and difficulty might have been expected to. For a start it is much less accessible than a number of other similarly prominent courses in Germany, such as Hamburger Falkenstein and Frankfurter. And then there is the depth of the forest and the narrowness of many of the fairways. There would be nowhere for spectators to stand on several holes, rather like Pine Valley in the United States. In fact, that narrowness has been made more severe as the trees have grown over the years, to the extent that a substantial course of rebuilding has had to be carried out recently to improve drainage and air circulation. A bunker reconstruction program has considerably altered the style of Bernhard von Limburger's originals.

The course today

We are not expected to play Garlstedter Heide (as the course is usually known) at the length Limburger initially created, but given the severity of the punishment meted out on even the slightest inaccuracy, 7,039 yards/6,436 m from the back tees is still a daunting prospect. That said, there are a few moments of respite, one of which comes right at the start, an accommodating drive-and-pitch hole. Immediately after that you are into the tough stuff, with a challenging par 5 on which you can easily perish in water on the drive or on the second shot. The 3rd is a stout par 3.

Another demanding par 5 is the 6th, which features alternative fairways over the latter part of the hole. But once you have made your choice you are committed to one route or the other, come what may. This option is repeated on the extraordinary 7th, the decision on which line to take this time being made on the tee.

On the back nine a feeling of claustrophobia may set in, for these are some of the narrowest holes imaginable. Stray from the fairway and your ball is almost certain to be lost. Go and look for it and you might yourself soon be lost! And a glance at the card shows that these are nearly all big, powerful holes. It is a great challenge, if a daunting one.

▶ The German Open has rarely been played at Garlstedt, but in 1971 it attracted a field that included former British Open champions, Roberto de Vicenzo and Peter Thomson. Neil Coles—who has likened the course to Augusta—set a course record 68 on his way to victory.

LEFT *The density of the forest is plainly to be seen in this view of the 16th, the joint longest par 4 on the course (with the 12th).*

CARD OF THE COURSE

Hole	Distance (yards)	Par
1	359	4
2	538	5
3	220	3
4	561	5
5	313	4
6	542	5
7	406	4
8	164	3
9	392	4
Out	3,495	37
10	563	5
11	177	3
12	453	4
13	409	4
14	341	4
15	536	5
16	453	4
17	212	3
18	400	4
In	3,544	36
Total	7,039	73

Hamburger Falkenstein

Falkenstein Course, Hamburger Golf Club, Hamburg, Germany

When golf course architect Harry Colt was called to the Hamburg suburb of Falkenstein in 1928 his heart would have leapt. Here was an inspiring piece of rolling heathland that might easily have been lifted directly from the heathlands of southwest London. He rewarded his clients, the Hamburger Golf Club, with a masterpiece, and it has remained so for 80 years.

Most of Colt's original course survives, and certainly his best holes, but a few alterations were made by the great German course designer, Bernhard von Limburger, in the 1960s. The two notable gains are offset by a couple of losses, but this course remains at the top of the vast pile of German golf courses 80 years after construction began. Colt routed the course superbly, using the hills and valleys expertly to provide a compact course that, nevertheless, maximizes the potential of this great piece of land.

Memorable tees and greens

Colt could have begun the course outside the clubhouse door, but this is a patch of flat, uninteresting land much better suited to its current use as a first-rate pitching and putting practice area. Instead, you climb a hill beyond to gain access to an elevated tee. It converts a potentially ordinary hole into a lovely dogleg, the green on high ground and cleverly defended by the trees on the left and its own special site. The 2nd and 3rd are Limburger holes, and among the best on the course: a stout par 5 with a well-chosen green site and a great par 3 played across a valley to a green angled behind cunning bunkers.

Few of the par 4s are of great length, but they are some of the most enchanting two-shotters even among Colt's distinguished repertoire. The 6th, for instance, beckons from the tee, inviting a strong drive toward a distant hill, the fairway moving insistently to the right as it climbs to a wonderfully sited hilltop green. Then the 7th plunges down a hillside toward a delightfully bunkered green. And there are few more engaging spots for a green than above the wooded valley that lies beyond the plateau 12th green. It is followed by another gem, the 13th, with a lovely drive over banks of heather to a sloping fairway followed by an uphill pitch to yet another brilliantly located green, on a hilltop, cleverly angled from the fairway. The 14th, too, tumbles downhill over heather from the tee before, again, climbing to a hilltop green. Repetition? No! Each hole is distinctive and uplifting.

Another Colt masterpiece awaits on the 17th, a short par 5, but a charmer nonetheless. The drive is tricky, semi-blind to a distant ridge beyond which the fairway turns gently to the left. It runs downhill toward the green, but most of the last 150 yards/137 m is occupied by a sea of heather. The challenge is on! Of course you can clear it with your second shot—but only if you have hit a cracking drive. Our vanity challenged, all too many of us somehow manage to find the heather despite our best endeavours not to!

▶ The Hamburger Golf Club staged the inaugural German Open in 1911 at its original course in Flottbek. It was won by Harry Vardon, six times winner of the British Open.

LEFT *Heather is a good hazard. You are likely to find your ball, but playing from it is an uncertainty. Colt used it expertly, as on the 17th.*

CARD OF THE COURSE

Hole	Distance (yards)	Par
1	321	4
2	549	5
3	233	3
4	474	5
5	399	4
6	410	4
7	354	4
8	177	3
9	421	4
Out	3,338	36
10	171	3
11	438	4
12	400	4
13	363	4
14	349	4
15	155	3
16	329	4
17	478	5
18	366	4
In	3,049	35
Total	6,387	71

"*Especially noteworthy is Falkenstein's complete absence of water.*"

TONY RISTOLA,
GOLF COURSE ARCHITECT

Sporting Club Berlin

Faldo Course, Sporting Club Berlin, Bad Sarrow, Germany

Before World War II, Germany could boast more golf courses than any other country in continental Europe. After the war the country was divided and the eastern part, the DDR, became aligned with Soviet Russia. Golf and Communism were not compatible, and a number of fine old courses were abandoned, never to be restored. As an island city, surrounded by Communist territory, Berlin could not expand. It boasted a single 18-hole course and there was no possibility of room being found for any other course within the western-controlled sectors.

The fall of Communism and the symbolic dismantling of the Berlin Wall provided a stimulus for the rapid development of new courses within easy striking range of the city on former DDR territory. Given that agricultural practices in the DDR were antiquated and that much farm work was still carried out using horses, it seems a pity that no developer thought to exploit those skills while they remained available in order to create a traditional course such as Colt or Simpson might have built. The results are so much subtler. Instead, developers have seen this as an opportunity to aim for the high-end market, and top of that list is the impressive resort at Bad Sarrow, Sporting Club Berlin.

RIGHT *A view of the par-5 10th hole on the Faldo Course at Bad Saarow. Faldo has a great affinity with links golf. It shows here.*

▶ The back nine of the Palmer-designed Champions Course runs into the woods and has been described as the most beautiful back nine in Germany.

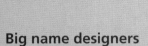

ABOVE *Escape from the bunkers on the Faldo Course needs strength, skill, commitment, and nerve. These are on the 17th.*

Big name designers

You can add millions of dollars to the construction bill for a new course if you persuade a famous golfer to put his name to the design. For that money you might get two or three single-day visits from the great man, the design work being carried out by the full-time architects in his team. Nick Faldo is something of an exception, taking a rather greater personal interest in the detailed design of "his" courses than most. His links-like course at Bad Sarrow has already attracted much favorable comment. It makes a fine contrast with the Arnold Palmer woodland course at the same resort. There is a third 18-hole course by Stan Eby, plus exemplary practice facilities.

The Faldo Course was intended to hold professional tournaments right from the start (it has hosted a number of German Opens), but Faldo was not to be tempted to make this course a long slog. Interestingly, he has included a number of shorter par 4s in the repertoire, and water—the seemingly obligatory element of any new design with championship aspirations—is blissfully absent, being a factor only on the par-5 1st and 10th holes. It could hardly be a links course without bunkers, and Faldo has seen to it that there are 133 of them, most of the deep pot-bunker variety.

Flat the land may be, but there are abundant features to the course, with angled greens such as at the 7th, narrow entrances to them such as at the 9th, and always the thought that if you finish in the wrong part of one of these bunkers you are almost bound to lose a stroke.

▶ SC Berlin is not just about golf. It is one of Europe's finest sports resorts, offering tennis, riding, sailing on the largest lake in Brandenburg, and excellent spa facilities.

CARD OF THE COURSE

Hole	Distance (yards)	Par	Hole	Distance (yards)	Par
1	548	5	10	559	5
2	414	4	11	570	5
3	186	3	12	376	4
4	379	4	13	233	3
5	213	3	14	415	4
6	533	5	15	391	4
7	439	4	16	360	4
8	382	4	17	193	3
9	447	4	18	458	4
Out	3,541	36	In	3,555	36
			Total	7,096	72

Biella

Biella

Golf Club Biella "Le Betulle", Magnano Biellese, Valcarozza, Italy

As in so many European countries, the British brought golf to Italy, the first club being established in Florence in 1889. They were also instrumental in the setting up of the Rome Golf Club in 1903, and several clubs in the cooler, mountain climate of the north of Italy. This was one of the few areas of Europe in which the great English course designer Harry Colt did not work, many of the early courses being designed by the gifted Irishman Peter Gannon. It was to one of Colt's former business partners, John Morrison, that the founders of the Biella Golf Club turned in the late 1950s when they sought to establish a championship-standard course of their own.

BELOW *Even when you can't see the mountains Biella is attractive, the trees giving privacy to each hole and a compulsion for unerring straight hitting.*

Morrison had been a gifted amateur player either side of World War I, joining Colt and Alison in the 1920s and becoming a partner and director of the firm in the 1930s. Biella (opened in 1958) was one of his last solo designs, and a magnificent job he did! A golf course does not have to be beautiful to be great, but beauty is a great bonus. At Biella the course runs over superbly rolling country through great forests of birches—*le betulle*. It could almost be an English heathland course. There are superb mountain vistas, too, and a round of golf here in the autumn, with the leaves golden brown and fiery red and the mountains covered in gleaming, freshly fallen snow, is one of life's great treats.

Stay focused on the golf

Take time to enjoy the surroundings, of course, but you will need to concentrate fully on the task in hand if you are to score well, for there is no denying the demands made by this exacting layout. A solid par 4 gets you under way, sweeping downhill and to the right. It sets the standard, with restrained bunkering but plentiful trouble should you stray into the trees and the threat of a stream or pond affecting many holes.

One of the strongest holes is the 3rd, which plunges downhill between the trees before turning sharply left and climbing beyond a stream to a well-placed green. In fact very few holes are straight, another strong dogleg on the way out being the 6th.

On such a site it is something of a feat to have engineered it so that both nines start and finish near the clubhouse, a happy result of this being that the holes interweave attractively. Two of the four par 3s exceed 200 yards/183 m. There are some fine two-shot holes on the back nine, particularly the 12th and 14th, and one of the most handsome holes of all is the par-5 16th, played to a falling fairway with a majestic mountain backdrop. It is part of a delightful finish, with a scenic par 3 and a tough par 5 remaining.

▶ Morrison worked alongside Colt on such designs as the East and West courses at Wentworth, Hamburg Falkenstein, Kennemer, and Utrecht, and was part of the restoration team at Prince's.

▶ At an altitude of some 2,000 feet/600 m, Biella has to close for the winter, but golf is usually possible from the end of March to the end of November.

CARD OF THE COURSE

Hole	Distance (yards)	Par
1	439	4
2	196	3
3	416	4
4	393	4
5	211	3
6	408	4
7	529	5
8	403	4
9	563	5
Out	3,558	36
10	220	3
11	510	5
12	412	4
13	376	4
14	422	4
15	372	4
16	539	5
17	188	3
18	510	5
In	3,549	37
Total	7,107	73

"A great test of golf in superb surroundings."
PEUGEOT GOLF GUIDE

Is Molas

Is Molas Golf Hotel, Is Molas, Pula, Sardinia, Italy

Given the hot and arid climate of most of the Mediterranean islands it is something of a surprise that there are any golf courses on them, let alone a number of good ones. Sardinia fares well, with two notable courses—Robert Trent-Jones's outstanding creation for the Aga Khan, Pevero, and the resort of Is Molas, with its 27 holes of captivating golf in a fine setting close to the Phoenician city of Nora.

The original course was built by the British partnership of Ken Cotton, Charles Lawrie, and Frank Pennink, the additional nine holes being contributed by the Gary Player design team. Four Italian Opens have been played on the course, beginning in 1976 with a native winner, Baldovino Dassù. Later winners were Mark James (1982) and Ian Poulter (2000) of England, and Frenchman Gregory Havret in 2001. It was victory in the 1989 Volvo Masters here that placed Vijay Singh on the international golf ladder for the first time.

BELOW *Golf at Is Molas is played against a backdrop of typically bare, Sardinian rocky hills and scrubby maquis. This is Mark Roe putting on the 16th during the 2001 Italian Open.*

GOLF ON THE MEDITERRANEAN ISLANDS

Sardinia is not the only Mediterranean island on which golf is played. Elba manages to provide room for the diminutive nine-hole course, Acquabona, and Mount Etna dominates Sicily's only (and rather attractive) course—Il Picciolo. The engaging nine-hole course of Royal Malta dates back to 1888. There are now three 18-hole layouts in Cyprus. Two of Greece's four courses are on islands—Rhodes and Corfu. On Corsica there is the Robert Trent-Jones course, Sperone.

Easy for the professionals

Is Molas may play to just over 7,000 yards/6,400 m, but for the professionals it is a stroll. The winning scores in the last two Italian Opens to be played there were 21 and 20 under par respectively. They expect to make a killing right at the start, and almost invariably they achieve their goal, with a par 5 easily in reach of two of their prodigious shots. Lesser players will find the next four holes quite challenging, with the 2nd a substantial par 4 climbing toward the green. Then comes a serious par 3, which calls for a tee shot that has sufficient power to make it up the slight rise to the green.

The 4th requires two hefty shots from most of us, although clever management of the dogleg brings the green within easier range. And there is still the punishing 5th hole to come. This is the most destructive hole on the course, with bushes, out-of-bounds, water, bunkers, a mid-fairway tree, a gully before the green, and a green perched on a rocky outcrop constituting the catalog of potential disasters lying in wait.

On the homeward nine three par 5s offer hope of clawing back strokes that had perhaps slipped away earlier. This time it is the Tintioni River that threatens to spoil the party, with a Sardinian dry-stone wall as another, if unusual, nuisance. A fine closing hole has been kept in waiting, with the green quite difficult to attack as it is narrow, raised, and angled. Twenty under par today, Sir? Perhaps not!

▶ The Phoenicians are thought to have founded Nora as a trading post in the 8th century BC. It later passed into the hands of the Carthaginians and Romans before falling into ruin on the departure of the Romans in the 4th century AD.

CARD OF THE COURSE

Hole	Distance (yards)	Par
1	502	5
2	431	4
3	214	3
4	464	4
5	403	4
6	362	4
7	215	3
8	422	4
9	389	4
Out	3,402	35
10	192	3
11	394	4
12	544	5
13	406	4
14	170	3
15	560	5
16	500	5
17	408	4
18	437	4
In	3,611	37
Total	7,013	72

Villa d'Este

Villa d'Este, Montorfano, Italy

Few will have heard of Peter Gannon, one of the most influential golf course designers in the early years of Italian golf. He was born in 1874 in Buenos Aires of Irish parents. In 1901 he was ordained as a Catholic priest in London and became secretary to the Bishop of Plymouth. But he was also an accomplished left-handed golfer, winning the national championships of Austria, France, and Italy. He forsook the cloth, got married and became a golf course designer!

Gannon had already completed modest but beautiful courses at Menaggio and Stresa in Italy, Karlsbad in Bohemia, and Engadine in Switzerland, when in 1926 he was commissioned to design a course at Villa d'Este near Lake Como. It is considered by many to be his masterpiece, but there are other contenders for that title including the Milan Golf Club at Monza and the Ugolino course he built for Italy's oldest club at Florence. He could hardly have been given a more beautiful canvas on which to work. Here was an undulating site, some 1,500 feet/457 m above sea level, with a glorious mountain backdrop. He responded by building a course that has more than stood the test of time.

Short but challenging

On paper Villa d'Este may look short by today's standards, but that does not take account of the hilly nature of the ground and the way in which Gannon routed the course. There is a delightful change of pace between long and short examples of one-, two-, and three-shot holes; you are required to play the ball from a variety of hilly lies with the ball sometimes above the feet, at others below, and there are all sorts of narrow openings through which the ball must be played from time to time. Each hole presents a fresh challenge.

It is unusual these days to encounter a course with six par 3s. It is refreshing, too, to find a course on which little attempt has been made to push tees back beyond each hole's natural length. As a result there remain several charming short par 4s, a species all too often neglected in contemporary golf design. The round kicks off, however, with a sturdy opener, a long par 5. From the much elevated tee the fairway presents a narrow target, and position off the tee is important on this gently but persistently curving hole. And with a sloping fairway the 2nd also calls for precision off the tee. Already it is apparent that you cannot bludgeon your way round. Clear thinking is the main requirement.

The back nine opens with a short hole taking you into the woods, and the 11th is tough with out-of-bounds to the right and a well-defended green. Also coming home two tough holes follow each other, the 14th and 15th, the former a long one-shotter demanding unwavering straightness. The approach shot to the 15th green is similarly unforgiving.

▶ Twelve Italian Opens have been held at Villa d'Este and, in total, 30 Italian Opens have been played on 7 separate Gannon courses. Every Italian Open from 1925 to 1949 was played on one of his courses, a remarkable record.

LEFT AND BELOW *Villa d'Este's course is not long, but it is rated among the most difficult par-69 courses in Europe, typified by the tricky 18th hole. Its raised green is deceptively contoured and tightly bunkered.*

CARD OF THE COURSE

Hole	Distance (yards)	Par
1	591	5
2	397	4
3	212	3
4	325	4
5	146	3
6	319	4
7	203	3
8	422	4
9	389	4
Out	3,004	34
10	196	3
11	421	4
12	369	4
13	538	5
14	223	3
15	466	4
16	181	3
17	528	5
18	344	4
In	3,266	35
Total	6,270	69

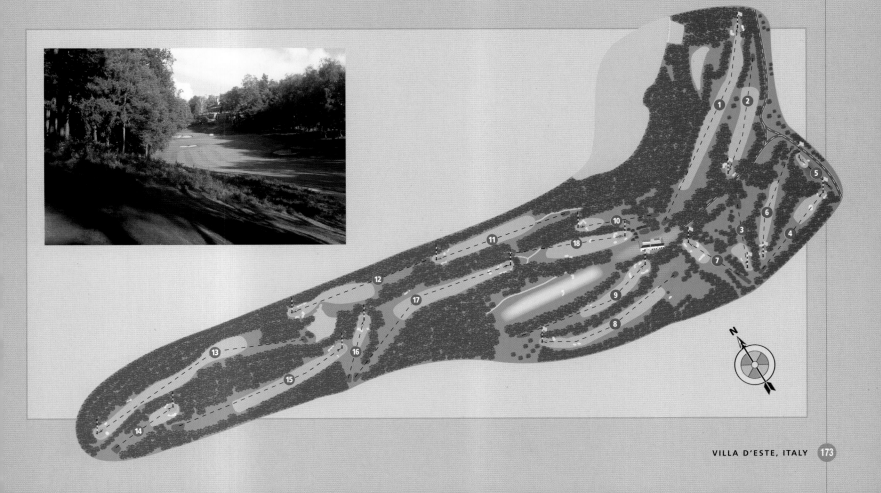

Hilversum

Hilversum Golf Club, Hilversum, Netherlands

Holland's links courses are becoming increasingly well known. What is less known outside the country is the strength in depth of its inland courses. The golfing experience at Hilversum is strikingly different from that at the more famous courses on the North Sea, where the holes are carved through the dunes and gorse in the same way as their Scottish counterparts. Hilversum too has the flavor of a British course but in this case more of an inland English course.

Approaching the club along its woodland driveway one is reminded of Surrey heathland, and the traditional design of the course itself is not dissimilar to a Sunningdale or Wentworth. Despite hosting numerous Dutch Opens, Hilversum has not been tricked up with modern features such as astronomical length or numerous artificial lakes. Instead, challenges come in the form of established trees and a design that calls for good planning to negotiate the carefully placed bunkers and fierce rough. One of the most interesting features is that there are blind shots, seemingly impossible in a country so notoriously flat!

COLT IN THE NETHERLANDS

That great English course designer, Harry Colt, worked extensively in the Netherlands, leaving a legacy of first-class classic courses around the country. He upgraded Hilversum, did superb work at Kennemer, and his links-like course at The Hague is a masterpiece. He created archetypal heathland courses at Einhoven and for De Pan at Utrecht, and also worked on De Dommel and Amsterdam Old Course. It is a remarkable catalog.

Heathland charms

The tree-lined fairways demand accuracy and a cautious approach. On the short 2nd, for instance, you should hit an iron from the tee to find the raised landing area. In traditional fashion the fairway is divided into two parts, separated by rough, thus limiting the distance you can take from the tee. Cleverly this leaves everybody with the same approach shot, where again accuracy is key, as the green is tucked away in the trees and almost surrounded by bunkers.

Provided you stay in play, the opening holes are relatively straightforward. However, despite its lenient appearance, the course will punish errant shots, notably on the birdieable par-5 4th, where heather grows into the fairway down the left. As many a golfer has found to their cost, with sprained wrists caused by trying to hack out of it, heather is far from the soft purple plant it appears. A different challenge is presented at the 6th, where you must smash a drive down the right-hand side to have any hope of reaching the green in regulation on this sturdy par 4. As with many of the holes, the subtle doglegs call for a specific line from the tee, otherwise towering trees will block out the approach shot. Though caution is recommended, it was never in the vocabulary of Seve Ballesteros, who shaped the ball magically around the trees to win the Dutch Open at Hilversum.

Undulations in different guises provide much of the challenge of the closing stretch: the green on the par-3 13th is a sea of slopes, while hills on the 16th and 17th fairways make for blind second shots. Throughout the round, one is treated to delightful approaches to greens nestled in the woods, where the ball is illuminated in flight against the foliage of the backdrop. A round at Hilversum shares all the charms of the great heathland courses.

▶ Hilversum has hosted the Dutch Open 24 times since 1923. Its most famous winner (in 1980) is Seve Ballesteros.

LEFT *The peace and tranquillity of Hilversum's charming golf course is not restricted to golfers. The paths through the woods are well used by cyclists and walkers.*

CARD OF THE COURSE

Hole	Distance (yards)	Par
1	486	5
2	339	4
3	383	4
4	407	4
5	208	3
6	436	4
7	478	5
8	136	3
9	329	4
Out	3,202	36
10	145	3
11	422	4
12	353	4
13	476	5
14	119	3
15	449	4
16	370	4
17	382	4
18	490	5
In	3,206	36
Total	6,408	72

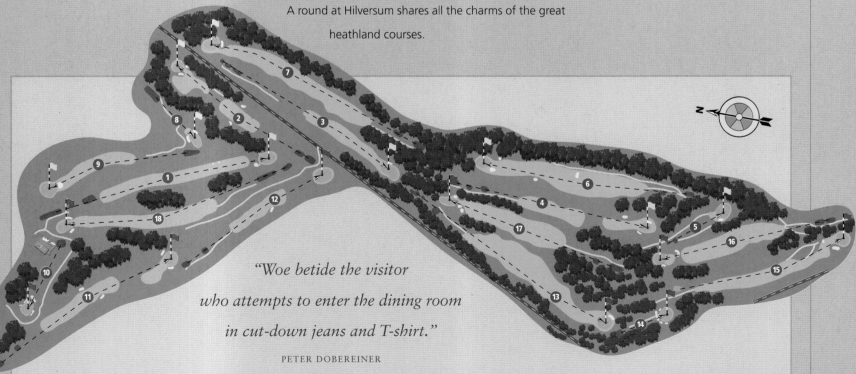

"Woe betide the visitor who attempts to enter the dining room in cut-down jeans and T-shirt."

PETER DOBEREINER

Kennemer

Kennemer Golf & Country Club, Zandvoort, Netherlands

It would be all too easy to assume that the Netherlands is entirely flat. True, much of it is, but there would be no Netherlands at all without a chain of sand dunes along its North Sea coast preventing the briny waves from invading the bulb fields and meadows on which much of the nation's wealth was founded. Three excellent courses are to be found in these dunes: The Hague, Noordwijk, and Kennemer.

In many ways Kennemer is rather like Royal Lytham and St. Annes on England's Lancashire coast. Both are actually a short distance inland from the sea, behind popular seaside resorts (Zandvoort and Blackpool), and both have the company of a railroad track for a few holes. There the resemblance ends, for Kennemer's dunes are wilder and more imposing than Lytham's. Nevertheless, there is something of a British feel to Kennemer due, in part, to the thatch-roofed clubhouse but, more fundamentally, to the fact that the course was designed by Englishman Harry Colt, who also designed Sunningdale and Wentworth.

WARTIME DEFENSES

It's something of a miracle that Colt's course survives, because during World War II Kennemer was a concrete jungle of anti-tank walls and anti-aircraft guns, part of a big defense area surrounding Amsterdam. Astonishingly, though, the course was not totally destroyed, and it was brought back into use as early as 1947. Key to this was the survival of the detailed correspondence between Colt and the club during construction.

Tumbling dunes and plateau greens

Holland's sand dunes are important not only sea-defensively but also ecologically, and there is a great feeling of being at one with nature when playing a round at Kennemer. Perhaps this is felt most while waiting on the 1st tee, a platform high on the dunes next to the clubhouse, with a rolling fairway far below making its way through dunes and scrub on either side to a distant green. This feeling continues on the 2nd, a short hole over wild country to a pinnacle green. One of the great vistas awaits on the 3rd tee, the fairway swinging left past bunkers and a tree-clad hillock en route to the green. Tracking back along the perimeter of the course on flatter ground, the next five holes, somewhat different in character, offer good scoring opportunities before the handsome 9th returns play to the heart of the dunes.

An exhilarating drive over a tumbling valley opens the back nine, and the pitch to a secretive green keeps up the fun. There is no shortage of length over the 11th and 12th holes, taking play to the far end once more. Pine trees give this part of the course more of a heathland feel, continuing through the 13th and 14th holes. Then comes the most individual hole of the lot, an extraordinary short hole played to a plateau green on top of a steep hill. There are no marks for being short, with the ball tumbling all the way down to the bottom of the hill! Three solid holes complete the round.

LEFT *The 14th green and beyond it the unforgettable short 15th, precariously perched on its hilltop with bunkers far below. In the background is Kennemer's attractive thatched clubhouse.*

CARD OF THE COURSE

Hole	Distance (yards)	Par
1	452	4
2	165	3
3	524	5
4	330	4
5	346	4
6	476	5
7	371	4
8	187	3
9	425	4
Out	3,276	36
10	361	4
11	460	4
12	546	5
13	373	4
14	385	4
15	163	3
16	480	5
17	168	3
18	398	4
In	3,334	36
Total	6,610	72

▶ A 17th-century painting of a young golfer hanging in the clubhouse at Kennemer is a reminder that golf in the Netherlands may well be as ancient as it is in Scotland.

▶ When the Dutch Open is played here a composite course is used, incorporating holes from the newer nine-hole Van Hengel Course, designed by Frank Pennink.

Noordwijk

Noordwijk

Noordwijk Golf Club, Zuid Holland, Netherlands

Dutch golf has a long history. It can be traced back to the 13th century, when records refer to a game called *colf* in which players hit a ball with a club to a particular target in strokeplay format. Contemporary golf began in the Netherlands in 1889 with a three-hole course at The Hague, closely followed by a course at Utrecht. Noordwijk has two additions to this epic golfing timeline, albeit of a peripheral nature.

First, at the 1976 Dutch Open, new European Tour rules meant that all participants must belong to a professional golfers' association, but the organizers of the event misunderstood and gave special invitations to three Americans who belonged to no PGA. Most of the field went on strike and refused to play the first round. As only a handful of local professionals and the three Americans played, that first round was canceled. Eventually the situation was resolved, though somewhat bizarrely: the Americans were technically withdrawn but played on for prize money from a separate prize fund.

The second of Noordwijk's additions to Dutch golfing history occurred when Seve Ballesteros won the 1986 Dutch

Open to become the first player on the European Tour to win £1 million in prize money. That occasion was marred by two of the greens being wrecked by anti-apartheid demonstrators, rendering them unplayable for one round.

A fusion of links and woodland

Perched upon the ridge that acts as Holland's protection against the North Sea, Noordwijk is as hilly as any seaside course. An expanse of Leviathan dunes seems to continue north to the horizon, making this a far cry from the rest of Holland's creaseless landscape. The small clubhouse is modest for such a venerable club. It sits on a crest of the dunes, overlooking green fairways winding through the folds of the

RIGHT *The short 3rd hole, one of those damaged by anti-apartheid demonstrators during the 1986 Dutch Open. Ballesteros won by a margin of eight strokes that year.*

land. From the 1st tee it becomes clear that Noordwijk is a true links, with the elevated tee leaving the shot perilously exposed to the wind. A perfect view of the slight dogleg on this par 4 shows the line of rough protecting the compact links turf of the fairway.

Noordwijk's location has a trick up its sleeve, because the sandy soil of this important region is actually held together by trees. As a result, the opening links holes soon lead into dense woodland, while retaining the legendary tight lies of a links. It is an interesting and unusual mix, where one hole can be totally exposed to the wind or protected by dunes, while the next could technically be termed forest golf.

Noordwijk's links holes are good looking, with ripples and mounds in the pristine fairways lined by mountainous dunes, but a stretch of holes in the woods provides some real gems. The entrance to the green looks minute on the par-3 6th. In fact it is just over ten paces wide, with further protection from trees and a large bunker. A 200-yard/183-m carry over trees—hardly links golf!—is the short cut for the bold on the 7th, allowing an easier approach to a magnificent raised green.

Noordwijk's fusion of different styles creates a wonderfully original experience with firm links turf backed by picturesque woodlands.

CARD OF THE COURSE

Hole	Distance (yards)	Par
1	386	4
2	598	5
3	166	3
4	463	4
5	412	4
6	184	3
7	362	4
8	404	4
9	557	5
Out	3,532	36
10	438	4
11	500	5
12	147	3
13	370	4
14	532	5
15	372	4
16	392	4
17	201	3
18	386	4
In	3,338	36
Total	6,870	72

"When the winds kick up, Noordwijk, like all classic links layouts, really gets tough."

GARY PLAYER,
*GARY PLAYER'S TOP
COURSES OF THE WORLD*

Praia d'El Rey

Praia d'El Rey

Praia d'El Rey Golf and Country Club, Obidos, Portugal

While the principal concentration of Portuguese golf courses is on the Algarve, there is a smattering of interesting courses in the Lisbon area sufficient to detain the visiting golfer. There is then something of a gap before a further outcrop of courses, much further north, in the region of Oporto, with Oporto Golf Club itself the oldest club in Portugal, dating back to 1890, as near to a links as you will find so far south in Europe. That gap between Lisbon and Oporto is not wholly golf-free. On the seashore to the west of Obidos can be found Praia d'El Rey and it, too, is links-like in many ways.

The course enjoys excellent seascapes and a string of holes that really do run along the shore. This may not seem remarkable at first sight, but in most real-estate developments these days it is the hotels and villas that face the sea—attracting premium rates—with the golf course inland, providing a selling feature for those rooms and properties that do not face the sea. Here the golf course comes first, which is to be commended.

BELOW *As close to links golf as you can get on Portugal's Atlantic coast. This is the short par-4 13th hole, 328 yards/300 m of old-fashioned seaside fun.*

LISBON COURSES

Robert Trent Jones's links-like Tróia, located on a sandy peninsula reached by ferry near Setúbal, is one of the best courses in the Lisbon area. To the west of Setúbal is the spacious and elegant Quinta do Perú. Many of Lisbon's best courses are around Estoril and Cascais, with Penha Longa the favorite of many. Mackenzie Ross's classic 1945 course at Estoril is short, but full of charm. It was a European Tour stop for many years.

Clever routing

The sea is a glorious companion to a golf course, but how do you maximize its proximity? The secret lies in the routing. As early as the 2nd hole you find yourself playing toward a backdrop of the sea, and the sense of anticipation grows. Sand dunes are a vital part of seaside golf and they form a framework for the short 3rd, but then you are sent off inland, having been given a taste of the sea only to be told not to be too greedy. The cream will come later. Get on with laying the foundation of a decent score!

By the 9th hole you are returning to the clubhouse, yet somehow you sense that this time you really are going to make it to the sea shore. Once again the anticipation grows over the 10th and 12th, cleverly moderated by the short 11th, running back. At last you have made it, and the 13th, 14th, and 15th are glorious oceanside holes. There is no disappointment in returning inland from here, because the 16th, 17th, and 18th are made of stern stuff—for tournament purposes they can be stretched to 1,482 yards/1,355 m between the three holes, the apparently never-ending 17th alone accounting for 623 yards/570 m.

LEFT *The par-5 10th hole overlooking the resort hotel and, beyond that, the Atlantic Ocean.*

CARD OF THE COURSE

Hole	Distance (yards)	Par
1	394	4
2	506	5
3	194	3
4	332	4
5	482	4
6	418	4
7	538	5
8	190	3
9	430	4
Out	3,484	36
10	503	5
11	200	3
12	433	4
13	328	4
14	164	3
15	410	4
16	427	4
17	623	5
18	432	4
In	3,520	36
Total	7,004	72

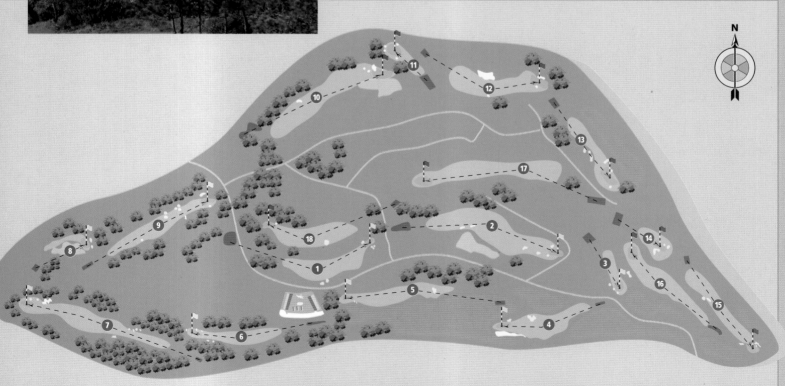

San Lorenzo

San Lorenzo Golf Course, Almancil, Algarve, Portugal

The Algarve is one of the most popular golfing destinations in Europe. It has the climate to be wonderfully attractive to Northern European golfers during the dark and cold winter months, yet Atlantic breezes help to prevent it from being unbearably hot during the summer. Golf courses litter the region—the choice is immense. But there is another side to it. The Algarve is now a maze of concrete, high-rise apartment blocks. To enjoy golf in the Algarve it is necessary to be very selective, and the course that has that little bit of edge over the others is San Lorenzo.

San Lorenzo dates from the late 1980s, a design by the American architect Joe Lee. What Lee had in his favor was a site that descends to the Atlantic Ocean, and he made full use of the advantage he was given. There is another plus, it must be said. Like all other Algarve courses, San Lorenzo is woven between real-estate developments. The developments here, however, are of Hollywood-style villas and mansions adorned with Moorish ornaments. They may resemble a film set, but they are far superior to the dreaded high-rise monstrosities elsewhere.

Nature's backdrop

It is not quite true to say that San Lorenzo descends to the Atlantic Ocean. More correctly, it descends to the banks of the estuary of the Ria Formosa, which is separated from the ocean by a low ridge of sand dunes. The shelter these dunes afford to the estuary ensures a safe haven for a wide range of species of swimming, diving, and wading birds. Happily, the whole area is designated a nature reserve.

While ornithologists may rush to the 6th and 7th holes, so do golfers, for it is at this point that San Lorenzo comes

into its own. Both holes enjoy elevated teeing grounds from which drives are made on to narrow strips of fairway bordering the waters. There are no marks for playing too safe—the chances of finding the ball on the tree-clad hills on the left are no better than 50:50. Both greens lie perilously close to the beach, that on the 7th, unusually, bunkered behind.

For the average golfer, the 8th is about keeping out of trouble and using any handicap shots available—it is, after all, Stroke 3. But for the big hitter it is an exciting hole, with water all the way down the right and hillocks encroaching from the left where you would rather they did not.

The back nine opens with a demanding drive over an arm of a lagoon to a rising, curving fairway, but from here on—until the 17th—the round is solid rather than spectacular, handicap golfers inventing their own problems. At the 17th, however, the prospect of a watery grave looms, or else dropping a shot by playing too safely away from the lagoon. The green is threatened by water. So is the 18th green, but this time there is no safe route for the timid. At some point at least one stretch of water must be taken on and conquered.

LEFT *San Lorenzo's final green, surrounded by water and sand, is a difficult target whatever the length of the approach shot—a touch of Florida in the Algarve.*

CARD OF THE COURSE

Hole	Distance (yards)	Par
1	540	5
2	177	3
3	365	4
4	372	4
5	143	3
6	422	4
7	377	4
8	574	5
9	400	4
Out	3,370	36
10	568	5
11	383	4
12	432	4
13	393	4
14	172	3
15	517	5
16	208	3
17	376	4
18	406	4
In	3,455	36
Total	6,825	72

▶ San Lorenzo has never sought to attract professional tournament golf, and has been spared the unnatural lengthening so often imposed on Tour courses.

▶ San Lorenzo is located within the Quinta do Lago estate, although it is not part of the Quinta do Lago portfolio, which includes the four Quinta courses and two Vale de Lobo courses.

San Lorenzo

PORTUGUESE RESORT GOLF

Portugal's rise in prominence from being an almost golfless country to that of being a major player in resort golf is quite remarkable. Suffice it to say that there were only three courses on mainland Portugal at the end of World War II. There are now over 50 courses and the number is rising steadily, even alarmingly. Yet this is almost entirely a business for tourists, and given the winter climate of northern Europe one understands why it should be so. In comparison with the number of golf courses there are few native players. The sad thing about this is that golf courses are developed in an "international" style for "international" golfers.

A comparison can be made with Vinho Verde, a Portuguese wine of no greatness, but the perfect accompaniment to *bacalhau*, that great Portuguese salt-cod dish. Have the real thing served to you in a pitcher and it is frothing, bone dry, and thirst-quenching. Drink the stuff made for tourists and it is semi-sweet, a little cloying, and bottled with a fancy label. It loses its character and its honesty. Portuguese resort courses need a little more distinctive character and rather fewer fancy labels.

RIGHT *The 6th green is found only after a perfect drive from an elevated tee to a low fairway bounded by a treacherous, scrub-clad hill and the Ria Formosa.*

ABOVE RIGHT *Unusual bunkering is a feature of the 7th green, its purpose, as much as anything, to deceive the eye into thinking the target is smaller.*

Vilamoura

Old Course, Vilamoura, Quarteira, Algarve, Portugal

It was Henry Cotton who first showed the world what golfing potential was on offer in the Algarve. His 1966 course in a former rice plantation at Penina, near Lagos, can be said to have started the explosion that has led to several dozen courses being constructed on the coastal strip between Lagos and Faro. Three years after Penina was completed, the pioneering course built by Frank Pennink among the umbrella pines and cork oaks at Vilamoura was unveiled. The resort of Vilamoura has grown out of all recognition since those days, but, happily, Pennink's gem remains largely unaltered: a beacon for those with eyes if something of a sleeper compared with some of the more brazen offerings being blatantly promoted today.

Pennink was a British architect of Dutch background, a fine amateur player, a connoisseur of all that is best in golf, and, incidentally, a gifted and stylish writer on all matters golfing. From the start, Vilamoura oozed class. It was not in Pennink's armory to resort to "eye-candy"—he was too honest for that. In fact Pennink's laid-back style was all about subtlety, which is why it is all the more pleasing that nobody has ever been brought in to "tart up" the course.

Trees, trees, trees

Vilamoura's fairways have become narrower over the years. The umbrella pines that line each fairway are undoubtedly attractive, but they are also constrictive, their spread increasing with each year's growth. Straight hitting is clearly essential to good scoring. With pines as the principal defense Pennink had little need for fairway bunkers, and throughout the round it is Pennink's restraint that shines through.

The course received a major overhaul in 1996, under the sensitive guidance of Martin Hawtree, with the overall conditioning being greatly improved.

The Old Course starts gently, with a short par 4, a par 5 reachable in two shots, and another short par 4. Then comes the only water hazard on the course (what a contrast to so many of the neighbouring courses!), a duck pond on the par-3 4th. It will trouble only a really terrible shot, the more pertinent obstacle being a tree on the direct line to the green. The par 3s are among the best holes on the course. Following this, the par-5 5th returns us to the clubhouse, a hole with fewer trees and consequently more prolific bunkering. Greater length of tee shot is required over the next three holes, and strong hitters will certainly fancy a crack at driving the 9th green, but its defenses are strong—Pennink was a wily golfer.

In the opinion of many, the 12th is the finest hole of the round, an admirable dogleg requiring perfect shot placement for success, and with no need for more than minimal bunkering. And a single fairway bunker is all that is required to turn the par-5 16th into a model exercise in control. Bring your brains to the Old Course. Take your brawn to its neighbors. Class will out!

LEFT *Pennink's honesty is shown in this aerial view of Vilamoura. He simply made the most of what he was given—natural undulations and umbrella pines.*

BELOW *The problems of excessive tree growth on an artificially watered course are plain to see in this view of the 11th hole.*

So prolific are the courses in this part of the Algarve that the Old Course is one of seven owned by Oceânico. Their new Faldo Course is described as having an Arizona desert style!

CARD OF THE COURSE

Hole	Distance (yards)	Par
1	339	4
2	476	5
3	354	4
4	178	3
5	531	5
6	232	3
7	430	4
8	458	4
9	290	4
Out	3,288	36
10	167	3
11	427	4
12	533	5
13	381	4
14	481	5
15	164	3
16	562	5
17	386	4
18	452	4
In	3,553	37
Total	6,841	73

El Saler

El Saler

Parador de El Saler, Valencia, Spain

Some 10 miles/16 km south of Valencia is a stretch of rippling sand dunes and pine forests on a narrow strip of land between the expansive wetlands of the Albufera National Park and the unspoiled beaches of this part of Spain's Mediterranean coast. In the 1960s, before golf tourism had taken off in Spain, it was decided to add a golf course to the facilities on offer at the luxury hotel, the Parador Luis Vives. Javier Arana, a gifted Spanish architect largely unknown outside his native country at that time, was called in to design the course. El Saler, his finest creation, remains, after his death, a magnificent testament to his talent.

Although there are a number of links-like holes in the dunes closest to the sea, El Saler is for the most part a pine-forest course with generous, undulating fairways and expansive greens. Arana's bunkers are in scale with the course, seriously proportioned, although their flat floors make escape relatively simple—that is until you perish in one of the deep bunkers in the dunes, very possibly through the back of the green when escape is made to a green running downhill, away from the shot, testing even for the best.

Golf at one with nature

An abundance of wildlife, particularly many species of birds of the forest and wetland, is found at El Saler, and a post-golf tour of the Albufera is heartily recommended. Such abundant flora and fauna suggest a healthy environment. In parallel, the course is maintained in a cultured condition, although the price to pay for this is slow greens—if they were kept fast-running they would disappear under the scorching, penetrating sun in no time at all.

Starting off amid the pines, the first four holes introduce us to most of the trademarks of Arana's style, with fairways characterized by deceptive ridges that make distance judgment and tee-shot placement subtly challenging—you have to think your way round here, not simply blast away unimpeded. Suddenly, on the 5th, the whole feel of the course changes with a tee shot uphill toward a distant ridge. And on the far side there is a most attractive panorama, with the fairway rushing downhill toward a green constructed in the dunes, and a wide seascape beyond.

From here to the turn this links-like atmosphere is maintained, with the sweeping, up- and downhill par-4 6th, one of the best holes on the course, and a monster dune on the 8th. These holes set El Saler apart from so many other Spanish pine-forest courses. That said, the 10th is a handsome way to return to the pines, with a characteristically sited green, raised up amid the pines and ingeniously bunkered.

After a somewhat pedestrian passage, the course revisits the dunes for a stunning finish, with the 17th green enfolded in sandy hills and treacherous chasms. From the final tee there is a marvelous seascape to the right, although a golfer's mind should be on the matter in front, for this is a difficult, sloping, curving fairway to hit, and there is serious trouble in the dunes to the right. For good measure the green is typically tricky, with many slopes to contend with should you fail to find the right part of it.

▶ El Saler has staged few professional tournaments, but these have included the Spanish Open, Turespaña Masters, and Seve Trophy. Bernhard Langer scored a remarkable 62 when winning the 1984 Spanish Open. His fellow competitors were so astonished that they suggested that he had left out two holes.

LEFT *There is no denying the links challenge of the drive at the last hole, with its distant, sloping fairway and all manner of sandy perils to the right.*

CARD OF THE COURSE

Hole	Distance (yards)	Par
1	428	4
2	376	4
3	532	5
4	189	3
5	515	5
6	442	4
7	358	4
8	359	4
9	156	3
Out	3,355	36
10	399	4
11	568	5
12	198	3
13	348	4
14	414	4
15	564	5
16	428	4
17	213	3
18	466	4
In	3,598	36
Total	6,953	72

Las Brisas

Real Club de Golf Las Brisas, Nueva Andalucía, Spain

There are, today, some 20 golf clubs in the Marbella area of Spain's Andalucían coast. What is not a golf course is more than likely to have disapperaed under villas, apartments, or hotels. But when Las Brisas opened in 1968 it had the place more or less to itself, and from the course you looked out over open country direct to La Concha, the dramatic Sierra Blanca peak. It was, and still is, fashionable and expensive.

Robert Trent Jones, the world's most prolific golf course designer, had already announced his imposing presence in Spain with Sotogrande, his first European course, in 1965. It was not the earliest course in the area—that honor belongs to Guadalmina (1959)—but it set the standard by which every subsequent course was measured. Unfortunately, it also set a style standard: that every golf course should look "American." With water coming into play on no fewer than 12 holes, Las Brisas, Jones's second Spanish course, clearly falls into that category.

BELOW *There's a golf course there somewhere! The unfortunate consequence of overdevelopment in Andalucía is that courses as good as Las Brisas become suffocated in concrete.*

A STAR-STUDDED WORLD CUP

Las Brisas was only five years old when it hosted the World Cup. A number of very powerful teams were present, not least the American pair of Jack Nicklaus and Johnny Miller, both in fine form. They won, of course, and Miller took the individual honors with a total of 277, 11 under par. He also set a course record of 65. The World Cup returned in 1989, and there have been a couple of Spanish Opens and a Mediterranean Open on the European Tour, but for the most part golf at Las Brisas is social.

A plethora of water hazards

The course begins gently with a straightforward par 4, but steps up a gear for the 2nd, a difficult driving hole with a narrow fairway turning to the right past a pond before climbing to a raised green, one of several that will be encountered during the round. There is plenty of length over the next few holes, not least the 582-yard/530-m 5th, until at the 8th we encounter a quite unusual challenge. A water hazard runs most of the length of the hole before crossing in front of the green. For the last 100 yards or so there is an alternative fairway on the far side of the water. It lies along the axis of the green and is the safer route to the putting surface, but for those chasing birdies or eagles, the shorter, more daring route over the water must be taken.

Another par 5 calling for heroics is the 12th, the birdie seeker having to carry a long stretch of water to find the green in two. In the World Cup, Nicklaus solved the problems of the 15th by eliminating the dogleg completely, driving over the trees and out-of-bounds nonchalantly, necessitating a clear carry of over 270 yards/250 m. There is a formidable water carry on the par-3 16th, and water in front of the 17th green has messed up the promising cards of many on this otherwise simple drive-and-pitch hole. It goes without saying that the final drive is also threatened by water.

LEFT *Las Brisas is beautifully presented. The water is there to intimidate the golfer, but whatever the outcome, the round is memorable for the conditioning of the course.*

▶ Nick Faldo won the 1987 Spanish Open at Las Brisas. The greens were particularly fast and testing that year, but Faldo found them to his liking and fought off a chasing pack.

CARD OF THE COURSE

Hole	Distance (yards)	Par
1	399	4
2	426	4
3	477	5
4	207	3
5	582	5
6	377	4
7	173	3
8	489	5
9	346	4
Out	3,476	37
10	395	4
11	206	3
12	511	5
13	370	4
14	395	4
15	418	4
16	222	3
17	318	4
18	396	4
In	3,231	35
Total	6,707	72

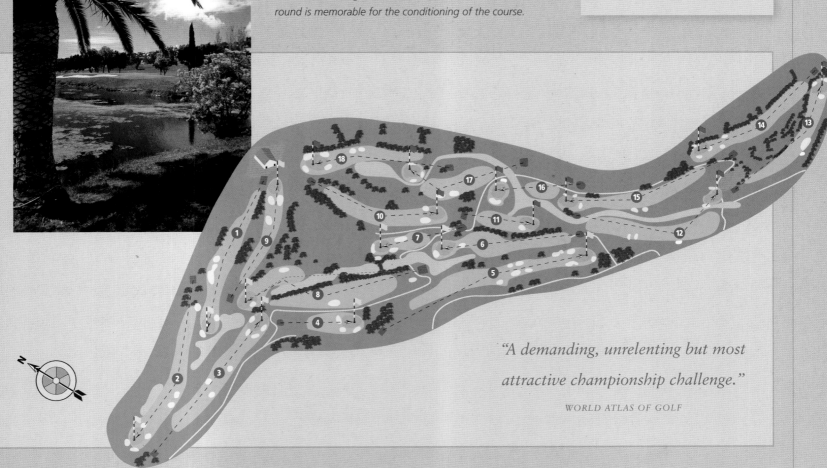

"A demanding, unrelenting but most attractive championship challenge."

WORLD ATLAS OF GOLF

Valderrama

Valderrama

Club de Golfe Valderrama, San Roque, Cadiz, Spain

Regarded by many as the top golf course in continental Europe, Valderrama is inextricably linked with the Volvo Masters, the European Tour's end-of-season flagship event. In 1997 it hosted one of the most closely fought Ryder Cups, with Seve Ballesteros's European team managing to withstand the comeback of the Americans on the final day to retain the Cup by a margin of one point. Despite its high profile, and the menacing reputation of the 17th, Valderrama prides itself on being playable by all skill levels. A large range of tees ensures not only widely differing yardages, but also different routings, to cater to various abilities. Credit must go to the inventive design of the course, which, interestingly, was designed twice by the same man.

Valderrama began its life as the New Course at Sotogrande, in turn becoming Las Aves, before being bought by rich Bolivian industrialist, Jaime Ortiz-Patiño. Keen to host high-quality tournament golf, Ortiz-Patiño called back the designer of the course—the prolific architect Robert Trent Jones—to make alterations. Most significant of these changes was to reverse the two nines so the hardest run of holes would become the finishing stretch. A massive drainage program was initiated and, later, a lake was introduced in front of the 17th green. Conditioning is always impeccable.

Shades of Augusta

Overall length has never been a priority at Valderrama, but the challenges are considerable. The course is hilly, wind is a constant factor—and a variable one, with two prevailing winds changing the characteristics of the course from day to day—and a proliferation of trees makes particularly high demands on straight hitting. The trees remove options from play. Usually there is only one specific route to the green, meaning that this is target golf.

One of Ortiz-Patiño's aims was to replicate the feel of Augusta, both in condition and design, and this is achieved well on the 10th. Despite its short length there is little room for error, as the tee shot must be faded past a lake on the right and short of a bunker that devours a tee shot hit too straight. From here one has a magnificent view of the green, surrounded by white sand bunkers and a ring of cork trees. But, like the 9th at Augusta, the approach must be hit positively, as a weak shot will roll backward off the green and often back down the fairway!

The environment plays an important role in the Valderrama experience, and the natural beauty of the course is a shining example to others. An active involvement in ecology means that there are twice as many species of plant and a third as many more types of bird on the course than in the surrounding countryside. While many courses resort to fertilizer, pesticide, and even dyeing the lakes blue, Valderrama has maintained quality without neglecting the environment. In fact, U.S. Ryder Cup captain Tom Kite claimed the greens to be among the best he had ever putted on.

▶ Huge sums are spent each year on maintaining the course in peak condition. Valderrama has 4,600 sprinklers, compared to the 600 for the average course in the United States.

LEFT *This view of the short par-4 10th shows why yardages are irrelevant, even at professional level, if the topography of the site and the intuition of the architect are in harmony.*

CARD OF THE COURSE

Hole	Distance (yards)	Par
1	389	4
2	399	4
3	173	3
4	535	5
5	381	4
6	163	3
7	461	4
8	345	4
9	441	4
Out	3,287	35
10	364	4
11	547	5
12	197	3
13	402	4
14	370	4
15	200	3
16	422	4
17	511	5
18	434	4
In	3,447	36
Total	6,734	71

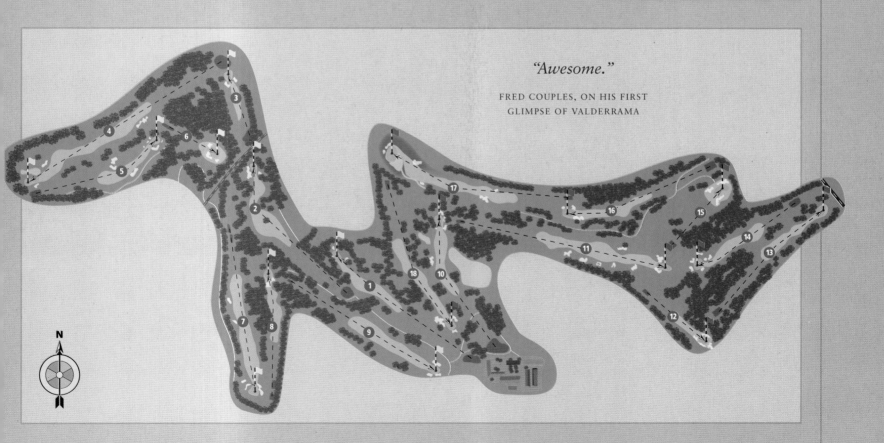

"Awesome."

FRED COUPLES, ON HIS FIRST GLIMPSE OF VALDERRAMA

NOTORIOUS 17TH

At 511 yards/467 m, the par-5 17th at Valderrama ought to be a picnic to the professionals, but this is actually one of the most controversial holes in golf. Like many of the holes on this course, it begins with a challenging drive to a bunker-adorned fairway lined by cork trees. After a slight dogleg right, the front of the green is guarded by a lake, with a steep mound behind the putting surface housing three bunkers. The controversy arises because the green slopes dangerously toward the water, as Tiger Woods found out with a triple bogey in the 1999 World Golf Championship. At the 1997 Ryder Cup, the 17th was criticized as the green was deemed unfair. Colin Montgomerie famously described it as "the worst hole in Europe," perhaps not the most tactful thing to say considering the hole was redesigned by the European captain, Seve Ballesteros! But the hole showed its undeniable strength: to create drama. It was an instant favorite with the emotional fans who swarmed on the bank behind the bunkers to witness the few who proved it could even be reached in two and managed to hold the green.

RIGHT *In the heat of the Ryder Cup or the pressure of other professional tournaments the 17th is a nervous moment for the players. It can make spectacular viewing for the gallery. But is it great architecture when seemingly perfectly played shots to the green are inconsistently rewarded?*

Falsterbo

Falsterbo Golfklubb, Falsterbo, Sweden

For many, their first sight of Falsterbo's haunting links is from an airplane flying into or out of Copenhagen Airport. It is only a matter of minutes away by air and with the new road bridge across the Øresund it is little longer by car. Falsterbo lies on the end of a peninsula at the southwestern tip of Sweden. Indeed Falsterbo was the venue for Sweden's first international match—against nearby Copenhagen Golf Club. That was in 1909, the year of the club's foundation.

It was the British professional at Copenhagen Golf Club, Robert Turnbull, who laid out Falsterbo's original nine holes. Not until 1930 did it become an 18-hole course, this time designed by a local doctor, Gunnar Bauer, and, with the exception of the 16th and 17th, which were created in 1934, that course remains the one we play today. The only change has been a recent updating of the putting surfaces and bunkers, generally very well received.

A genuine links

Falsterbo is undeniably flat, and it is also undeniably a genuine links course, one of very few in continental Europe. The course is dominated by an old lighthouse that stands proudly beside the 13th fairway, surrounded by trees, and behind the 14th green. It comes as no surprise, then, to find that the course runs alongside the sea on two sides, with an inland excursion toward a marsh, where some of the best holes are.

The start is strict, with a long par 4 running inland beside a wood. It is followed by a well-bunkered short hole and a par 5 on which out-of-bounds is a serious threat. Then comes a really testing hole, the 4th. Into the wind it can be a devil. There is water all down the right and serious rough to the left. What is more, the green is angled out into the water, calling for steady nerves on the approach. The 5th is hardly any easier, with water on both sides of the fairway and a brilliant green complex. Two great two-shot holes. Respite of a kind comes at the 7th, an almost drivable par 4, but its closely bunkered green is zealously guarded.

As the back nine begins the golf returns to the marsh, with water all round the 11th green. Fortunately it is not a long par 3. Play then continues around the lighthouse, with the 13th and 14th each adding substantially to the course length, before the 15th heralds the start of Falsterbo's famous finish. It is a reachable par 5 with its green protected by yet another pond. While the 16th takes play to the very tip of Sweden the 17th runs parallel to the beach, its fairway narrowing awkwardly at the length of a good drive. And to finish there is a tempting par 5 played from a tee overlooking the beach, the fairway angled from left to right, increasing the pressure on the tee shot the further you attempt to drive.

On a still day Falsterbo is idyllic. When the wind is up it can be a bruiser.

▶ Europe is full of one-dimensional professional Tour courses of inordinate length; 6,652 yards/6,083m of Falsterbo is worth 7,652 yards/6,997 m of such courses in terms of subtlety.

LEFT *This happens to be the short par-4 7th hole, but it is typical of the whole course at Falsterbo with its keen bunkering and subtle undulations.*

CARD OF THE COURSE

Hole	Distance (yards)	Par
1	449	4
2	191	3
3	558	5
4	443	4
5	405	4
6	170	3
7	317	4
8	197	3
9	421	4
Out	3,151	34
10	383	4
11	159	3
12	406	4
13	563	5
14	230	3
15	514	5
16	388	4
17	377	4
18	481	5
In	3,501	37
Total	6,652	71

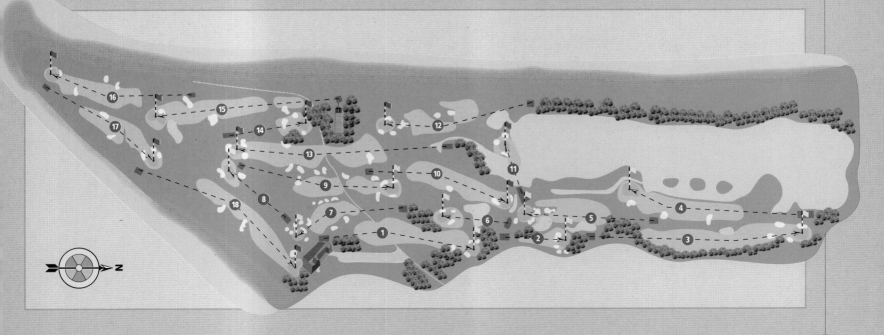

Halmstad

North Course, Halmstad Golfklubb, Tylösand, Sweden

Halmstad's hosting of the 2007 Solheim Cup put the club on the map for many, but what Swedish golfers have known for many years is that this is one of the finest courses anywhere, not just in Sweden. It lies slightly inland behind the little seaside resort of Tylösand on Sweden's west coast in an area of sandy woodland and is known popularly as Sweden's Wentworth. This title is not as far wide of the mark as might be imagined, for the course designer, Rafael Sundblom, had worked alongside Harry Colt during construction of the East and West courses at Wentworth, drinking in the old master's techniques and philosophies at the same time.

BELOW *Halmstad's traditional strength lies in its long two-shot holes. But it would be wrong to overlook its short holes. The 4th bears a superficial similarity to Wentworth's 2nd.*

The club started life in 1930, playing its golf on military training grounds in Halmstad before moving to its newly built 18-hole course at Tylösand in 1938. In 1963, an additional nine-hole course was constructed, with Nils Sköld as the architect. Nine further holes were constructed in 1975, to the designs of Frank Pennink. Sköld's nine holes were added to the back nine of Sundblom's course to form the North Course, while Pennink's were joined with Sundblom's outward nine to make up the South Course. They are a formidable pair, in their different ways worthy of comparison with Wentworth's historic East and West courses.

Dense woods

At Halmstad the woods are so dense that there is little need for rough. The fairways are wide enough not to cause the golfer undue concern, and the bunkering is sparing. But that does not mean that the golfer can play unthinkingly. On the 1st, for instance, it is necessary to play to the right of the fairway from the tee in order to open up the green. Play too far left and a tree blocks out the second shot. Then on the enormously long 5th the tee shot must find the gap between two trees eating into the fairway from both sides, otherwise you are playing catch-up golf for the rest of the hole.

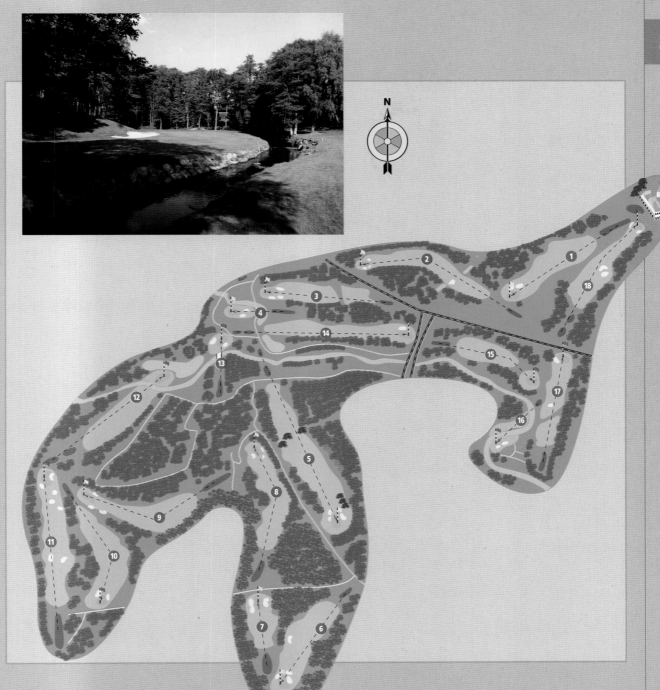

ABOVE RIGHT *The stream running through the course has been put to good strategic use. This is the 16th.*

▶ In the 2007 Solheim Cup at Halmstad the Europeans led the Americans 8½–7½ going into the final 12 singles matches, but they ended up losing 16–12.

▶ Laura Davies, Britain's outstanding female golfer, won the 1999 Chrysler Open at Halmstad at 15 under par, eight shots ahead of English golfer Alison Nicholas.

CARD OF THE COURSE

Hole	Distance (yards)	Par	Hole	Distance (yards)	Par
1	434	4	10	394	4
2	544	5	11	510	5
3	383	4	12	439	4
4	166	3	13	172	3
5	600	5	14	558	5
6	356	4	15	337	4
7	213	3	16	179	3
8	423	4	17	353	4
9	455	4	18	395	4
Out	3,574	36	In	3,337	36
			Total	6,911	72

There are many doglegs on the course, and you will be required to play them bending to the left and the right. The sequence through the 8th, 9th, and 10th holes is particularly rewarding to the player who enjoys shaping shots.

The manner in which the North Course was formed from the work of two different architects is apparent when comparing the front and back nines. Whereas the outward nine is painted with a broad brush, the back nine is shorter and generally rather tighter. There is greater emphasis, too, on the use of the stream that runs through the course as a strategic hazard. There is a particularly demanding approach to the 12th green, for instance, and a watery grave awaits the inaccurate on the 16th.

A diagonal ridge some 200 yards/183 m out must be cleared from the 17th tee, and the green is angled, but the hole is not overlong. As long as the fairway bunkers are avoided at the last it should be possible to hang on to a slight lead successfully.

Crans-sur-Sierre

Golf Club Crans-sur-Sierre, Valais, Switzerland

The European Masters and, before it, the Swiss Open have attracted quality fields to Crans-sur-Sierre every year since 1948, plus the one prewar Swiss Open held at Crans in 1939. It has produced some famous winners: Garcia, Donald, Els, Romero, Westwood, Montgomerie, Ballesteros, Olazábal, Stadler, Faldo, Woosnam, Price, Locke, Rees, Nagle, and Charles to name but a few. They enjoy playing here: they like the place; they like the atmosphere; they like the winner's cheque; they like the golf course. After all, it usually produces very low scoring.

The first course at Crans was set up in 1905, opening the following year with a nine-hole layout, which was expanded a few years later to 18. It did not survive World War I. A second attempt at establishing a course, again of nine holes, was made in 1921. That was superseded by an 18-hole course that opened in 1929. It was designed by an Englishman, Harry Nicholson, and remained largely intact until 1997, when Seve Ballesteros was commissioned to rebuild the greens, add a little difficulty around the course, and create some new back tees.

LOW SCORING

It was at Crans-sur-Sierre in 1971 that the Italian golfer, Baldovino Dassù, carded a 60, the first time anyone had achieved it on the European Tour. Against the par of the day this worked out at an astonishing 13 under par. Colin Montgomerie holds the 72-hole scoring record for Crans at 260. He closed with rounds of 61 and 63 to win by four shots.

RIGHT *The 7th is one of the easiest holes on the course, a drive-and-pitch hole of only 331 yards/303 m, but who could not be exhilarated by such a spectacle!*

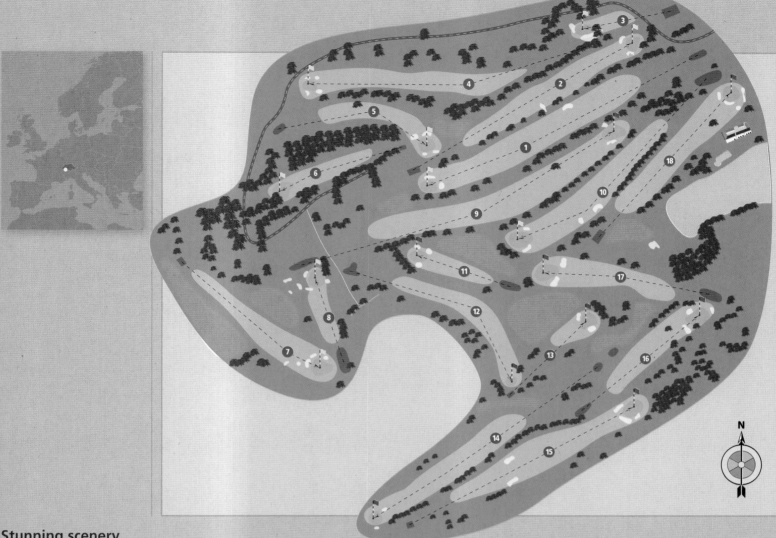

Stunning scenery

If you were to set down the Crans course in the middle of flat farmland it would attract little attention. It is perfectly good but nothing remarkable in itself. What sets it apart—very much apart—is the ravishing scenery. It is not every day that you get to pitch to a skyline green backed by a towering, snowy, Alpine peak. Against such massive backdrops the golf course can seem minuscule. In fact it is far from minuscule, measuring a healthy 6,937 yards/6,343 m from the white tees, with a par 5 stretching to 629 yards/575 m and the longest par 4 being 503 yards/460 m. That said, the course sits at an altitude of some 5,000 feet/1,500 m, which enables longer hitting.

The course opens with a reachable par 5 before doubling back for a sturdy two-shot hole, followed by a short hole along the course boundary. In the past, the 4th was played as a par 5, but now it is a super-long par 4, and even from the visitors' tees it measures a healthy 487 yards/445 m. Length is less significant on the dogleg 5th, pine-enclosed 6th, wide-open 7th, and well-bunkered 8th, but then comes the extraordinary 9th, wending its way relentlessly to its green near the clubhouse.

On the back nine there is another sharply doglegged hole, the 12th, and back-to-back par 5s. You and I play the 16th as a short par 4, but for the European Masters it is shortened to a 235-yard/215-m par 3, bringing the overall par down to 71. Two straightforward par 4s then bring us home.

> There is a second, nine-hole, course at Crans, designed by Jack Nicklaus. It is hoped eventually to extend this course to 18 holes.

> Crans is possibly the best example of a place where the course map, or course statistics, tell least of the golfing experience.

CARD OF THE COURSE

Hole	Distance (yards)	Par	Hole	Distance (yards)	Par
1	540	5	10	405	4
2	439	4	11	205	3
3	191	3	12	410	4
4	503	4	13	200	3
5	339	4	14	595	5
6	324	4	15	516	5
7	331	4	16	346	4
8	175	3	17	386	4
9	629	5	18	403	4
Out	3,471	36	In	3,466	36
			Total	6,937	72

▶▶▶ Courses 82–89

▶▶▶ Middle East & Africa

Resort golf may be new to the Middle East and Africa but golf has been played there for many years. The great problem for all but the southern part of Africa was climate. Grass would not grow at all in the arid climates of north Africa and the Middle East. Grass would grow in the hot and wet equatorial lands, but it was impossible to grow fine grasses. Golfers had to improvise.

The easy bit was simply to carry a carpeting mat around with you. You could stick a tee peg in it for the drive and treat yourself to a perfect lie for subsequent shots. Greens were a greater problem and the solution found was to have sand greens, rolled flat and then oiled so that the surface did not blow away. It provided a remarkably true putting surface and was easily repaired. Such greens are still in use here and there and were common in the southern states of the United States until scientists developed grass strains capable of producing an acceptable surface even in fierce heat.

In the Middle East the water required to grow the grass is more expensive than oil!

Emirates

Emirates

Majlis Course, Emirates Golf Club, Dubai, United Arab Emirates

The Emirates Golf Club was dubbed "The Desert Miracle" when, in 1988, it became the first grass course in the Middle East, and it is easy to see why. Sheikh Mohammed bin Rashid Al Maktoum, of the Dubai ruling family, donated the property and urged that the course should reflect the natural state of the land. Karl Litten's design was an instant success, creating lush Bermuda-grass fairways of a kind more usually associated with Augusta National, while protecting them with the natural desert dunes.

Not only has the course succeeded in bringing grass to the desert, there are also abundant water hazards. Desalinated water is transported to the course from a nearby factory at huge engineering expense. It is achievement enough that any golf course has been constructed in such an inhospitable environment, but the fact that the course is a fine one almost makes it deserving of the accolade of a "miracle"!

Instant recognition

The quality of the course was instantly appreciated when the European Tour chose the Majlis for the Dubai Desert Classic just one year after its completion. As a result the course can

already boast a considerable history for one so relatively young. Drama is often created around the excellent 18th, a long par 5, which doglegs around a lake. A simple layup is sensible, but the temptation is to cut the corner and risk finding water. Then the approach shot is also over a stretch of water that has claimed the errant shots of many a great player. Both Ian Woosnam and Tiger Woods have lost the championship from near-certain victory by finding water with approaches at 18. But it is a rewarding hole if played well, perfectly demonstrated by Ernie Els, who struck a majestic 6-iron to 22 feet/7 m and rolled the putt in for eagle to claim victory by one shot in 2005.

▶ Ernie Els holds the course record 61, which helped him to victory in the 1994 Dubai Desert Classic. He also won the tournament in 2002 and 2005.

▶ Tiger Woods won the 2008 Dubai Desert Classic in stunning fashion, taking just 31 strokes on the back nine to catch and overtake Els in the final round.

LEFT *Linking the lush green of the fairways and greens of the Majlis Course with the barren desert beyond, the remarkable clubhouse is styled after Bedouin tents.*

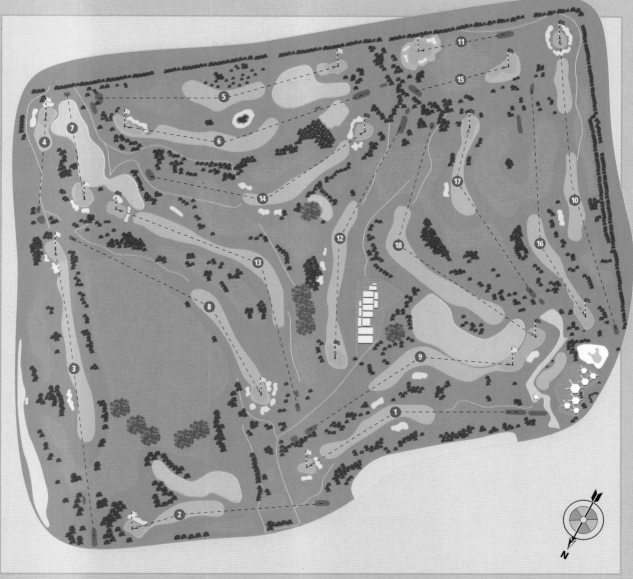

CARD OF THE COURSE

Hole	Distance (yards)	Par	Hole	Distance (yards)	Par
1	458	4	10	549	5
2	351	4	11	169	3
3	530	5	12	467	4
4	188	3	13	550	5
5	436	4	14	434	4
6	485	4	15	180	3
7	184	3	16	425	4
8	434	4	17	359	4
9	463	4	18	547	5
Out	3,529	35	In	3,680	37
			Total	7,209	72

Like the 18th, many holes require a strong nerve and a great deal of accuracy to play over the picturesque oasis-like lakes, but the best-looking hole on the course is the stunning 8th. The fairway doglegs around the desert on this difficult par 4, creating a captivating view from the tee, as lush green fairway is contrasted with desert scrub. Equally impressive is the approach shot, played to a raised green backed by the dramatic clubhouse.

The clubhouse is an extraordinary sight, built in white concrete and glass; it resembles a Bedouin tented village, providing a unique backdrop for a beautiful course. Hospitality is a matter of pride at the club, and this extends beyond the superbly equipped clubhouse. Golfers are looked after out on the course as well, even provided with air-conditioned refreshment huts—it is in the desert, after all, and temperatures range from 86–122°F/30–50°C.

In 2006 the second 18-hole course, the Wadi, was redesigned by Nick Faldo. This course is also appealing, incorporating the "wadi" (Arabic for "valley") into the design, which, along with Faldo's trademark fairway bunkering, creates an interesting course requiring disciplined course management.

The Cascades

The Cascades

The Cascades Golf & Country Club, Soma Bay, Egypt

It is hard to believe that this peaceful course was until recently an Egyptian military base that saw wartime conflict with Israel—land mines had to be removed before construction of the course could begin. Fortunately those days are in the past and the Cascades of today, completed in 1999, is one of the most serene places imaginable.

Picturesque fairways are backed by the tranquil Red Sea while the cascading lakes, from which the course takes its name, reinforce the Zen-like atmosphere. The whole 5-star resort complex is designed with relaxation in mind, with extensive spa facilities, and it is also particularly popular for scuba-diving, as the waters of the Red Sea are fabulously clear. It seems a world away from the sinister barracks that previously occupied this area.

The course itself is testing enough not to allow a totally hassle-free experience. As with most desert courses, the

Gary Player design effectively uses the sands as a natural defense for wayward shots—Player was one of the finest bunker players of all time—but there are also lakes to contend with on a couple of holes. The Red Sea makes a beautiful backdrop to the 4th green, an attractive prospect from the elevated tee, but it also comes directly into play on four holes. Jutting out into the sea, the 5th is inevitably the signature hole, a mid-length par 3 played over a continuous bunker to the green, the prevailing wind adding length to an already daunting carry.

RIGHT *The 4th green and, beyond, the 5th hole, where multiple tees allow all skill levels to enjoy the challenge of the course's signature hole.*

Desert beauty

Stunning views accompany every hole, with waterfalls, distant mountain ranges, the deep blue sea, and lush fairways making this one of the most distinctive courses in the world. There is a good variety of holes. Considering the location it might have been all too easy to design each hole as a variation of the same thing and let the view do the work. But diversity is here in abundance.

The 2nd is a muscular par 5, with well-positioned fairway bunkers to make you think about your second shot. There are a couple of good, short, two-shot holes as well, including the 6th, which, at 339 yards/310 m from the very back, is drivable but requires nerve, as a big slice will be lost to the ocean. Course management is key to success on many holes, as effective fairway bunkering (and even a split fairway on the 12th) requires golfers to select and play to a line according to their individual abilities.

Gary Player also designed the accompanying nine-hole par-3 course, which, as one would expect considering the quality of the par 3s on the championship course, is full of well-designed short holes. But be warned, what seems a perfect way to relax in the evening sunshine may turn sour on the difficult 154-yard/141-m 9th, where one must hit over a lake to a tiny island green.

▶ This is the first championship course in the Gulf region designed by one of the "Big Three"—Arnold Palmer, Jack Nicklaus, and Gary Player.

▶ Hurghada, the nearest town, was formerly an impoverished fishing village. The golf resort has helped to turn it into a leading tourist center.

CARD OF THE COURSE

Hole	Distance (yards)	Par
1	425	4
2	614	5
3	427	4
4	438	4
5	207	3
6	339	4
7	384	4
8	190	3
9	540	5
Out	3,564	36
10	480	5
11	426	4
12	355	4
13	547	5
14	186	3
15	358	4
16	184	3
17	470	4
18	426	4
In	3,432	36
Total	6,996	72

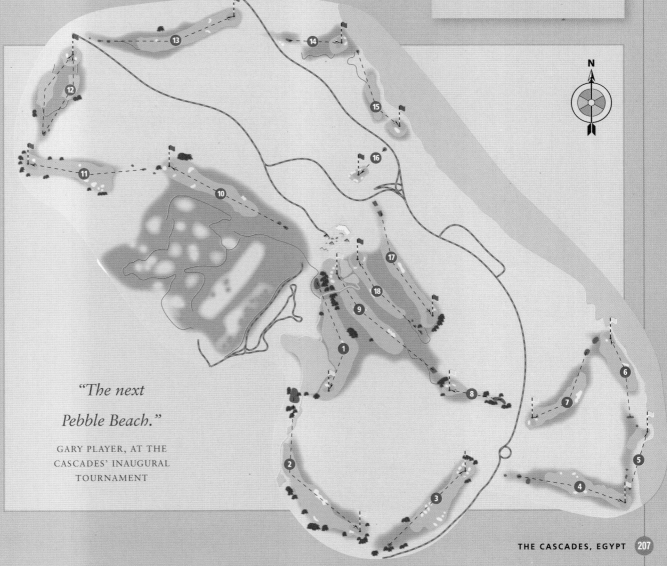

"The next Pebble Beach."

GARY PLAYER, AT THE CASCADES' INAUGURAL TOURNAMENT

Royal Dar Es Salam

Red Course, Royal Golf Dar Es Salam, Rabat, Morocco

As golf course designer Robert Trent Jones said, "The king, to put it kindly, is a golf nut." He was speaking of King Hassan II of Morocco, who commissioned Jones to build 45 holes of golf at Rabat between 1970 and 1974. North Africa is a place of enormous contrasts, not least between wealth and poverty. The sensitive golfer cannot fail to feel enormously privileged to play at Royal Rabat, for this is very much more than a mere oasis. It is a horticultural wonderland. Had these courses been around in classical times they might have given the Hanging Gardens of Babylon a run for their money in the Seven Wonders league table.

Trent Jones made his mark in the golf design world not only by being so prolific, but also by "building" courses—building in the sense of moving thousands and thousands of tons of earth. At Rabat, Jones was given a site overflowing with cork oaks. It still does overflow with them, and the wayward golfer will rapidly discover their golf-ball-stopping properties. Those fortunate enough to stay on the fairways will find them immaculately groomed, the greens manicured to perfection, deep blue waters in the lakes and ponds, and ravishing wild flowers in the lush rough.

The Red Course is seriously demanding and seriously long, with three of the par 3s over 200 yards/183 m and all but two of the par 4s in excess of 400 yards/366 m. However, the 10th, at a mere 481 yards/440 m, must be viewed as a compulsory birdie (and possibly an eagle) for the good player. And good players have graced these fairways frequently, for the Moroccan Open was a regular part of the European Tour for many years. Howard Clark's course record 66, achieved in 1987, has occasionally been threatened but never beaten.

Royal Dar Es Salam

▶ Robert Trent Jones and King Hassan II became friends, and it was in 1971 while Jones was attending the king's birthday party (held at a palace with a golf course!) that a coup was attempted. It failed, but Jones was held at bayonet point for an hour or two—not the sort of thing you expect to happen as part of your work building golf courses, though it's a good story to dine out on.

LEFT *It all looks so peaceful and gentle! But this island green, the 9th, is totally surrounded by water and is no easy target even from the most forward tee.*

"Surely the best course on the continent outside South Africa."

ROBERT GREEN,
CLASSIC GOLF HOLES

CARD OF THE COURSE

Hole	Distance (yards)	Par	Hole	Distance (yards)	Par
1	400	4	10	481	5
2	232	3	11	467	4
3	443	4	12	526	5
4	404	4	13	384	4
5	566	5	14	206	3
6	440	4	15	391	4
7	420	4	16	424	4
8	582	5	17	226	3
9	188	3	18	552	5
Out	3,675	36	In	3,657	37
			Total	7,332	73

Penal approach

Jones's philosophy is penal. You are either in the ideal spot on the fairway to attack the well-defended greens or hopelessly struggling for that miracle rescue shot. Take the 1st hole, for instance, whose narrow fairway curves to the left along its avenue of oaks. It is hard enough to shape the tee shot through the bend, but two big bunkers further narrow the fairway where you would prefer they did not. In fact bunkers in the landing zone are a recurring feature throughout the round. Jones expects you to drive with arrow-like precision, allied to plenty of length, or pay the penalty.

He is no less compromising around the greens. Look at the bunkering on the 16th! Successfully overcome the bunkering from the tee and you then have to clear a green-front bunker on the direct line, avoid others either side, and stop the ball on a shallow putting surface. In fact, every single green is bunkered and most fairways are bunkered in the landing zone.

Karen

Karen Country Club, Nairobi, Kenya

Whatever the rights and wrongs of the colonization of Africa, there is one lasting legacy of former times that is more apparent in Kenya than in other such countries—a golf infrastructure. Kenya's geography and climate suit the growing of tea and coffee, and many of the golf clubs were founded in the early years of the 20th century by estate owners and farmers. Golf courses were not confined to any specific region. They were to be found all over the country.

First came the Nairobi Golf Club, started as a nine-hole course in 1906. It was given the Royal prefix by King George V and is now an expansive 18-hole course. Up-country courses soon followed, with Nyeri leading the way in 1910. The Indian Ocean coast was also a promising golfing region, and the Mombasa Golf Club dates back to 1911. Not far behind was the primitive Kisii course (1914) in the Western Rift Valley/Lake Victoria region, although the pick of the club names in that part is surely the enticing Nandi Bears Club, formed by tea farmers in 1928. Happily, the golf tourism industry in Kenya flourishes and visitors are treated to some enchanting golf in wonderful locations.

BELOW *At an altitude of 5,400 feet/1,646 m, conditions for golf at Karen are not as overpoweringly hot as might be imagined. Here golfers putt on the 12th green.*

Literary origins

The essence of Kenya in those years before World War II is captured in the novel *Out of Africa* by Baroness Karen von Blixen. It was on part of her former coffee estate, in the area now known as Karen, that one of Kenya's top courses was begun in the 1930s. Karen Country Club was the product of hard work by a young banker, Remi Martin (nothing to do with the Cognac house), who was in charge of acquiring the land for the course, setting up the company to build it, and developing the real estate, which was to be particularly attractive to investors because the golf course would have grass greens—as opposed to "browns"—at that time largely

unknown in Kenya. Such investment has paid off with a course that is maintained in fine condition, good enough to host annually the Kenyan Open on the European Challenge Tour.

Karen's golf course is as pretty as a picture, its flourishing wildlife (both flora and fauna) encouraged by an active policy of nature and wetlands conservation and promotion. Everywhere there is color and beauty. There is also considerable variety in the nature of the golfing challenges.

The course retains the layout it has had for many years, and still plays to more or less the same length it did over 30 years ago. It has not needed to be lengthened inordinately to withstand the onslaught of today's young professionals. All that has been done is to drop par from 72 to 71, with one of the members' par 5s (the 3rd) being played as a tournament par 4. A surviving par 5 is the 2nd, a demanding hole that turns through almost a right-angle at the length of a decent drive.

▶ In the early years of the club, natural hazards included cobras (one interrupted the official opening of the club in 1937), baboons, zebra, and elands— and above all lions.

CARD OF THE COURSE

Hole	Distance (yards)	Par
1	350	4
2	580	5
3	538	4
4	387	4
5	203	3
6	489	4
7	185	3
8	384	4
9	443	4
Out	3,559	35
10	362	4
11	395	4
12	301	4
13	457	4
14	137	3
15	561	5
16	195	3
17	458	4
18	559	5
In	3,425	36
Total	6,984	71

RIGHT *A fire destroyed the clubhouse in 1977 and almost caused the club to be closed. Its replacement was built in the style of a game park lodge.*

Durban Country Club

Durban Country Club

Durban Country Club, Durban, Natal, South Africa

The Durban Country Club is one of South Africa's great golfing institutions. It has hosted 16 South African Opens, more than any other South African club, and is generally regarded in the golfing world as one of the few genuinely world-class courses in South Africa—in all Africa for that matter.

It came into being in 1922 because the Durban Golf Club (later Royal Durban) was at that time in a bad way, being waterlogged and with little prospect of immediate improvement. For the new Durban Country Club a site was found on well-draining, sandy, high ground overlooking the Indian Ocean. Two fine South African golfers, George Waterman and Laurie Waters, laid the course out in such a way as to maximize the potential of the two types of ground at their disposal: tumbling dunes, exposed to the ocean winds, and a lower, flatter, partially wooded area. While there have inevitably been some changes through the years, the general routing and nature of the course remains remarkably intact, testament to the sound design of Waterman and Waters.

The wind factor

It is not uncommon to hear golfers at St. Andrews or Lahinch describe the conditions on the course thus: "It's a three-club wind today." By that they imply that the wind is of such a strength that a shot that would normally be played with a 6-iron is today a 3-iron or a 9-iron, depending on whether the shot is into the wind or with it. The winds affecting the conditions at Durban can be just as extreme and might well vary enormously within a matter of an hour or two. Waterman and Waters had to ensure that their course remained playable during such winds yet would withstand free scoring on those days when the wind was absent. You need to play the course in a variety of different wind conditions to appreciate the skill with which they did their job.

CARD OF THE COURSE

Hole	Distance (yards)	Par
1	387	4
2	188	3
3	512	5
4	181	3
5	459	4
6	352	4
7	372	4
8	501	5
9	434	4
Out	3,386	36
10	560	5
11	480	4
12	156	3
13	339	4
14	527	5
15	194	3
16	417	4
17	401	4
18	274	4
In	3,348	36
Total	6,734	72

▶ Gary Player set a record score of 273 in winning the 1969 South African Open at Durban. That score was matched in 1998 by Ernie Els.

ABOVE RIGHT *Durban Country Club at tournament time. A small crowd gathers round the 1st green.*

LEFT *Seaside golf at its most fun: the huge undulations that define the character of the 18th are the main factor making this such a good short par 4.*

Some of the best holes come at the start of the round, with an opening hole that demands authoritative striking, with out-of-bounds on the right, a sloping fairway, an uphill approach to the green, and much trouble to either side of the putting surface. It is followed by a beautiful short hole with fine views of the ocean. Many would nominate the 3rd as one of the best par 5s in the world, a hole requiring the straightest of hitting. The 4th plays down from the dunes to a green on the lower ground, while the 5th is a very tough two-shot hole with an undulating fairway.

A brief return is made to the dunes on the 8th, but it is the final two holes that make particularly telling use of them. The 17th is an engaging hole, played along a valley with a bouncy fairway toward a plateau green. In theory the 18th is drivable, but misery lurks off the fairway if the tee shot is pulled or pushed in an attempt to make the distance. And even if the shot seems to be on target, there is always the potential of the wind to spoil things.

"The player is not shown everything at a glance but is given the thrill of anticipation and uncertainty."

BOB GRIMSDELL, GOLF COURSE ARCHITECT

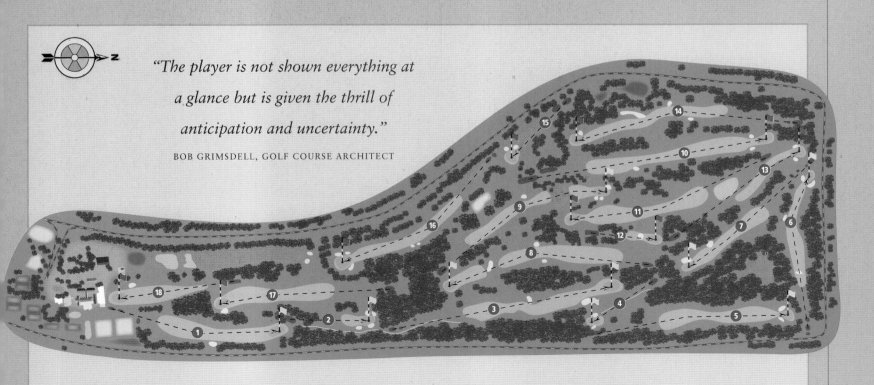

Fancourt

Fancourt

The Links at Fancourt, Fancourt Hotel and Country Club Estate, George, South Africa

Late on November 23, 2003, the Links played host to one of golf's greatest duels. The U.S. and International teams of the President's Cup, tied at the end of four days of golf, sent one player each to settle the match with a head-to-head, sudden death play-off. An estimated 800 million people worldwide watched Ernie Els and Tiger Woods battle for the cup as darkness fell on the picturesque course.

With the first two holes halved, both players faced long par-saving putts on the third play-off hole. Tiger holed out from 15 feet/4.5 m to leave Els with a putt of 8 feet/2.5 m to keep the match alive. Opposing captain Jack Nicklaus later said, "There wasn't anybody in the world who wanted to see you miss that putt," and Els duly rose above the pressure and holed out. Captains Nicklaus and Player epitomized the spirit of the game by agreeing to a tie and sharing the cup.

Designed by Gary Player, this strikingly beautiful course sweeps through mounds at the feet of the Outeniqua Mountains, the dunes creating a links-like experience. These mounds are often assumed to be natural because they seem so in keeping with the surrounding mountains, but they are actually the result of a huge amount of earthmoving. In fact, from the mounds down the right of the 13th, there is a good view of the flat farmland that is the land's more natural state. But natural or not, the course plays like a links, those carefully created mounds enveloping the fairways and fierce pot bunkers protecting tough greens.

BELOW *The clubhouse at Fancourt reflects the atmosphere of the Manor House, the hub of the resort, where fine dining is the order of the day.*

Risk and reward

Player's trademark design features—risk and reward and playability to all skill levels—exist throughout the course. Powerful hitters have opportunities to make long carries on most holes, and there is temptation to drive both short par 4s, the 6th and 14th. However, the drives must be perfect as the holes are cleverly designed, with large pot bunkers and thick rough on the dunes ready to gobble up wild shots.

Multiple tees successfully keep the course interesting to all golfers, so an exciting contest will arise between a long hitter and a short accurate player. On all too many other courses the holes are consistently too tight for the long hitter, or too long for the player relying on accuracy. It is this element of the design that made the course perfect for the matchplay of the President's Cup, as one player could lay up safely in the fairway, allowing his partner to take on the aggressive lines.

The long par-4 15th is reminiscent of the 18th at Sawgrass, doglegging left around marshland. However, the unsung hero is the par-3 17th. With a stone-walled burn short and left, most golfers play out to the right, leaving themselves a tough chip across a slick green. Trees behind the green add confusion about wind direction. This is when you should turn for advice to one of the caddies at Fancourt, said to be among the best in the world.

FANCOURT'S FOUR COURSES

The Links is the highest profile of four courses at Fancourt. The Montagu has recently been upgraded by David McClay Kidd, designer of Bandon Dunes in Oregon, U.S.A., while the Outeniqua is a 7,000-yard/6,400-m Gary Player design. To play these courses you must stay at the resort. The public-access course is Bramble Hill, designed by Player to give "golfers of every level a Fancourt experience."

CARD OF THE COURSE

Hole	Distance (yards)	Par
1	396	4
2	236	3
3	469	4
4	494	4
5	549	5
6	341	4
7	476	4
8	202	3
9	609	5
Out	3,772	36
10	408	4
11	161	3
12	481	4
13	533	5
14	361	4
15	477	4
16	584	5
17	186	3
18	616	5
In	3,807	37
Total	7,579	73

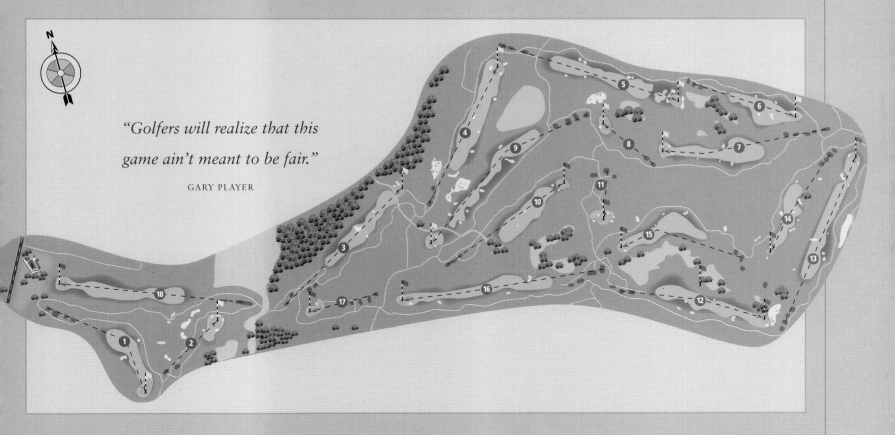

"Golfers will realize that this game ain't meant to be fair."

GARY PLAYER

GETTING IT RIGHT

In order to get the links feel just right, Player (rumored to be the world's most traveled athlete) revisited a number of links courses in Scotland and Ireland. Writing about Fancourt, he said, "It has been designed to make golfers feel as though they were at Ballybunion, Dornoch or St. Andrews, with rolling fairways, pot bunkers, big greens, high rough, and a seascape appearance."

ABOVE *The 17th, viewed here from left of the tee, is reckoned to be one of the toughest par 3s on all four courses. The humps and bumps designed to give the course an authentic links appearance are clearly visible in the background.*

RIGHT *Key to producing a links-like playing experience is scaling the artificial undulations so that they are not overwhelmed by the mountain background, aptly demonstrated here on the 12th hole.*

Gary Player Country Club

Gary Player Country Club, Sun City Resort, South Africa

Gary Player is one of golf's hardest competitors; he won his first major at 23, was the first non-American winner of the Masters, and won the Grand Slam at 29, the youngest player to do so at that point. But when the man nicknamed "The Black Knight" stood at the site for the proposed course in 1978, he almost threw in the towel. His brief was to build a course capable of hosting the world's richest golf tournament, to be held at the Vegas-style Sun City Resort, but the location did not exactly lend itself to golf.

To start with, the site chosen used to be a volcano. The land is naturally rocky and arid, and, unfortunately, there is no running water. A comparatively minor problem was that the land was covered with cattle, manure, and barbed-wire fences. If the challenges of the land itself were not enough, there was also the fundamental dilemma of combining, in one course, a championship course capable of testing the world's best golfers and a resort course ordinarily played by vacationers. But developers of resorts on this scale are not easily put off, and an adequate budget was provided to allow Player's team to move as much earth as they required.

Multiple tees

Player's solution has been to create effective changes in distance through the use of multiple tees, so that the fairway bunkers that catch the high-handicapper will also affect the likes of Ernie Els playing from the back tees. Although this course is one of the longest in the world from the back tees, over 7,800 yards/7,132 m at full stretch, the different tees allow the setup to change according to the requirements of the day. Altitude, of course, means that the course does not play quite as long as the card suggests, but there are some very substantial two-shot holes, nevertheless.

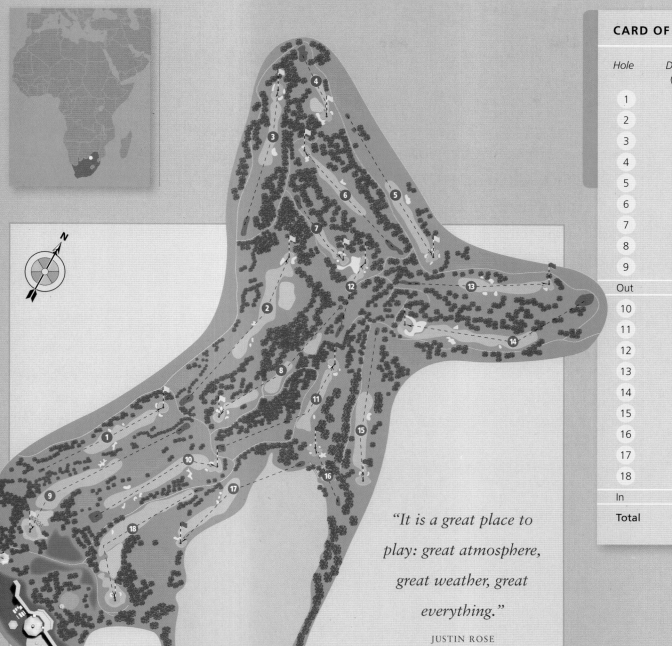

CARD OF THE COURSE

Hole	Distance (yards)	Par
1	441	4
2	569	5
3	450	4
4	213	3
5	491	4
6	425	4
7	225	3
8	492	4
9	596	5
Out	3,902	36
10	547	5
11	458	4
12	219	3
13	444	4
14	602	5
15	472	4
16	211	3
17	478	4
18	502	4
In	3,933	36
Total	7,835	72

"It is a great place to play: great atmosphere, great weather, great everything."

JUSTIN ROSE

▶ "The 18th is one of the greatest finishing holes I play all year. I love it: the crowds, the lake . . . this hole seems to improve every year." Ernie Els

LEFT *Player described the 9th as "a heroic par 5, even though it is regularly set up to allow players to reach the green on their second shot."*

Throughout the round the strategy is one of risk and reward. It is possible to play conservatively, but to score well you have to take risks. The best example is on the signature 9th. Although it is 596 yards/545 m from the back tee, the hole is generally played from forward tees—average golfers play this par 5 at 508 yards/464 m—and the hole naturally plays shorter due to a slight dogleg. A good drive will encourage players to go for the island green in two to set up a birdie, but the green is more receptive to a short iron shot and may not hold a fairway wood. Contoured greens offer a variety of pin positions, from easy to hard.

Gary Player once said: "If I am one of the greats, it's for one simple reason: no bunker shot has ever scared me and none ever will." With his legendary talent, it is no surprise that he makes good use of both fairway and greenside bunkers. Another theme is the emphasis on accuracy. Poor drives will find dense bush, and the slick greens will generally not hold approaches from the rough; the severe contours relentlessly roll mediocre approaches off the green altogether. Although the course can be brutal, especially the massive par-4 8th and nail-biting 18th, the course is fair and the player with guile and accuracy will generally succeed here.

Leopard Creek

Leopard Creek

Leopard Creek Country Club, Malelane, Mpumalanga, Transvaal, South Africa

Leopard Creek is a very private country club in the African bushveld, so private that membership is by invitation only. But Leopard Creek came very much into the public eye during the 2007 Alfred Dunhill Championship, when Ernie Els, seemingly cruising to victory for the fourth time in the event, dumped two balls consecutively into the water surrounding the final green, ran up an eight, and handed the trophy to the little-known English professional John Bickerton.

The man behind Leopard Creek was Johann Rupert, who engaged the wise old man of South African golf, Gary Player, to lay out his dream course. Player was no stranger to this environment, having already designed championship tests such as the Gary Player Country Club at Sun City. At Leopard Creek, however, there were special difficulties to be overcome: those of the Kruger National Park, its habitat, and its inhabitants. Clearly, this was much more than just ensuring that fertilizers or pesticides did not find their way into the unpolluted waters of the park. Rupert wanted his guests to be able to enjoy the fabulous wildlife. Yet it would hardly do if a hungry crocodile occasionally lunched on a member. The design had to be such that it was elevated sufficiently above the Crocodile River that hippos might splash about unconcernedly and golfers might at the same time be able to concentrate on their yardages without always having to keep an eye out for ambush. The course opened in 1996 and was altered a few years later, with the lowering of some of the tees and greens and the removal of a wall behind the 13th green in order to open up the views beyond.

RIGHT *It is now almost obligatory to contrive that finishing holes should play to an island green, as here at Leopard Creek, scene of Els's misfortunes in 2007.*

Expansive design

In laying out Leopard Creek, Gary Player and his team utilized as many natural features as they could. It is, therefore, a spacious course and yet there are some very demanding shots, such as the drive at the 3rd. With bunkers on the left and trees on the right, straightness is of the essence. Length, however, is also imperative, with a stream crossing the fairway short of the green. Water is used extensively throughout the design, not least on the parallel 9th and 18th holes with their greens threatened by a lake. For the Alfred Dunhill these two holes are interchanged, so that it is the 18th hole that finishes on an island green.

For drama, though, it is hard to beat the par-5 15th, which skirts a river all the way to the green perched above a lake to give stunning views of the Kruger Park and its teeming wildlife. Nor has the fun ceased, because on the short 16th the tee ball is played over this lake to a green almost surrounded by water. The 17th provides a rare dry interlude.

▶ There are many fine views of the Kruger National Park from the course, but few better than that from the elevated 12th tee—a distraction for the golfer who is about to play a testing, steeply downhill tee shot to a green surrounded by bunkers.

RIGHT *The 13th green, adjoining Crocodile River. This must be one of the hardest courses in the world on which to concentrate on golf, with this sort of scenery and proximity to wildlife.*

CARD OF THE COURSE

Hole	Distance (yards)	Par
1	419	4
2	542	5
3	448	4
4	427	4
5	164	3
6	319	4
7	215	3
8	480	4
9	541	5
Out	3,555	36
10	432	4
11	375	4
12	192	3
13	552	5
14	413	4
15	598	5
16	208	3
17	448	4
18	476	4
In	3,694	36
Total	7,249	72

"Playing while hearing a hippopotamus snort or seeing a lion near the fence is unique."

GARY PLAYER

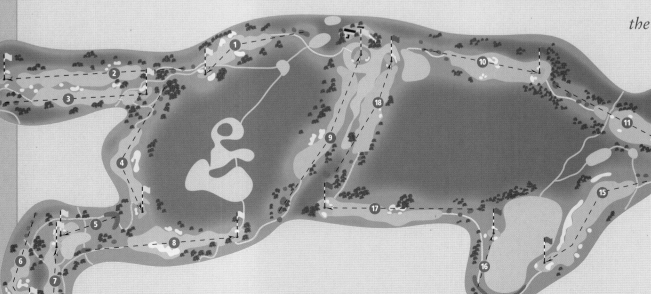

▶▶▶ Courses 90–101

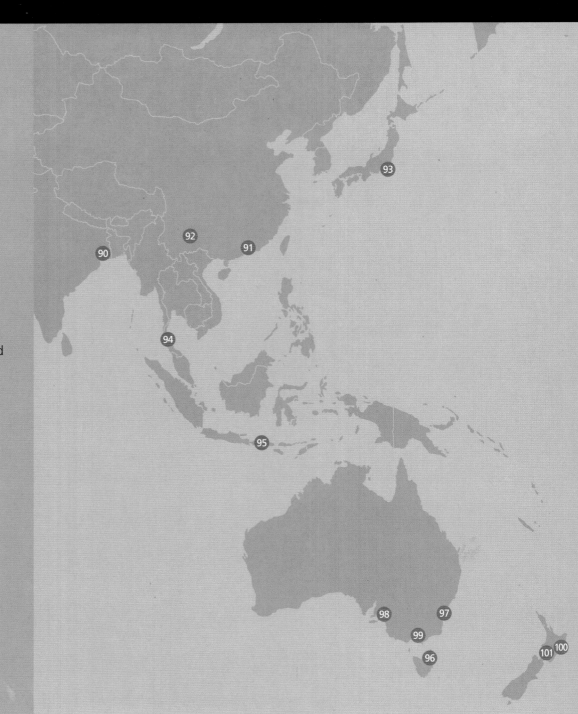

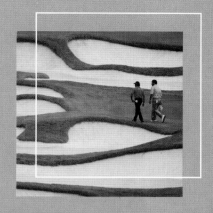

▶▶▶ Asia & Australasia

Golf in Asia is booming. Its players, men and women, are among the most competitive and successful on the U.S. and European Tours. Golf tourism is growing at unprecedented rates, and new courses are being built in quantity. At last China has taken hold of the sport and, with political support, golf is simply exploding there, with Mission Hills building no fewer than 12 courses: St. Andrews is only halfway there after six centuries! But golf is hardly new to Asia, Royal Calcutta being the oldest club in the world outside the British Isles. On the whole, golf was played where European countries had colonies or around the great trading posts. Japan, in particular, took up golf at a high level, in the interwar years.

Australia and New Zealand, with their traditional links to Britain, have been well stocked with good courses, many of them truly world-class. As in Asia, new course building is proceeding apace, and the quality of design is so high that any of 20 modern courses might have been included in this book, and there are many mature courses that can give them a run for their money.

Royal Calcutta

Royal Calcutta Golf Club, Kolcata, India

The Royal Calcutta Golf Club is the oldest in the world outside Great Britain, founded as the Dum Dum Golf Club in 1829. It was some 12 years before another Indian golf club was established, this time in Mumbai, and between them the two clubs fostered the game in the subcontinent. Indeed, Royal Calcutta (it became Royal at the time of the visit of King George V and Queen Mary to India in 1911) was so influential that it had a status similar to the R&A in that it was the custodian of the rules and etiquette of the game in India. The club also set up the Amateur Championship for India.

Under British rule, Royal Calcutta excluded Indian members. Happily that is no longer the case, although the club still retains its strong links with the R&A and also with a number of British clubs with which it shares reciprocal courtesy of the course. Less happily, however, the club could not afford to retain all of its former 36-hole grounds, selling off that portion further from the clubhouse to the Bengal government. What remains, however, is a formidable 18-hole test.

Unseen dangers

At first sight, Royal Calcutta appears to be benign, with flat fairways and few bunkers. What the eye has not seen is a whole network of ponds and pools and interconnecting ditches criss-crossing the course below the level of the fairway. They were created when earth was dug out to form the greens and tees and, as they are now used to store water, are known as tanks. Their positions cannot be predicted and there may be several forced carries over them on any hole.

One of the hardest holes on the course is the 7th, a solid par 4 running along the course boundary, driving out of a chute of trees toward a fairway curving to the left past water, before another tank cuts the fairway off abruptly. With the length of the drive limited, the second shot is substantial. Another strong hole on the way out is the 3rd, curving this time to the right, with a serious carry over a tank to find the fairway.

Royal Calcutta is a long course, but this is largely because, like the Old Course at St. Andrews, there are only two short

RIGHT *The splendid clubhouse, which has been the spiritual home of Indian golf since 1829. It still carries with it a sense of grandeur and formality.*

holes. The par 5s are not particularly long by today's standards, but there are enough longer par 4s to keep mid- and long-irons in work. A good example is the 10th, which, yet again, involves a second shot that must carry water in front of the pear-shaped green. And so it goes on, tank after tank, until suddenly, on the last hole, there is water-free fairway. Surely there must be one more hidden tank lurking to catch the incautious somewhere before the green! But no, a single fairway bunker and a couple of greenside ones are all that remain to trap the unwary.

▶ The Cashmere Cup, presented by Royal Calcutta Golf Club to the R&A in 1882, became the trophy for the world's first handicap tournament, now known as the Calcutta Cup.

RIGHT *Sheep sheltering from the heat of the sun in a bunker at Royal Calcutta. Sheep sheltering from the wind in Scotland created many of the very first bunkers.*

CARD OF THE COURSE

Hole	Distance (yards)	Par
1	359	4
2	141	3
3	436	4
4	525	5
5	426	4
6	422	4
7	415	4
8	413	4
9	398	4
Out	3,535	36
10	432	4
11	410	4
12	369	4
13	194	3
14	409	4
15	502	5
16	362	4
17	371	4
18	430	4
In	3,479	36
Total	7,014	72

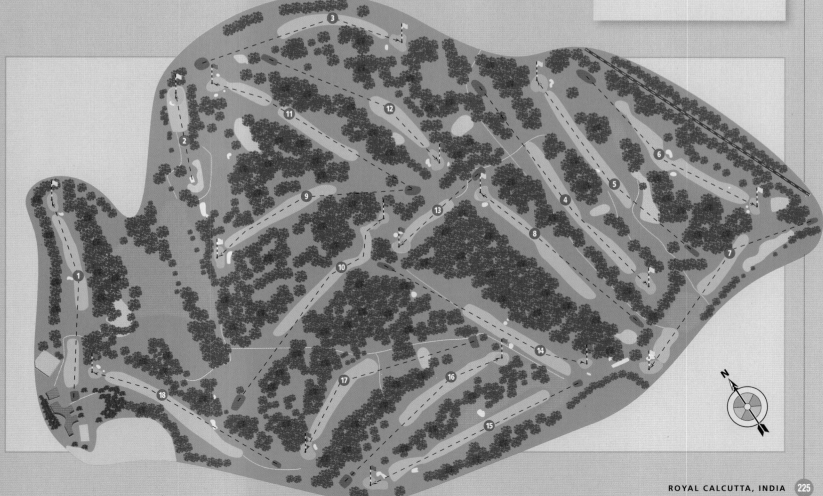

Mission Hills

Mission Hills

Olazábal Course, Mission Hills Golf Club, Shenzhen, China

With 216 holes of golf stretched over 12 courses, each one carrying the name of a great golfer, Mission Hills is already established as the largest golf resort in the world. The names—or most of them—trip off the tongue: Annika, Duval, Els, Faldo, Leadbetter, Nicklaus, Norman, Olazábal, Ozaki, Pete Dye, Vijay, and Zhang Lian Wei. The Nicklaus Course hosted the World Cup of 1995, the first time a Chinese course had been accredited by the U.S. PGA. The tournament returned in 2007, but this time it was to be the first of 12 World Cups to be staged annually at the resort.

It is astonishing to see the way in which China has embraced golf. Whether charging in, building courses and resorts at an alarming rate, will be good for Chinese golf is yet to be seen, but its enormous tourism potential must be obvious to all. Mission Hills has the desirable asset of being a mere 20 minutes from Hong Kong, and the transport links necessary to get the numbers of visitors required to make a resort on this scale viable are excellent. Another great asset is the climate, which is good for golf all year round, as players in Hong Kong have known since golf arrived in 1889.

Long and heavily bunkered

For the 2007 World Cup the Olazábal Course was selected as the host. Olazábal has never been the longest (or most accurate) driver on tour, although he is an exceptionally gifted iron player. So it is something of a surprise to find that the course that bears his name is the longest of all 12 courses at Mission Hills. On this occasion it produced Scottish winners (for the first time since the tournament began as the Canada Cup in 1953) in Colin Montgomerie and Marc Warren, who had finished second in the previous year.

The long 6th, with its narrow fairway in the driving area, is probably the toughest of the par 4s. Like so many holes here the jungle background is impressive. There is a chance to enjoy this from the elevated tees of the 8th, a long and difficult par 3, and the 9th, a very heavily bunkered par 5. Olazábal is an impressive bunker player and this is reflected in the number of bunkers on the course—around 150. A large number of them appear on the 10th, the great majority of those littering the left side of the short but uphill par 4.

These days it is almost obligatory to provide a so-called signature hole. On the Olazábal Course this is the 15th. It is an all-out skirmish with the water that runs down the left of the fairway, giving the brave (or stupid) several options for cutting the corner to turn a regular par 5 into a death-defying two-shotter. This style of hole is becoming commonplace, as are imitations of the final hole at TPC Sawgrass, and there is a striking resemblance to this template with the last hole on the Olazábal Course, water again threatening throughout on the left.

▶ When Olazábal visited his course during construction in 2002 he was told that his and four other courses had to be finished within one year. They were—some 3,000 workers and 600 machines were brought in to do the work.

ABOVE LEFT *The 16th green on the Faldo Course bears a striking resemblance to the 17th at TPC Sawgrass.*

BELOW LEFT *Designers have been given almost free rein—this is the imaginative 6th hole on the Ozaki Course.*

CARD OF THE COURSE

Hole	Distance (yards)	Par
1	447	4
2	175	3
3	548	5
4	405	4
5	176	3
6	476	4
7	566	5
8	214	3
9	573	5
Out	3,580	36
10	404	4
11	568	5
12	457	4
13	241	3
14	401	4
15	580	5
16	432	4
17	197	3
18	460	4
In	3,740	36
Total	7,320	72

"This is truly a wonderful course."
COLIN MONTGOMERIE

SPOILED FOR CHOICE

With 12 courses available, visitors are spoiled for choice at this astonishing resort. Notwithstanding the appeal of the Olazábal Course, many will want to sample the Nicklaus Course, which hosted the World Cup in 1995. Possibly the toughest is the Norman Course, rated one of the hardest in Asia. The Sorenstam Course, designed by the first female professional to play against the men of the PGA Tour, is quite long enough to keep even them in check. David Leadbetter has a reputation as one of the foremost teachers in world golf. No, his course is not an "academy course." It is every bit as long and demanding as the rest.

ABOVE *On the 10th, on the Olazábal Course, it is better to be on the left side of the fairway, skirting these prolific bunkers, to open up the approach to the green.*

RIGHT *Sand is present on the 15th—the signature hole on the Olazábal Course—in profusion, too, but in most cases the bunkers will save the ball from finding the water.*

Spring City

Spring City

Mountain Course, Spring City Golf and Lake Resort, Kunming, China

Kunming, in the south of China, is blessed with an ideal climate of springlike weather all year round. Spring City, taking its cue from the climate, stands at an altitude of 7,000 feet/2,134 m, surrounded by mountains and overlooking Lake Yang Zong Hai. With two golf courses, the Mountain designed by Jack Nicklaus and the Lake designed by Robert Trent Jones Jr., it has entered the resort golf market at the high end. It is easily reached by air and the extra-golfing facilities are all you might expect of a resort of this kind.

Golf in such circumstances can be idyllic, but there is a price to pay—real estate. A large membership is necessary to pay for the construction and ongoing maintenance of two courses designed by such big names, so the resort has built many villas, lodges, and apartments, whose residents automatically become members of the golf club. Many of the holes are therefore bounded by housing, albeit of an attractive kind, and golfers are not always so much at one with nature as they might wish to be. That said, there are many great views and moments to savor on both courses.

THE LAKE COURSE

Robert Trent Jones Jr. was given first choice in deciding on which part of the estate he should build his course. He chose the lower site, but with it came the problem of the 150-foot/46-m drop to the lake. In order to keep the golf holes reasonably flat there are a number of substantial changes of level between holes during the round, and as a result buggies are a necessity.

RIGHT *Elaborate bunkering is a feature of the Mountain Course's 11th hole—a short par 4, and one of the most attractive, too.*

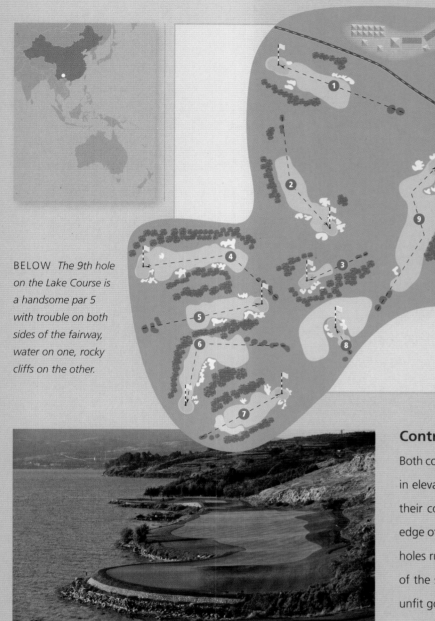

BELOW *The 9th hole on the Lake Course is a handsome par 5 with trouble on both sides of the fairway, water on one, rocky cliffs on the other.*

Contrasting courses

Both courses make use of the topography intelligently. With a significant change in elevation available to both designers, they have approached the routing of their courses in very different fashion. Where Jones takes play down to the edge of the lake in the middle of the round, Nicklaus leaves it to the end. Most holes run along the hill, rather than up or down it, so, despite the hilly nature of the site, much of the golf is flat and, therefore, not too strenuous for the unfit golfer, although most visitors ride buggies.

Nicklaus's 1st hole is a prime example, playing along the side of a hill with a drop beyond the fairway on the right and a rocky hillside on the left. It is routed into the prevailing wind and, from the back tee, is no gentle starter. There are five sets of tees for each hole, which make a considerable difference to the length of the course, allowing the course to be played by golfers of all handicaps. However, everybody must be on top form over the closing two holes, long par 4s playing into the wind, plentifully bunkered and with a ravine severing the final fairway just short of the green. Whatever the score, the views through the trees over the lake are impressive.

Where Nicklaus's routing takes play to most points of the compass, Jones's involves a series of almost entirely parallel holes. Inevitably there are steep hillsides on either or both sides of most holes. In places it can be intimidating, such as the 11th, which calls for the drive to carry a long way in order to clear a deep canyon in front of the tee. Such a site brings with it the reward of many splendid views and some exciting green positions, such as at the 13th, the green being perched on top of a precipice.

CARD OF THE COURSE

Hole	Distance (yards)	Par	Hole	Distance (yards)	Par
1	448	4	10	437	4
2	452	4	11	387	4
3	180	3	12	573	5
4	600	5	13	205	3
5	460	4	14	378	4
6	431	4	15	628	5
7	416	4	16	194	3
8	155	3	17	447	4
9	597	5	18	465	4
Out	3,739	36	In	3,714	36
			Total	7,453	72

Kawana

Kawana

Fuji Course, Kawana Golf Resort, Ito City, Shizuoka, Japan

A golf journalist once described Japan as the "golfingest country on earth." It is true that the Japanese are passionate about their golf. The only problem is that there are too few golf courses in Japan to grant access to more than a fraction of its aspirant golfers. Most of the best courses, such as the venerable Hirono near Kobe, are strictly private, and the nearest most Japanese golfers will get to playing there is to read about them. There is however one exception—Kawana.

BELOW *A stunning hole on a stunning course – the par-5 15th. It is a great hole in its own right, with a brilliant green.*

The Fuji Course at Kawana is one of the most beautiful courses in Asia, especially the ultrascenic 15th, running along the clifftops overlooking Sagami Bay. You might, at first glance, think that this was a modern course, using state-of-the-art earthmoving equipment to bludgeon a spectacular course out of the ground, but it is not. This is a product of that golden age of golf course architecture between the two World Wars. It was designed by Charles Alison, an Englishman who became the design partner of the great Harry Colt. Alison did most of the company's work outside Europe. He came to Japan several times in the 1930s, and his courses there are some of the most revered in the country.

Kawana actually boasts two courses, the Fuji and the shorter Oshima, which already existed when Alison came to Kawana. It is equally beautiful, but it is the Fuji Course that keen golfers will wish to test themselves against.

A dream start

There are few opening holes quite as inviting as that on the Fuji Course. It simply plunges down a hill, the fairway's edge clearly defined by the mature woods on either side. In the background is the ocean. A golf course may not have to be ravishing to be great, but it certainly helps.

Alison was a master craftsman in the art of bunkering. His bunkers are things of beauty, staring you in the face, challenging you to clear them, yet welcoming you into them with a siren smile. There are a fistful of them on the corner of the 450-yard/411-m 3rd, which plays as a par 5 because it climbs steeply uphill. Those bunkers must be cleared if there is to be any hope of reaching the green in two—even for the mightiest of hitters.

One of the best holes is the 7th, a downhill two-shotter with an amazing roller-coaster fairway and a narrow approach to the green through an avenue of bunkers. Once again, the ocean provides a glorious backdrop. And there is another higgledy-piggledy fairway on the 9th, a good test of your driving. On this course of contrasts, the diminutive 10th gives way immediately to a monster of a par 5. Yet this hole is 619 yards/566 m of fabulous views. And we have not even mentioned Mount Fuji yet! As if this place were not already scenic enough, Japan's highest and most symbolic mountain looks down like a god on the mortals enjoying their golf on earth.

▶ Where golfers in Europe and the United States might dash to the bar straight after their round of golf, in Japan it is customary for golfing partners to share in the ritual of a communal bath.

CARD OF THE COURSE

Hole	Distance (yards)	Par
1	415	4
2	411	4
3	450	5
4	482	5
5	181	3
6	434	4
7	393	4
8	150	3
9	367	4
Out	3,283	36
10	143	3
11	619	5
12	404	4
13	395	4
14	416	4
15	470	5
16	185	3
17	410	4
18	366	4
In	3,408	36
Total	6,691	72

Blue Canyon

Blue Canyon

Canyon Course, Blue Canyon Country Club, Phuket, Thailand

Thailand is awash with golf courses, some good, some very good. The most celebrated of them all is Blue Canyon, a country club with two brilliant courses, situated in a heavenly spot looking out on to the blue waters of the Andaman Sea, with the Phang Nga mountains creating an inviting terrestrial backdrop. It is fabulously beautiful, but it was not always so. In former times this was a tin mine and rubber plantation.

When it was decided to develop a golf course here, Yoshikazu Kato was engaged as course architect, with a brief to keep the shifting of earth to a minimum and to utilize the natural features of the property. He had been given a helping hand with honoring his brief because huge quantities of earth had already been moved in the tin-mining days, and the abandoned workings had filled with the rainwater that falls so abundantly in Thailand to form a network of lakes and ponds. In this climate the rapidly growing vegetation also assists in softening the once stark features. Kato began with the Canyon Course, which was built in 1991. The Lakes Course followed in 1999 and more than lives up to its name—there are water hazards on 17 of the 18 holes.

TIGER TRIUMPHANT

The 1994 Johnnie Walker Classic was played on the Canyon Course. Greg Norman stormed round the course on the final day in 64 for victory. Finishing in a tie for 34th place was a young amateur, Tiger Woods. Woods, now a professional, returned to Blue Canyon for the 1998 Johnnie Walker Classic. He began the last round nine shots behind the leader, Ernie Els, dug deep and caught up with Els on the final green. Woods won the play-off. It was an immensely popular victory, not least because Tiger's mother is herself from Thailand.

The Canyon Course

After a reasonably straightforward opening hole, water is encountered for the first time on the 2nd hole, a par 3 of some length. On the 3rd a huge calabash tree, standing in the middle of the fairway, confronts the golfer. Which way round it do you go? Accuracy off the tee and precise approach shots to tiered greens are called for on the otherwise fairly short par 4s going to the turn, while the stiff par 5s are a foretaste of the challenges ahead.

The sea views from the 10th tee are superb, while the hole itself is a manageable dogleg to the left. Then comes a 600-yard/549-m monster of a par 5, with water adding complications for the long hitter. Water is present on the next hole as well, and there are strategic decisions concerning water to be made on the par-3 14th, with its kidney-shaped island green, and the 15th, too. The 17th, squeezed between trees to the left and water to the right, is an outstanding short hole, while the water-troubled 18th ensures that the pressure is kept up right to the very end of this delightful course.

LEFT *The 14th is a deceptive hole, playing shorter than you think because of the big drop from tee to green, and it can be complicated by crosswinds.*

BELOW *The strong finishing hole, with its drive over water and cunningly sloped green.*

"One of the best I have ever played on."

TIGER WOODS, JOHNNIE
WALKER CLASSIC, 1998

CARD OF THE COURSE

Hole	Distance (yards)	Par
1	390	4
2	218	3
3	449	4
4	407	4
5	398	4
6	556	5
7	205	3
8	412	4
9	561	5
Out	3,596	36
10	392	4
11	600	5
12	440	4
13	390	4
14	194	3
15	586	5
16	357	4
17	221	3
18	403	4
In	3,583	36
Total	7,179	72

N

Nirwana Bali

Nirwana Bali

Nirwana Bali Golf Club, Bali, Indonesia

The island of Bali is a popular tourist destination. Indeed, tourism is the island's biggest industry, with so-called "congress tourism" a major player. Nirwana Bali Golf Club is the principal attraction at the Nirwana Bali Resort, set on cliffs overlooking Bali's most famous temple, Tanah Lot. Tourists and locals gather in the evening to witness the breathtaking sunsets that frame the temple, perched on a rocky outcrop and cut off from the mainland at high tide.

Golfers owe a debt of gratitude to the presence of the temple, which, it is said, is protected from earthly influences by the highly poisonous sea snakes that swim in large numbers in these waters. Partly out of respect for the holiness of the temple and partly because of the sea snakes, the resort's developer decided not to build the resort too close to the water. Instead, he gave that piece of land to be developed into the golf course, to act as a buffer between resort guests and the dreaded snakes.

The course bears Greg Norman's name, but it was Norman's chief designer, Bob Harrison, who carried out the bulk of the work. He relished the opportunity of being able to build a course so close to the sea. Harrison decided that he would route the course in such a way that seaside holes would be encountered on both nines. For the rest, the course weaves its way through jungle and rice fields. These, and a few streams and ponds, are hazards enough, so bunkering has been applied sparingly.

▶ The rice fields incorporated into the course are tended by local farmers who are encouraged to plant the seed in succession, ensuring year-round harvesting.

LEFT *Of the sea holes it is the 7th that visitors never forget— for both the challenge of making the carry to the green and the extraordinary setting.*

"If you get a site like this, you don't want to muck it up!"

BOB HARRISON, ON BUILDING THE COURSE.

Double helpings of ocean

Avoiding a rice plantation is the first obstacle to be overcome as the round gets under way, heading inland. Rather more pertinent, however, are the bunkers on the left of the sloping fairway. The short 2nd takes us farther from the sea, the 3rd runs across the top of the property, then the next three holes speed across the middle of the site, each of them doglegs.

On the 7th everything changes. This is the first of the sea holes and it is quite stunning. As it is a par 3 all you have to do is knock the ball on to the green, but the green is 214 yards/196 m away on the far side of a stretch of the Indian Ocean, full of sea snakes! To the left stands the temple, but the golfer's attention needs to be firmly focused on the wind speed and direction. This is not the place to come up short! The 8th then begins the journey back to the clubhouse, the 9th completing the task with an exciting pitch across a deep valley to find the green.

On the back nine one of the best holes, fortuitously, returns us to the ocean. The 12th green, built on a rocky promontory, is lovely to look at but difficult to hit. On paper the next hole looks simple enough, but it is actually remarkably tricky and is played alongside the ocean. If you are playing from the back tees,

that on the 14th is almost totally surrounded by water, the shot being over the beach to a clifftop green. From here it is back inland, but the excitement is kept up to the very end, with a death-or-glory approach to the last.

CARD OF THE COURSE

Hole	Distance (yards)	Par	Hole	Distance (yards)	Par
1	383	4	10	445	5
2	188	3	11	211	3
3	400	4	12	381	4
4	439	4	13	337	4
5	441	4	14	186	3
6	501	5	15	447	4
7	214	3	16	431	4
8	544	5	17	349	4
9	388	4	18	520	5
Out	3,498	36	In	3,307	36
			Total	6,805	72

Barnbougle Dunes

Barnbougle Dunes, Bridport, Tasmania, Australia

One of the most exciting golf courses to have been built in Australia in recent years is unexpectedly far from the usual tourist resorts, being located on Tasmania's north coast on what was an otherwise unusable stretch of land on an extensive potato farm. Its owner had no interest in golf, but a young man called Greg Ramsey spotted the potential of this thin strip of duneland and, after much persuasion, convinced the owner that a great course might be built there. The lot fell upon vogue designer Tom Doak to realize the land's potential, which he has done brilliantly.

ABOVE *A great short par 4, the 4th is a fine example of Tom Doak's skill in creating wonderfully appealing holes that, nevertheless, have a sting in the tail.*

The ground on which Barnbougle Dunes is built is a very narrow plot reminiscent of the traditional 18-hole out-and-back courses such as Royal Aberdeen or the Old Course at St. Andrews. However, here, rather than the clubhouse being located at one end it is built in the middle, thereby providing two loops of out-and-back nines. Every hole, except the 2nd, has thus been provided with a border of sea and/or dunes on both sides of the fairway. Fortunately, Doak's style is to create wide fairways with enough space for the high-handicapper to cope with the demands of omnipresent wind, but also to offer multiple playing options to the golfer proficient enough to be able to utilize them.

Such options are particularly appealing when the architect has been confident enough to employ them on a short par 4, such as the 296-yard/271-m 4th. You cannot preplan how to play this hole. You have to wait until you get there, find out what the wind is up to and where the pin has been cut and start plotting back from there, taking into account your own strengths and weaknesses. Holes of this length and of such distinction are rare. Let us hope it is never lengthened, whatever developments of club and ball may lie in the future. The par-3 5th, too, is timeless, calling for a tee shot that rolls on landing, letting the contours feed the ball to the pin.

▶ Barnbougle Dunes is unusual for a contemporary, world-ranked course in having two par 4s (4th and 12th) measuring under 300 yards/274 m from the very back tees.

▶ Accommodation for visiting golfers is provided, not in some hugely expensive hotel, but in a row of charming cottages in the style of traditional beach huts.

RIGHT *The double fairway of the 8th is not an invitation for free hitting. You have to plan your route to the green according to the pin position.*

CARD OF THE COURSE

Hole	Distance (yards)	Par	Hole	Distance (yards)	Par
1	554	5	10	447	4
2	417	4	11	520	5
3	371	4	12	278	4
4	296	4	13	206	3
5	220	3	14	556	5
6	417	4	15	351	4
7	120	3	16	167	3
8	489	4	17	438	4
9	438	4	18	440	4
Out	3,322	35	In	3,403	36
			Total	6,725	71

Architectural brilliance

What makes Tom Doak one of the outstanding architects of our time is his willingness to be unconventional if it results in the right hole for the right place on the course. There is a prime example at the 13th, a substantial par 3 of 206 yards/188 m. With modern equipment this is well within reach of a mid-iron for most, but what sets the hole apart is the green. It is so imaginatively contoured that the normal high, stopping shot is simply not right for here. Control of length and shape of shot is required, with a need to feed the ball into the correct part of the green to allow the extraordinary contours to carry the ball on to the section of putting surface on which the pin is located for the day. Because of Doak's vivid imagination, golfers are required to respond with equal imagination in the way they tackle each hole.

At Barnbougle Dunes Doak was joined by Michael Clayton, a tour golfer turned course designer with an equally original architectural mind. We should expect more mold-breaking courses to emerge in Australia in the future.

"I hated those dunes. It was just land where I couldn't grow potatoes."

RICHARD SATTLER,
OWNER OF BARNBOUGLE DUNES

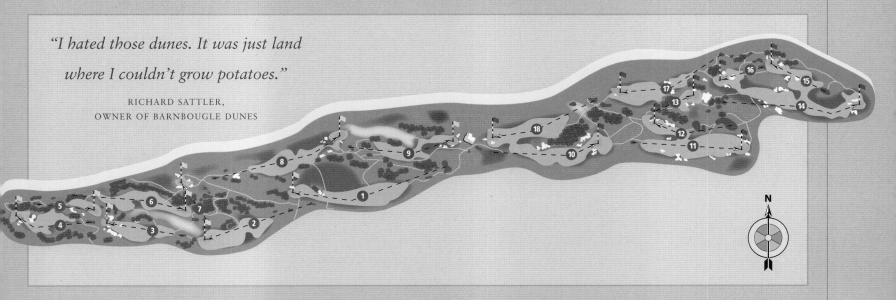

New South Wales

New South Wales Golf Club, Matraville, New South Wales, Australia

Australia's largest city, Sydney, is blessed with surprisingly few great courses. The one really exciting course it possesses is to be found high on the cliffs overlooking Botany Bay, at the New South Wales Golf Club. The views are stupendous, the course is rugged, and when the wind is up (as it usually is) it can be an absolute brute. But who could begrudge a course its difficulty when the experience is undeniably so uplifting?

Impatient golfers cannot wait to reach the seaside holes, but getting there is no easy matter, with the 2nd a tough par 3 and the 3rd a mystifying hole played blind over a huge sand dune. In an era of golf made easy by the overuse of bulldozers and earthmovers, it is heartening to find such a throwback to the past left intact.

Australia's Pebble Beach?

Although the New South Wales course cannot compete with Pebble Beach for the number of seaside holes it possesses, the quality of them is comparable, starting at the 5th. A magnificent seascape awaits the golfer arriving on this tee, and the player's prowess is immediately called into question. Can you clear the ridge crossing the fairway a driver's length away? If you cannot, you will be faced with a daunting second shot played blind across the ridge with an unknown fate on the far side. Those with the strength to clear the ridge from the tee will enjoy many precious yards of extra roll beyond it, bringing the green in easy reach of two shots. Whatever your golfing ability, and your score on this hole notwithstanding, you would be an unfeeling golfer if you left this green without a spring in your step.

RIGHT *The 6th, viewed from behind the green, is played from a tee on the rocks stretching into Botany Bay, where Captain Cook landed in April 1770.*

New South Wales

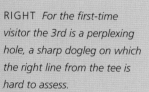

▶ The name Alister MacKenzie stands out from the credits list at New South Wales, but MacKenzie was quite restrained in his alterations here, for the original routing was excellent. For that vision, Australian Eric Apperly, an accomplished amateur golfer, must be given due prominence.

RIGHT *For the first-time visitor the 3rd is a perplexing hole, a sharp dogleg on which the right line from the tee is hard to assess.*

CARD OF THE COURSE

Hole	Distance (yards)	Par	Hole	Distance (yards)	Par
1	321	4	10	394	4
2	202	3	11	163	3
3	416	4	12	527	5
4	428	4	13	410	4
5	512	5	14	353	4
6	194	3	15	407	4
7	411	4	16	441	4
8	552	5	17	167	3
9	372	4	18	548	5
Out	3,408	36	In	3,410	36
			Total	6,818	72

The 5th is followed by a short hole surpassing any at Pebble Beach for its dramatic setting, played from a tee low on the rocks over the pounding ocean waves to a green set in a fold of ground on the far side. Golf does not get much better than this!

The most demanding golf, however, is still to come. A stretch of tough par 4s from the 13th to the 16th has the ability to wreck a promising scorecard, so late in the round that there is no chance of rehabilitation. The raised 13th green is extraordinarily hard to attack, while the 14th is one of those rare short par 4s that are rendered little easier by the advent of modern clubs and balls. On the 15th it is the tee shot that puts fear into the heart of many golfers, with an uncompromising drive and no room for error. Any skirmish with the dunes on the 16th is likely to lead to at least one dropped shot.

This stretch may well be the toughest sequence of holes in Australia, particularly so when the wind probes the golfer's technique and resolve, remorselessly revealing the slightest defect. The short 17th is very exposed to the wind, too, while the final hole rewards the stronger hitter.

Royal Adelaide

Royal Adelaide Golf Club, Seaton, Adelaide, South Australia, Australia

Many courses, particularly long-established British ones, have the company of a railroad track for at least some of the holes. Royal Troon, Wentworth, Carnoustie, Prestwick come to mind. Others, such as the Old Course at St. Andrews and Royal County Down, lost their companion rail tracks years ago. In its early days Royal Adelaide enjoyed its very own railroad station, where members could alight from the train and walk straight out on to the 1st tee. The station has gone, but the railroad is still active, and it forms an unusual hazard on the 2nd and 14th holes where the drive is made from one side of the track to the other.

The club moved to its present site in Seaton, in the Adelaide suburbs, in 1904, golf having been played in the city on and off since 1869. A local golfer, Cargie Rymill, was largely responsible for the layout, and much of this remains intact despite a visit from Alister MacKenzie in 1926. MacKenzie presented the club with detailed plans for an improved (and considerably altered) course, but only some of his ideas were adopted and implemented.

Royal Adelaide is blessed with two excellent short par 4s that continue to excite golfers despite the advent of new and ever more powerful clubs and balls. At 291 yards/ 266 m, the 3rd might well be driven by long hitters, but there is trouble on the right in the form of a treacherous sand dune, and the green itself is long and narrow, demanding arrow-like straightness even from close range. The other memorable short par 4 is the 11th, known as the Crater Hole. On this the fairway is interrupted by a sandy waste at the length of a decent drive, so everyone is forced to lay up short of this before playing a testing approach shot over the sand to a saucer-like green cradled in the arms of a sand dune. Pine trees used to clad the dune, but these have been removed to improve the putting surface.

RIGHT *Royal Adelaide's 14th hole is probably its toughest. The drive is testing enough, but particularly so is the approach to the green over a swale.*

▶ The railroad track on the 2nd hole is deemed an integral part of the course and a ball landing on the track must be played as it lies, or dropped under penalty.

▶ Royal Adelaide, venue for the 2008 Eisenhower Trophy, has hosted 9 Australian Opens and 16 Australian Amateur Championships.

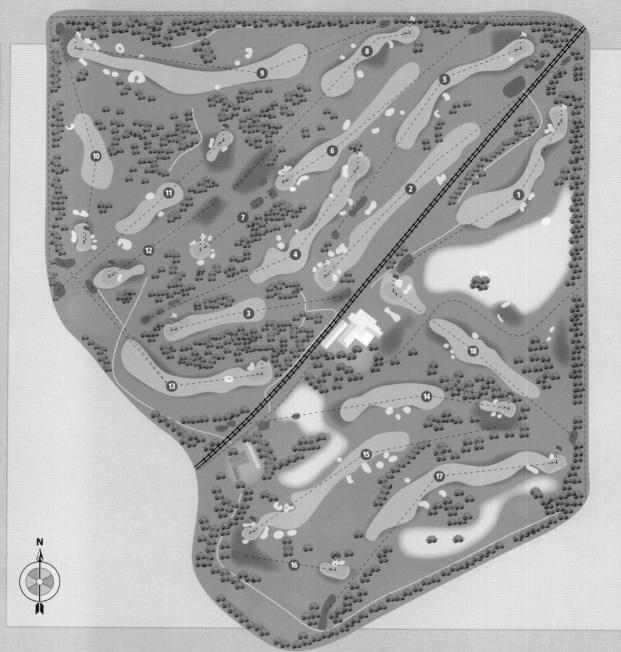

CARD OF THE COURSE

Hole	Distance (yards)	Par	Hole	Distance (yards)	Par
1	381	4	10	377	4
2	547	5	11	386	4
3	291	4	12	224	3
4	449	4	13	432	4
5	459	4	14	487	4
6	459	4	15	498	5
7	191	3	16	181	3
8	392	4	17	517	5
9	542	5	18	419	4
Out	3,711	37	In	3,521	36
			Total	7,232	73

Sand is plentiful at Seaton and in many ways Royal Adelaide plays like a links course, with fast-running fairways and slick greens calling for experience of the ground game and a solid chipping technique.

Three great par 3s

Perhaps the best holes on the course are the three short holes. The 7th is the only par 3 on the outward nine and has recently been lengthened. In fact it usually plays longer than its official yardage, as it is slightly uphill and into the prevailing wind. Green-front bunkers emphasize the need for a full carry. Even longer is the 12th, running to a healthy 224 yards/205 m. The last of the three is the 16th, quite possibly the best of the lot. It has a domed green that rejects anything but the most truly struck of iron shots. This hole vies with the par-4 14th for being the most challenging on the back nine, both holes having wonderfully sited greens. Only two excellent shots on the well-bunkered, dogleg 14th will find the heart of the elusive green.

Royal Melbourne

Royal Melbourne

West Course, Royal Melbourne Golf Club, Black Rock,
Victoria, Australia

The Royal Melbourne Golf Club has been—and still is—the most influential golf club in Australian golf. The man who made it so was a visitor, none other than Dr. Alister MacKenzie. He had been sent by the R&A following a request from Royal Melbourne seeking advice on the laying out of a new course. MacKenzie arrived in October 1926, staying for two months, during which time he also visited a number of other courses, making suggestions for improvements to these courses, too.

MacKenzie's lasting influence was his recruitment of 1924 Australian Amateur champion and Royal Melbourne member, Alex Russell, and the club's greenkeeper, "Mick" Morcom. MacKenzie was not going to be in Australia long enough to oversee the changes he suggested for so many clubs, nor would he be around to supervise at Royal Melbourne. Russell and Morcom quickly assimilated MacKenzie's architectural principles and were able to carry out a revolution in strategic design—and bunker design in particular—that has lasted to this day, especially in the Melbourne sand belt.

Model bunkers

Some years ago, when Nick Faldo, then just starting out in the golf design business, was in Australia to play in a number of tournaments, he was not to be found on the practice range in his down time. He was seen, instead, standing in, walking around, photographing, and measuring many of the bunkers at Royal Melbourne, so impressed was he by their enormous variety and the huge influence they still exert on playing strategy, even though modern professionals are so expert at bunker play.

RIGHT *Both courses intertwine engagingly at Royal Melbourne. Viewed from the back of the 2nd green on the East Course, the famous 6th on the West can be seen stretching into the distance on the right.*

The bunkers are only part of the story, for the real genius of the West Course is the way MacKenzie routed the course to take maximum advantage of the topography of the site. Take, for instance, the sequence of holes from the 3rd to the 10th, which makes brilliant use of two big sandhills and two smaller ones. The 4th is a magnificent hole, whether played as a short par 5 or ultra-long par 4, with a drive over cavernous bunkers to a distant hilltop, followed by a long second shot, very likely played from a hanging lie, along a curving fairway to a heavily bunkered, distant green. Then comes the 5th, as gorgeous a short hole as you could wish to find, and the 6th is one of the world's great two-shot holes, with a drive over serious bunkers to set up an approach shot to a deliciously bunkered, ledge green cradled in the dunes of one of the bigger hills.

Little attention is usually given to the short 7th, which is a better hole for being routed up a hill rather than over an adjacent pond, while the 8th green is unreceptive, being sloped down toward the back and attendant bunkers. A mid-length par 4 follows, with a tricky pitch uphill to the green, and then comes the fabulous 10th, as wonderful a short par 4 as you could hope to find, tempting the long hitter to drive the green and punishing even the slightest failure mercilessly. It remains a great hole despite our superior clubs and balls.

▶ For tournaments, a composite course is drawn from the West and East Courses, keeping play within the boundaries of the main club grounds and avoiding road crossings.

▶ Royal Melbourne's founders included a number of Scots: John Bruce, Tom Finlay, and Hugh Playfair, from St. Andrews, and William Knox and Tom Brentnall from Musselburgh.

CARD OF THE COURSE

Hole	Distance (yards)	Par
1	429	4
2	480	5
3	354	4
4	470	5
5	176	3
6	428	4
7	148	3
8	379	4
9	416	4
Out	3,280	36
10	305	4
11	455	4
12	476	5
13	147	3
14	366	4
15	467	5
16	221	3
17	439	4
18	433	4
In	3,309	36
Total	6,589	72

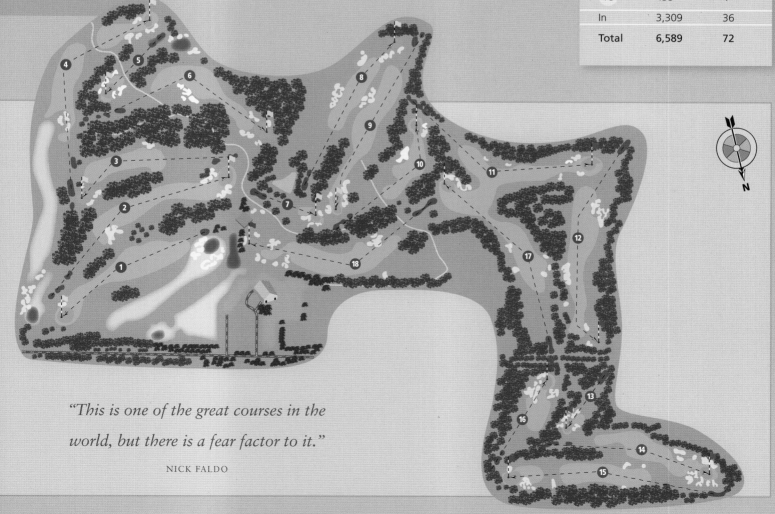

"This is one of the great courses in the world, but there is a fear factor to it."

NICK FALDO

THE EAST COURSE

In addition to the five Australian Opens played on the Composite Course and two on the West, there have also been two Opens contested on the East Course. It is a very fine course in its own right, and was laid out by Alex Russell and Mick Morcom in 1930–31. They were clearly influenced by Alister MacKenzie's visit in 1926, for stylistically it has much in common with the West Course, most particularly the bunkering. Russell and Morcom obviously had something of MacKenzie's gift for identifying great green sites, and both courses are superb tests of approach play. The short holes are particularly appealing, the 201-yard/184-m 4th being as tough as any short hole on the West. It plays long as it runs uphill through serious bunkers.

ABOVE *The hilltop 7th (West) green is narrow and angled across the line of flight. With bunkers through the back, this is not a green to overshoot.*

RIGHT *A great par 3, the 5th (West) involves a tee shot across low ground to a heavily bunkered green with a pronounced slope to the putting surface.*

Cape Kidnappers

Cape Kidnappers Golf Course, Hawke's Bay, North Island, New Zealand

For many years New Zealand has been something of a golfing sleeper. Given the natural advantages of climate and setting, few courses realized their true potential, Paraparaumu Beach being one of the exceptions. Now there are two spectacular modern courses—Kauri Cliffs and Cape Kidnappers—that have raised the bar enormously, just as their American developer, Julian Robertson, has raised the bar in golf tourism in New Zealand.

The name, Cape Kidnappers, is sufficient to suggest that here are to be found stunning seascapes and any number of fabulous holes exploiting them. But the key to maximizing the potential of a site of this kind is what you do with the rest of the course. It would be disappointing to have to play dull holes on dull ground simply as a means of getting to the exceptional holes. By choosing Tom Doak as the designer, Robertson was on to a winner, for Doak is a master at routing a golf course, ensuring that every hole is of golfing interest, that there is a good balance between sorts and styles of holes, and that the entire course is memorable. He and his team walked the site many times before setting to work, taking in the enormity of the task, getting to know every inch of the ground, and simply coming to terms with the magnificent canvas he had been given. Doak was able to exploit his talent for locating stunning green sites.

RIGHT *On the edge of the earth, the 12th green is just one of a number of stunningly sited targets presented to the golfer during the round.*

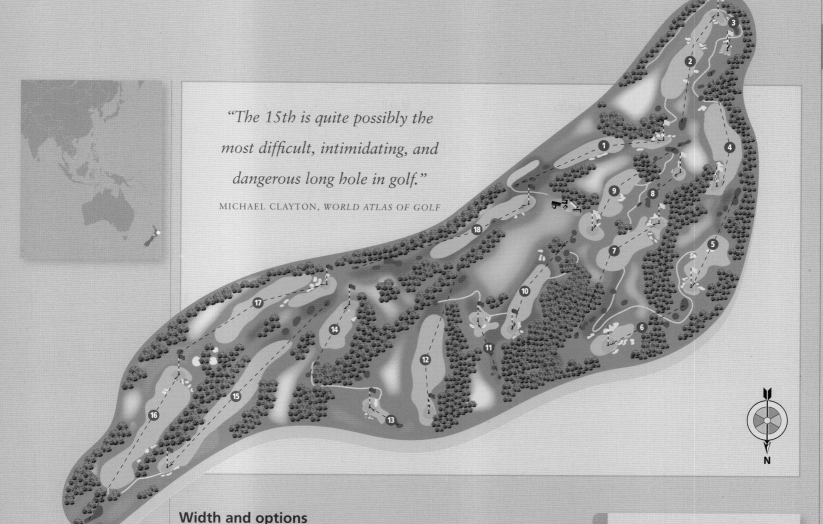

"The 15th is quite possibly the most difficult, intimidating, and dangerous long hole in golf."

MICHAEL CLAYTON, *WORLD ATLAS OF GOLF*

Width and options

Doak has rebelled against the "total" architecture of many of his contemporaries: not for him narrow fairways that call for target golf on every shot. Instead, where possible, Doak gives you width, just as Alister MacKenzie did in the early 20th century. And, just as MacKenzie's greens were defended cleverly so that you had to conjure up a different kind of approach shot depending on where exactly you were on the fairway, Doak requires you to use your imagination by giving you choice.

You are, for instance, given a lovely wide fairway on the 1st, tempting you into a big drive. But the green is angled across the line of the fairway and cleverly bunkered. Unless you are in the correct part of the fairway you may find you have no shot to the green. You have to do your homework—on every hole: you cannot blast your way round here.

Cape Kidnappers would be a fine course even if it consisted solely of holes comparable with the early ones, but it is at the 12th that it becomes exceptional, with a string of breathtaking clifftop holes. And that 12th green— sitting on the skyline twixt heaven and hell! It is followed by a short hole on the very edge of the cliffs and a clever drive-and-pitch hole made particularly devilish by a demon of a pot-bunker. This gives way to a 650-yard/594-m par 5 of incredible beauty and great treachery: to the left a vertiginous drop to the ocean; to the right a ball-swallowing ravine. Although a stroke might be rescued at the 16th, the two closing holes are decidedly tough, with Doak making you think until the very last putt has dropped.

▶ In 2007 *Golf Digest* magazine rated Cape Kidnappers the 10th best course in the world outside the United States—some accolade for a course opened as recently as 2004!

▶ The name Cape Kidnappers was given to this spot in 1769 by Captain Cook, following a Maori's attempt to abduct his cabin boy from his ship, HMS *Endeavour*.

CARD OF THE COURSE

Hole	Distance (yards)	Par
1	440	4
2	540	5
3	215	3
4	544	5
5	420	4
6	225	3
7	453	4
8	182	3
9	403	4
Out	3,422	35
10	430	4
11	224	3
12	460	4
13	130	3
14	348	4
15	650	5
16	500	5
17	463	4
18	480	4
In	3,685	36
Total	7,107	71

ROBERTSON'S VISION

Julian Robertson's other contribution to state-of-the-art golf in New Zealand is Kauri Cliffs on the North Island. As at Cape Kidnappers there are stunning seascapes from this clifftop course, which was laid out by David Harman, the Florida-based golf course designer. No fewer than 15 holes look out to sea, although some of the best holes are inland, such as the par-5 4th. The first skirmish with the ocean comes at the par-3 7th, an all-or-nothing carry over an abyss. There is an invigorating sequence of clifftop holes on the back nine, too, from the 14th to the 17th. Obviously, there are similarities between the two courses, because of their spectacular locations, but what makes a fascinating comparison is in the fine detail work of the two very different architects.

RIGHT *The spectacular setting of the stretch of holes from the 14th to the 17th is wonderfully captured in this aerial photograph. The 14th and 17th greens are in the foreground.*

Paraparaumu Beach

Paraparaumu Beach Golf Club, Kapiti Coast, North Island, New Zealand

The traditional sandy soil with its quick-draining properties, close-cropped fairway grass, fast greens, and deep bunkers of links golf are rare commodities away from the coastline of the British Isles. You cannot get much farther away from Britain than New Zealand, but at Paraparaumu Beach there is the real thing, a genuine links course, and of world class to boot.

Golf was first played here in 1929 on a nine-hole course, which was extended to 18 shortly before World War II. Already plans were afoot to turn it into a great course, and Alex Russell, the Australian who had worked with Alister MacKenzie at Royal Melbourne, was engaged to do the job. He finished the task in 1949 and little has changed since.

Not too short for today's stars

With a card length of a little over 6,600 yards/6,035 m, Paraparaumu Beach appears too short for the likes of Michael Campbell and Tiger Woods, just two of the world stars who have played the course recently in deadly earnest. But the course is well defended, and the slightest error is often punished more severely than you might imagine. Take the 5th, a short hole of modest dimensions, without a bunker to its name. If you hit the green and manage to keep the ball on the putting surface, fine. Miss it and the surest touch is required to ensure that the third shot is a putt, for this green sits high above its surroundings, the downslopes shaved punitively. Even shorter is the 16th, but it, too, is a fine demonstration that length is not necessary to create a great one-shot hole. Fail to make this green and the brilliance of the design is made all too apparent.

Short holes alone do not constitute a great course, and there are several longer holes of note, too. For instance, the 3rd and 4th are parallel, long par 4s playing in opposite

directions, maximizing the effect of the wind. The definitive hole is perhaps the 13th, a 446-yard/408-m par 4 with a wildly undulating fairway, the last part of which is some way below the level of the green. To make the long carry to the green from the higher part of the fairway is a considerable task. On the other hand, even though the shot is much shorter, the shot up from the lower level needs great precision.

The 17th, too, is a marvelous hole, its fairway on two levels, split diagonally by a ridge. It offers a choice, but the apparently easier option may prove the wrong choice, depending on your skill and nerve. The lower fairway level is simpler to reach, but you will be left with a long and arduous approach to a green angled away from you with bunkers on the right and another shaved slope on the left. A much tighter and longer tee shot is required to reach the higher level of the fairway, with no marks for failure. However, it follows that the approach shot is then made with a much shorter club, although the same perils await should your shot be inaccurate.

▶ At the 2002 New Zealand Open (played at Paraparaumu Beach) a 13-year-old Korean schoolboy, Jae An, won the qualifying competition to become the youngest boy to play in a professional tour event. He made the cut, only two shots behind Tiger Woods.

LEFT *What a wonderful green site for a long par 4! Alister MacKenzie would surely have warmly approved of his protégé Alex Russell's routing of the 13th hole at Paraparaumu Beach.*

CARD OF THE COURSE

Hole	Distance (yards)	Par
1	403	4
2	197	3
3	464	4
4	446	4
5	162	3
6	325	4
7	500	5
8	371	4
9	393	4
Out	3,261	35
10	310	4
11	427	4
12	545	5
13	446	4
14	146	3
15	372	4
16	138	3
17	442	4
18	550	5
In	3,376	36
Total	6,637	71

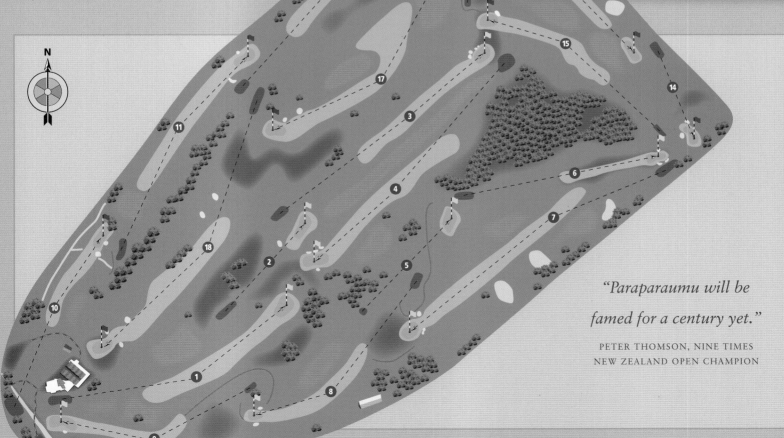

"Paraparaumu will be famed for a century yet."

PETER THOMSON, NINE TIMES
NEW ZEALAND OPEN CHAMPION

▶▶▶ Index

Acknowledgments

The publishers would like to thank the following for permission to reproduce copyright material:

Sean Arbie, p 58.

Barnbougle Dunes Golf Club, pp 238, 239.

Michael Calderwood/Peninsula Papagayo, p 136.

Celtic Manor Resort, p 56

Corbis/Tony Roberts, p 133.

Getty Images, p 78; /David Alexander, pp 12, 13, 96; /Stan Badz/PGA, p 104; /David Cannon, pp 2, 6, 6–7, 7, 8–9, 16, 20, 26, 28, 29, 32, 34, 48, 49, 50, 52, 54–55, 60, 61, 64, 70, 86, 92, 100, 108, 110, 112, 114, 115, 156, 158, 159, 176, 180, 196, 198, 199, 200, 222, 230, 231, 240, 241, 244, 246–47, 248, 250–251, 252; /Chris Condon/PGA, p 102; /Stuart Franklin, pp 174, 218; /Richard Heathcoate, pp 44, 223, 228, 228–29; /Harry How, pp 74, 78–79, 79, 90; /Image Source Black, p 4–5; /Craig Jones, p 92–93; /Ross Kinnaird, p 104–05; /Warren Little, pp 23, 154, 155, 212, 213, 220, 221; /Steve Munday, pp 11, 38, 170; /PGA of America/Stringer, p 111; /Paul Severn, p 194–95.

Hotel Transamérica Ilha de Comandatuba, pp 140, 141.

Kapalua Resort, p 82.

Karen Country Club, pp 210, 211.

Kiawah Island Golf Resort, pp 84, 85.

La Dehesa Golf Club, p 142.

Ed Lopez/Vista Vallarta Golf Club, pp 134, 135.

Iain Lowe Photography, p 30–31.

Master Golf Club, p 152.

Brian Morgan, pp 22, 72, 122, 127, 132, 146, 160, 161, 168, 172, 173, 224, 225, 232.

Ran Morrissett/GolfClubAtlas.com, pp 116, 117, 121, 138.

Mark Rowlinson, p 188.

Rungsted Golf Club, p 150.

Frank Sauve/St. George's Golf & Country Club, p 118.

Phil Sheldon Golf Picture Library, pp 10, 36, 37, 40, 46, 66–67, 75, 76, 80, 94, 95, 97, 98, 106, 124, 125, 190, 191, 195, 203, 204, 214, 242; /Liz Anthony, pp 14–15, 18, 42, 68, 88; /Bob Atkins, p 62; /Richard Castka, pp 226 above, 226 below, 235, 236; /Patrick Eagar, p 208; /Karina Hoskyns, pp 184–85, 185; /Jan Traylen, p 178.

Stefan von Stengel, pp 120, 126, 128–29, 130, 131, 144, 145, 148, 162, 164, 166, 167, 181, 182, 186, 187, 192, 202, 206, 216, 216–17, 234.